The Frameworks of English

2002/86

D0321501

Related titles:

Introduction to English Language	*Norman Blake and Jean Moorhead*
English Grammar: An Introduction	*Peter Collins and Carmella Hollo*
Linguistic Terms and Concepts	*Geoffrey Finch*
How to Study Linguistics	*Geoffrey Finch*
Varieties of English (2nd edition)	*Dennis Freeborn*
Meaning in English	*Lesley Jeffries*
An Introduction to English Language	*Koenraad Kuiper and W. Scott Allan*
An Introduction to Linguistics	*Stuart C. Poole*

THE FRAMEWORKS OF ENGLISH

Introducing language structures

KIM BALLARD

palgrave

First published 2001 by
PALGRAVE
Houndmills, Basingstoke, Hampshire RG21 6XS and
175 Fifth Avenue, New York, N.Y. 10010
Companies and representatives throughout the world

PALGRAVE is the new global academic imprint of
St. Martin's Press LLC Scholarly and Reference Division and
Palgrave Publishers Ltd (formerly Macmillan Press Ltd).

ISBN 0–333–65913–9 paperback

This book is printed on paper suitable for recycling and
made from fully managed and sustained forest sources.

A catalogue record for this book is available
from the British Library.

10   9   8   7   6   5   4   3   2
10 09 08 07 06 05 04 03 02

Printed in Malaysia

In memory of my grandparents

Ronald Elston Dell
&
Ivy Charlotte Dell

Contents

List of Tables

List of Figures

Part I
INTRODUCTION

Part 1
INTRODUCTION

1 Introduction

1.1 A VOYAGE AROUND THE ENGLISH LANGUAGE

In 1967, a science fiction film was released entitled *Fantastic Voyage*. In it, a team of scientists in a kind of space capsule are shrunk small enough to be injected into the human bloodstream and journey around the body exploring the lungs, stomach, heart and so on. The fascination of the film at the time was the way it showed the supposed workings of our anatomy from the inside, and the extraordinary perspective this gave on the human body. Human language is a subject of equal fascination and the aim of this book is to make a journey around the English language and get an inside view of how it works. Because language is something with which we are very familiar and which we are all very competent at using, it is easy to make the assumption that it is a relatively simple phenomenon. This is very far from the truth. Human language – be it English or any other tongue – is as complex in its own way as any of the bio-chemical and anatomical functions of the human body.

To take a relatively straightforward example, look at the following string of words: *whole scoffed the Kate cake greedy has.* They are clearly not a meaningful English sequence as they stand, although without any difficulty you could no doubt rearrange them into *greedy Kate has scoffed the whole cake.* This might strike you as an extremely simple task, but in fact the knowledge about the English language which you would draw on in order to reorganise the words into a permissible sentence is highly complex. If you asked any number of other speakers of English to do this, they would all come up with the same response. This is not a coincidence. All native speakers of English share a set of mental rules which guarantee that they will know how to group the words into meaningful units – *greedy Kate / has scoffed / the whole cake* – not, for example, *Kate cake / whole the has / scoffed greedy,* and that these units have to be arranged in a particular order so that a combination such as *has scoffed greedy Kate the whole cake* would not occur. Not only do we employ knowledge about the rules of word order here, but we are also using knowledge about meanings (for example, knowing that *greedy* could describe *Kate* but not *cake*). If you had heard these words read out instead of reading them on the page, you would need to use quite subtle information about the sounds of the language in order to distinguish between *Kate* and *cake,* which sound very similar.

Clearly, then, in order to make sense of that random string of words, you would need to employ specific knowledge about the English language. If you are reading this book, you are presumably interested in finding out how the English language works. Subconsciously you already know this because you are able to use the language effectively. However, your present knowledge about the patterns and rules which underpin English is **implicit**. In other words, you possess this knowledge, but only at a subconscious and instinctive level. The aim of this book is to help you make your knowledge **explicit** – in other words, to explain to you what exactly the nature of that knowledge is. Because you learn your first language instinctively from birth, it may come as a surprise later on to discover that you have mastered speaking it without consciously learning the rules on which it is based. This is one of the most extraordinary things about speech and language. But it is possible to distance yourself from your first language to see how it works and how it is structured: to take a voyage around it and understand it more closely.

1.2   FRAMEWORKS AND LEVELS

A framework is a structure which holds something together. Knowing the frameworks of a language enables you to understand how that language is structured and what rules operate to produce that structure. Without these patterns and rules, the language would be haphazard and would not be an effective means of communication.

This book is subdivided so that Parts II, III, IV and V each deal with a different aspect of the frameworks of English. Just as a book on the human anatomy might be subdivided into sections such as the skeleton, the nervous system, the digestive system and so on, in a similar way this book is organised according to four different aspects of the language, namely

lexis	the words of the language
grammar	the way words are combined into sentences
discourse	the way sentences are combined into texts
phonology	the sounds and the sound patterns of the language.

This voyage around the English language begins in Part II, Lexical Frameworks, with words, which may be regarded as the basic building blocks of language. We will look at ways of dividing all the words into family groups or **word classes** according to the features which characterise them and then move on to look at how English words are structured and the different strategies employed to create new words. Part III considers the ways in which words can be combined – first into phrases, then into clauses and finally into sentences – and the way in which words are modifed in certain situations by the addition of special endings or **inflections** (for example, by adding a plural ending to cat when we talk about *three cats*). The range of inflections and the principles of word order or **syntax** are together covered by **grammar**, so Part III deals with the grammatical frameworks of English. This is the most substantial part of this textbook. If you consider for a moment that there is an infinite number of possible sentences which we might compose in English (or any language, for that matter), then there must be a considerable range of ways to construct these sentences. It follows that there are many rules which ensure that the sentences we compose are both natural and meaningful. It is difficult to reduce a survey of these rules to anything much shorter, although it would be possible to go into even more detail on grammatical and other aspects of the language if the scope of this textbook were greater.   The largest unit of construction in grammar is the sentence. Part IV, Discourse Frameworks, gives an overview of some of the ways in which we combine sentences into what is known as **text** or **discourse**.

While Parts II, III and IV cover the words of the language and the way they combine into larger and larger units, Part V, Phonological Frameworks, looks at the English language from a rather different angle by considering the sound system of the language. First we will examine the set of distinct sounds which are used in English and then look at the way these sounds combine to form strings of sounds including syllables. Finally we will look at what are known as the **prosodic** features of language which often operate across groups of words and which include aspects such as the **pitch** and **intonation** of our voices.

The different aspects of language which we are studying here are sometimes referred to as **levels of language**. So Part II which deals with lexical frameworks is looking at language on a lexical level, Part III is looking at English on a grammatical level and so on. We need to have a methodical way of exploring the language and we must therefore rely on the levels of language to map out our journey. However, it would be a mistake to give the impression that these levels are completely separate. As you gradually absorb the material covered here, you will see how the different levels overlap and your understanding of how the language works will become more sophisticated.

A further level of language not mentioned so far is the **semantic level**. **Semantics** is the study of meaning. It is a crucial aspect in that the purpose of language is to convey meaning. The problem (if it is a problem) with semantics is that meaning is not an aspect of language which can be delimited in quite the same way as, for example, a study of the lexis of the language.

Meaning operates in a different dimension from the other levels and also operates in conjunction with them all. For example, as far as the sounds of English are concerned, it may at first seem that individual sounds such as the *'b'* at the start of *bat* have no intrinsic meaning but there is a correlation between sounds and meanings in some words – beyond what can be considered coincidental. For instance, one dictionary lists the following words which all begin with the same *gru-* sound:

grub	*grubby*	*grudge*	*gruff*
grumble	*grumpy*	*grunt*	

It is not unreasonable to propose that, since five out of the seven words listed above carry suggestions of impatience or irritability, there is some semantic link between those negative associations and the sound *gru-* at the beginning of *grudge, gruff, grumble, grumpy* and *grunt*. It may even be that this meaning of *gru-* has come about because we clench our teeth when we feel irritated and *gru-* is a natural sound to produce in this position.

At the other extreme, we can see how sentences can colour the meaning of adjoining or associated sentences. Consider, for example, *My best friend has just played a trick on me*. If you heard or read this sentence in isolation, the likelihood is that you would assume the trick in question was a harmless prank of some kind. You would think this first because the expression *play a trick* suggests this kind of playfulness and secondly because you are told that the person playing the trick is the speaker's best friend and you wouldn't expect a best friend to do something unkind. If the sentence were followed with a further comment such as *I laughed so much I cried* then you would be confirmed in your initial assumption. However, if the follow-up comment to *My best friend has just played a trick on me* were something like *A dirty, rotten trick* then you would have to rethink your interpretation of the first sentence since the trick in question was clearly far from harmless.

The above is an example of how meaning is constructed and reconstructed as more information is received and how this happens using large linguistic building blocks, namely sentences. You can see that meaning is not a unit of construction in the same way as other aspects of language are. A further consideration is that meaning is often dependent on context. We may not be able to interpret something accurately unless we know the context in which it is spoken or written. For example, if a person you meet at a business occasion introduces someone else as their partner, you would assume a professional relationship between these two people. On the other hand, if you were introduced to someone's partner at a social occasion, you would probably assume a more personal relationship such as boyfriend and girlfriend.

Semantics, then, is an aspect of language which is very diverse in that it operates at all linguistic levels. Because of this, and because meaning can be constructed either by language which is free from contextual consideration or by having to consider the context or situation in which language is used, semantics would prove an extremely demanding area to classify or describe comprehensively within the scope of this book. As mentioned before, explaining meaning is not really the same kind of process as describing the frameworks on which a language is constructed. On the other hand, it is impossible to look at the frameworks of English without frequently making reference to meaning of various kinds. For this reason, rather than presenting semantics as a separate topic or chapter, meaning is discussed at various points throughout this book where it is relevant to a full understanding of the frameworks. Inevitably, this will be frequently, but often the exploration of meaning is implicit to the discussion rather than a separate part of it.

1.3   SPEECH AND WRITING

Language can be spoken or written. (Some users also employ signing as a mode of communication.) Speech is the primary mode of communication. This is because all humans learn to speak as part of their natural biological development. Learning to speak is not something we choose to do: it is an instinctive process. By contrast, we have to make a conscious effort if we are to acquire the ability to write our language and not all language users develop the same facility for doing this. In our society, writing is highly valued for a variety of reasons, including its permanence and the way it embodies our social and cultural codes, such as our laws and our literature. However, other cultures do not depend so heavily on the written language as we do, and there are many people in the world who have not learnt to write.

This book is about the frameworks of English and to a large extent it is irrelevant whether we are talking about the language in its spoken or written form. Although we employ special conventions for writing our language (namely, using an alphabet, a standardised system of spelling and a set of punctuation marks), the vocabulary and the grammatical structures we use for speaking and writing are essentially the same even though writing is often more polished than speech. For example, we might say *If you're er going to the er to the shops, could you get me um a paper?* whereas in an e-mail message the hesitations (*er, um*) and the recycling (*to the ... to the shops*) would be absent. However, the opposite can also be true. Sometimes speech is free of the non-fluency that often characterises this mode, while someone who is writing in a hurry may not bother about fluency or correct spelling and punctuation. In fact, an interesting feature of many e-mail messages is that, because they are often swift responses composed online, writers don't always bother to tidy them up before sending them.

When we explore the lexis and grammar of English in Chapters 2 to 8, the material covered will be applicable to both the spoken and written modes of language. Only in the last three chapters is specific attention given to the primary mode of speech.

1.4   WHICH ENGLISH?

This may seem a rather strange heading in the sense that asking *which English?* implies that there is more than one. When we talk about the frameworks of English, we think of English as a specific language as opposed to the French language or the German language and so on. So far this introduction has simply referred to 'English' on the assumption that the reader knows what is meant by this term. However, you are probably already aware that English can take many different forms. For example, the English spoken in America varies in several ways from the English spoken in Britain. And within Britain, there are many regional variations in the pronunciation, vocabulary and grammar of English, just as there are many variations in America.

When analysing the lexical and grammatical frameworks of English, linguists find it helpful to use just one variety in order to find out what typifies or characterises the language. They can also use that variety as a yardstick or model with which to compare other varieties. It is perhaps unfortunate that there has to be such a yardstick, as this can mislead people into thinking that the selected variety of English is in some way intrinsically better as a means of communication than all the other varieties. This is not the case, but it is nevertheless valuable to have the set of reference points that the chosen variety provides. The 'yardstick' variety which linguists use – and therefore which is used in this textbook – is **Standard English** and because this book is designed primarily for readers living in the British Isles, it is specifically **Standard British English** which is used. Although you may not speak Standard English yourself, you are certain to be familiar with it as it is the English of national newspapers, of most news broadcasting on national television and radio, and the English which is used in textbooks. Standard English is also the variety of English which foreigners learn (which adds weight to the notion that it in some way represents or typifies the language).

Standard British English is a **dialect**. By dialect, we mean the lexis and the grammar of a particular language variety. (This is in contrast to **accent**, which is the pronunciation used, a matter which is considered in Chapter 9.)

A dialect may be spoken or written. Whereas a relatively small percentage of the British population speak Standard English (possibly as few as 10 per cent), virtually everyone is aware of the standard variety because it is used so widely in the written mode as well as in national broadcasting.

Another important point to make when defining exactly which English is being described here is that we are only concerned with contemporary English – English as it is spoken at the turn of the new millennium. The frameworks of any living language do not remain the same over a period of time but change in a variety of ways, some of those changes taking place slowly, others more rapidly. It is beyond the scope of this book to chart such changes – a full comparison of English in the year 2000 with, say, Shakespeare's English of 1600 would be an enormous task – but we will occasionally touch on the history of the language when this has some bearing on what English is like today.

The business of this book, then, is to describe those features and patterns of the language which characterise English as it is currently used. Simply because this book describes the grammatical rules of Standard English, it does not mean that the grammatical rules (or the lexis) of other varieties such as the Yorkshire dialect are inferior or incorrect. The term 'rule' can be misleading. It is essential to understand 'rule' as referring to a principle of construction rather than a way of judging correctness. This book, then, takes a **descriptive** rather than a **prescriptive** approach. This is important because we want to avoid being judgemental about language varieties.

1.5   USING THIS BOOK

Section 1.2 above explained how this book is divided up according to four levels of language, Part II dealing with lexis, Part III with grammar, Part IV with discourse and Part V with phonology. At the back you will find a reference section which contains a glossary and a list of phonetic symbols. Phonetic symbols (which are shown between slant brackets) are used as a way of referring in writing to particular sounds of the language. It is perfectly simple to tell which sounds many symbols refer to: /b/ for example refers to the sound at the start of *bat* and /z/ to the sound at the start of *zip*. However, others are less transparent such as the /æ/ at the start of /ænd/ (*and*). Although the phonetic symbols are explained fully in Chapter 9, other chapters do make occasional use of them and you can check the sounds which they represent by referring to the list at the back.

The glossary contains an alphabetical list of all the linguistic terminology used in this book, with a definition for each term. When a new term is introduced (or reintroduced) in the text, it is in bold print. This also indicates that it is one of the terms listed in the glossary. At the end of some of the sections in Parts II, III, IV and V, you will find entries such as the following:

☐ **connected speech** ⇨ 10.6

What this means is that the subject of connected speech has been touched on in another section and to find out more about that topic you should turn to section 6 of Chapter 10. These cross-references are designed to help you link certain aspects across the frameworks.

There are a range of other symbols which are used in this book. An asterisk (*) placed in front of an example, be it a word, phrase or sentence, indicates that the example would not normally or naturally occur in English. A question mark (?) at the beginning of an example indicates that it might occur, but it may not be accepted by all speakers. The null sign Ø indicates that a word or phrase has been omitted and is understood, as in

Fred went to the shops and Ø bought a loaf of bread

where Ø stands for *Fred*, or to indicate an empty position.

Various types of bracket are used and it is important not to confuse them. Phonetic symbols (representing phonemes) are contained within slant brackets, angled brackets < > are used for letters of the alphabet, and square brackets [ ] are used to mark out phrases. (Square brackets are also used for a detailed phonetic transcription but we will only occasionally be using them for this purpose.)

In a study of this kind there has to be a degree of selection and simpli-fication. This is a concession to the sheer complexity of the language. It is not impossible that you will come across some differences in the way the frame-works are described if you look at other textbooks. This kind of variation is inevitable when the subject matter is so vast and complex: it is unlikely that any two linguists will agree totally on how to describe English – or any other language for that matter. The aim is to give you as clear and coherent a description as possible: you will find that other textbooks you consult will concur with this one on the majority of points. If you encounter differences, you need to make up your own mind which description or interpretation you find most appropriate.

Part II
LEXICAL FRAMEWORKS

2 Word Classes

2.1 WORDS: THE BUILDING BLOCKS OF LANGUAGE

If you were to ask someone what they considered language to consist of, the most likely answer you would receive is 'words'. Most of us, whether or not we have made a close study of language, perceive words as the building blocks of language. Often, when we talk about language, we talk about it in terms of words – 'actions speak louder than words', 'mark my words', 'in other words' and so on. Of course, there is much more to studying a language than simply studying it on a **lexical** (or 'word') level. We can look at the units which make up words and which are therefore smaller than words, and we can look at larger units by exploring how words are grouped together in strings to form phrases, clauses and sentences and much longer texts too. Nevertheless, words are a very good place to start when studying a language and this is where we will therefore begin.

There is no doubt that the concept 'a word' has psychological reality for all users of the English language. Any definition of 'word' has to be, in some respects, specific to a particular language because words do not behave in the same way in all languages. This is often noticed when you try to translate from one language to another. If you were translating from Russian into English, for example, you would find that many single words in Russian can only be translated using several English words.

In some respects, defining 'word' in English is a relatively straightforward task because we can make recourse to the written language in order to clarify what we mean by a word. For example, speakers of English will agree that the following sentence contains ten words:

Old fat cats like to sleep in quiet sunny places

The reason why identification of words seems straightforward here is because in writing we normally leave a space between them. It is therefore possible to count the number of words in a sentence or text. For many speakers, their concept of 'word' is reinforced by the written conventions of their language.

Nevertheless, there are some problems with word identification or word definition which cannot be solved simply by stating that a word is a linguistic item which is written with a space on either side. One of these concerns **compound words**. These are words such as *world-class* (as in *world-class cricketer*) or *world war* made up of two existing words, which might be written with a hyphen or with a space between them. In the case of *world war*, most speakers think of it as a single lexical item despite the way it is written. In English there are also many verbs (known as **multi-word verbs**) which consist of more than one element. They can normally be defined with a single alternative word. Examples include *put off* (meaning either *deter* or *postpone*), *run up* (meaning *incur* or *make*) and *take on* (meaning *employ* or *challenge*). Again, speakers instinctively feel that although these multi-word verbs consist of more than one element, in terms of meaning they are a single unit.

This idea can be taken one step further when we consider **idioms**. Idioms are little groups of words whose meaning is not retrievable from the individual parts which make up the idiom. In a sense, the multi-word verbs we have just mentioned are idioms (*run up* in *run up a debt,* for example, does not have the literal meaning it has in *run up a mountain*), but there are many more groups of words in the language which, as a fixed expression, have a distinct meaning. A clear example of this is the expression *to pay through the nose*. This does not literally mean that money is passed down the nostrils when paying for something. This is clearly ridiculous, but it is impossible for a speaker to deduce without some contextual clues that *to pay through the nose* means 'to pay an excessive amount of money for something'. Another interesting feature about idioms, and another reason to treat them as single entities, is that they are fixed expressions and it isn't possible to make adjustments to them. *To pay through the nose*, for example, could hardly be adjusted to *to pay down the nose* or *to pay through the nostril*. This fixedness lends weight to the notion that although we might be dealing in these idiomatic examples with two or more words, we are nevertheless dealing with single items of meaning.

Despite the problem just outlined, there are some features of words which we can regard as fairly typical and which go beyond the initial observation that words are linguistic items written with a space either side of them. For one thing, a word can typically occur as a **minimal free form**. What is meant by this is that a word in isolation can be a complete utterance. Some examples might include:

Stop!
Here!
No
Possibly

Often these items are uttered in response to a question or other comment. For example, *possibly* might be uttered as a response to *Can you come to the cinema on Saturday?* Nevertheless, it is difficult to imagine some words - such as *the*, *by* and *their* – occurring in isolation in this way.

A further approach by which we might consider words as free-standing units is by considering the ability of one word to be substituted by another word, but not by anything less than a word. Thus we could replace *feeling* in the first example below with *premonition* but not with *pre-*:

> *She had a feeling that there would be an accident*
> *She had a premonition that there would be an accident*
> * *She had a pre- that there would be an accident*

In these examples, *pre-*, while having a discernible meaning (namely 'before' as in *preview* or *prejudge*), can neither replace a word nor can it be a free-standing and complete linguistic item. We accept that *pre-* can only be part of a full word.

Another feature typical of words is that, in addition to being free-standing, they also have a mobility which parts of words do not have. Compare these two examples:

> *I can't stand hypocrisy*
> *Hypocrisy, I can't stand*

It is possible to rearrange the first sentence by moving *hypocrisy* to the beginning as in the second sentence. Similarly, we can place additional words between existing words:

> *I admire the poetry of T. S. Eliot*
> *I <u>really</u> admire the poetry of T. S. Eliot*

However, in both cases, it would be impossible to carry out these operations on parts of words:

> * *I can't hypo <u>stand</u> crisy*
> * *I ad <u>really</u> mire the poetry of T. S. Eliot*

Words are typically minimal free-standing units which cannot be interrupted. When dealing with combinations such as *world-class* and *world war* which we mentioned earlier, this basic principle will often still apply:

> * *I thought he was a world <u>truly</u> class cricketer*
> * *There were fears that there would be another world <u>terrible</u> war*

However, this is a more problematic area given that there are other constraints on the order in which some items can occur and given that items such as multi-word verbs can be divided:

> *Dave <u>put off</u> the meeting until the following week*
> *Dave <u>put</u> the meeting <u>off</u> until the following week*

Both these examples are acceptable, and seem to contradict our sense that words are uninterruptible. Nevertheless, we would still instinctively wish to signal the existence of multi-word verbs as identifiable items which merit a separate definition.

This takes us a little nearer to a solution to our problem. Just as we might treat *put off* in the sense of 'postpone' as a separate item so, conversely, we are unlikely to treat *cats* in our much earlier example of *Old fat cats like to sleep in quiet sunny places* as a separate word from *cat*. *Cats* is plural while *cat* is singular. Most speakers would accept that *cats* is simply a variant form of *cat*. This leads us to the notion that many items of the kind we have been discussing have both an abstract, representative form and an actual spoken or written form. For example, *cat* is an abstract form for both *cat* singular and *cats* plural, while *put off* is an abstract form meaning 'postpone' whether that form occurs as two consecutive elements (*<u>put off</u> the meeting*) or not (*<u>put</u> the meeting <u>off</u>*). At this point, it is helpful to posit the existence of abstract forms which can encompass single words as well as combinations such as *put off* and *pay through the nose*. These abstract forms are known as **lexemes**.

The distinct advantage of bringing lexemes into the picture is that it solves our problem of how to account for items which are made up of more than one word, but which we feel are sufficiently distinct to merit entry in a dictionary. In fact, the forms which are given in dictionaries (what are known as **citation forms**) are in a sense lexemes, although you need to remember that a lexeme is an abstract entity. Nevertheless, we need to be able to classify the lexemes in our language and dictionary citation forms are the closest we can come to doing this. That is why a dictionary will have *cat* as an entry but not *cats*: the citation form (together with the information that *cat* is a noun) is sufficient indication that there is a lexeme *cat* which could also have a plural form *cats*.

Further factors about lexemes are usually reflected in the way that entries in dictionaries are organised. If, for example, you look up *host* in the dictionary you will see that *host* can mean someone who is holding a party of some kind, or a large number (as in *a host of angels*) or the bread used in the Christian church to signify the body of Christ. However, these three meanings are unrelated to one another and it is appropriate that each meaning should have a separate entry in the dictionary. In other words, there are three separate lexemes which are represented by the **word-form** *host*. This is an example of **homonymy**: a **homonym** is a word-form which just happens to be the same as another word-form even though their meanings are unrelated. By contrast, some lexemes have more than one meaning. A good example of this is *mouse*. First and foremost, *mouse* is defined as 'a small rodent', but we are also familiar with *mouse* as an item of IT hardware. Since the latter meaning is clearly derived from the former (a computer mouse supposedly resembles an actual mouse), we are unlikely to claim that *mouse* and *mouse* are separate lexemes. Instead we would probably suggest that they are related meanings of the same lexeme. This is an example of **polysemy**: in other words, one lexeme has two or more related meanings.

There is a value then in positing an abstract form, the lexeme, which helps us to get round some of the difficulties of defining 'word'. Later we will see how there are similar abstract concepts for looking at the smaller units which make up words and those units of speech which make up the sound system of the language. From now on, 'lexeme' is used if this term is appropriate, but 'word' is used for convenience and when it is unlikely to cause any misunderstanding.

Before we progress any further, it may be valuable to explain other terms used for discussing words in general. We use the term **vocabulary** to talk about words collectively. For example, we may say of someone that they have a large vocabulary or we may have to learn some vocabulary to develop our knowledge of a foreign language. In linguistics, a term which is often used in preference to vocabulary is **lexis**. Lexis is a collective term for words in general or for the vocabulary of a specific language. You may also come across the term **subject-specific lexis** (a set of specialised words relating to a particular topic) or you may find instances of 'lexis' being modified in some way: for example, 'polysyllabic lexis' or 'scientific lexis'. When we examine language in relation to its lexis, we are examining it on a **lexical level** (a term already used at the beginning of this chapter). A **lexical item** is an alternative way of referring to a lexeme and a **lexical set** is a group of closely related words of the same word class (for instance, the names of fruits form a lexical set). You may also encounter the term **lexicon**, which refers to the vocabulary of a language (for example, the English lexicon) but is sometimes used to refer to a type of dictionary.

□ **compound words** ⇨ 3.5
□ **multi-word verbs** ⇨ 3.6

2.2 WORD CLASSES

The previous section has shown us that in talking about words the concept of a lexeme is a very useful one in that it covers items which are not typical words and therefore goes some way to solving any problems involved in defining 'word'. Another issue which we need to consider when discussing words (or lexemes) is that all words belong to a particular category. Many people know that a particular linguistic item is, say, a noun or a verb although they may not be aware of the full range of categories into which words can be subdivided. These categories are known as **word classes**. There are nine major word classes and two minor ones. The major ones are **nouns, verbs, adjectives, adverbs, pronouns, determiners, auxiliaries, prepositions** and **conjunctions**. These classes are useful because they group words together according to particular characteristics which they share and give us more precise labels to use when referring to certain words or lexemes.

There are two minor word classes and they require a brief mention. The first of these is the class of **interjections**. These are the little exclamations such as *ouch* or *wow* or *mmm* with which spoken language is peppered. The reason, however, that interjections are only a minor word class is that they do not enter into grammatical structures, unlike words of the classes listed above. They are often, in fact, uttered in isolation as a response to a comment, question or event. The other minor class is the group of **particles**. This class consists of just a handful of words of which the most notable are the particle *to* as in *to be or not to be,* and the negative particle *not*.

One group of words which is treated in different ways by linguists is the group of **numerals**. It includes both **cardinal numerals** – *one, two, three* and so on – and **ordinal numerals** such as *first, second,* and *third* as well as **fractions** such as *a quarter, two-thirds* and *five-eighths*. Sometimes numerals are treated as a separate word class and sometimes they are seen as subsets of the major classes of pronouns and determiners. The latter approach is adopted here.

- ☐ **nouns** ⇨ 2.4
- ☐ **verbs** ⇨ 2.5
- ☐ **adjectives** ⇨ 2.6
- ☐ **adverbs** ⇨ 2.7
- ☐ **pronouns** ⇨ 2.8
- ☐ **determiners** ⇨ 2.9
- ☐ **numerals** ⇨ 2.8, 2.9
- ☐ **auxiliaries** ⇨ 2.10
- ☐ **prepositions** ⇨ 2.11
- ☐ **conjunctions** ⇨ 2.12

2.3   OPEN AND CLOSED CLASSES OF WORDS

One question which students sometimes ask is, how many words are there in the English language? If we're used to using and referring to dictionaries, we probably have a notion that it is possible to count how many words there are in our language. Dictionaries usually proclaim how many entries they contain and it is tempting to believe that, if we possessed the largest dictionary, we would be in possession of all the words in the language. It doesn't take much thought, however, to realise that it is impossible to know precisely how many words there are in the language or to produce a comprehensive and accurate list of them. For one thing, the language is constantly changing: new words enter the language and other words become obsolete all the time so even the most recent dictionary (be it in book form, or on CD-ROM or on the Internet) is out-of-date the moment it appears. Then, it is arguable whether obsolete words, which exist in texts such as the plays of Shakespeare (which are still performed of course), should be included in the count or not. A further problem is when to include new words, especially if they are slang (words which tend to have a short linguistic shelf-life) or from a foreign source. Should very specialised medical and scientific words be counted? Additionally, old words are given new meanings. At what point can we say that an additional or alternative meaning for an existing word has resulted in a new word or the replacement of an old one? The problems involved in 'measuring' the lexicon seem endless.

What we can do, however, is tackle the question in a slightly different way in order to achieve something approaching a satisfactory answer. We have seen above that we can label all words in terms of the word class they belong to. Clearly, this means that the words in each class possess particular characteristics and properties which differ partly or totally from those of words in other classes. One observation that we can make in fact is that it is much easier to come up with a fairly accurate total number of words in some classes than in others.

Look carefully at the following random collection of words, which are drawn from all nine major word classes.

pig	*autumn*	*me*	*explain*
they	*which*	*sing*	*suddenly*
from	*today*	*biology*	*and*
truth	*could*	*the*	*extraordinary*
since	*hot*	*announce*	*in*

Now try to divide these words into two separate groups. These two groups will not necessarily be of equal size. It is probably best to be guided by your instinct in making this division: don't worry about trying to explain your rationale in deciding which word goes into which group.

When asked to do this same experiment, speakers most typically and without any prompting or assistance divide the words as follows:

group one
pig, autumn, explain, sing, suddenly, today, biology, truth, extraordinary, hot, announce

group two
me, they, which, from, and, could, the, since, in

The words in the first group appear to be different from those in the second group in a number of ways. First, the words in the first group are longer on average than those in the other group (not just in terms of letters but more significantly in terms of syllables as well as units of construction such as in *suddenly* which consists of *sudden + ly*). Second, they are far more specific in meaning than those in group two. For example, *hot* has a specific and imaginable meaning in the way that an item such as *the* definitely has not. Third, words in group one could be linked together to make what would be a rather odd but nevertheless meaningful string such as *today autumn hot extraordinary* or *pig announce truth,* whereas no matter how hard you try the items in group two allow no such process, since the words in this group have little meaning except in relation to other words of the group one variety.

The words in group one are all either **nouns** (*pig, autumn, biology, truth*), **verbs** (*explain, sing, announce*), **adjectives** (*extraordinary, hot*), or **adverbs** (*suddenly, today*). Nouns, verbs, adjectives and adverbs are **open class** words. The words in group two consist of **pronouns** (*me, they, which*), a **determiner** (*the*) and an **auxiliary** (*could*), **prepositions** (*from, in*) and **conjunctions** (*and, since*). Pronouns, determiners, auxiliaries, prepositions and conjunctions are **closed class** words. The reason for these particular names is that the open classes form an extremely large group and it is the extent of the open classes which makes it virtually impossible to count the number of words in the language, especially since the words in this group are constantly changing. By contrast, the closed classes form a much smaller group and it is possible to make a finite list of its members. The words in closed classes change very slowly: new words rarely enter these classes and existing words rarely change their meaning or become obsolete.

The words in the open classes are known as **lexical words** or **content words** and those in the closed classes as **grammatical words** or **function words**. We noted that the lexical words in our earlier list were longer than the grammatical words. This is not a coincidence: lexical words may be **monosyllabic** but they are equally likely to consist of two, three or even more syllables. (We can use the term **disyllabic** to refer to a word of two syllables and **polysyllabic** to refer to one of three or more.) Grammatical words, on the other hand, typically contain just one or two syllables. In addition, the lexical words are drawn from a very wide range of languages which have influenced English. These include Latin, Greek, French and many, many more, probably over a hundred. Although some lexical words have been in English since its earliest stages, new lexical words have entered the language throughout its history and of course still do so. The vast majority of grammatical words are of either Old English or Old Norse origin. If they derive from Old English, they have been part of the language from the outset. Old Norse had a very strong influence on English in its early centuries and there are a number of grammatical words derived from this language of the Viking invaders, so these have existed in English for a very long time, most of them appearing in written form before the year 1100.

Another striking difference between lexical and grammatical words is the frequency with which we use them. Whereas there may be some lexical words which we will only use very occasionally, hardly an utterance goes by without using little grammatical words like *the* or *and*. You might think that such frequency of usage would jar on a listener but we give very little sentence stress to grammatical words when we speak and in some respects listeners barely notice them.

So, to answer the question of how many words there are in the English language, we might give the following response. The open classes are very extensive and contain hundreds of thousands of words. Not only this but, because language change affects these classes much more than it affects the closed classes, it is impossible to count the number of words in the open classes. By contrast, the number of words in the closed classes is far fewer and change is very slow. It is therefore possible to count the number of words in the closed classes, should we wish to, and we would find the closed classes to contain only several hundred words.

In the following sections, we will work through the word classes, beginning with the open classes, and look at the features which characterise them and at ways of determining which class any individual word belongs to. There is actually a great deal to say about the members of each group, but for the time being we will mainly concern ourselves with simple ways to identify word class. Sections 2.4 to 2.7 explain how to identify words which belong to any of the open classes. As far as possible, these sections show you how to assign words to the correct category chiefly by looking at their grammatical properties – where they occur or how they combine with other words. When we move on to the closed classes (sections 2.8 to 2.12) fairly comprehensive lists and tables of the words in each class will be given (something which would be impossible for the open classes) although there will also be some exploration of the functions of the various groups. As you progress through this book, you will find that you gradually understand more and more about the characteristics of each word class. If at any stage you are in doubt as to which word class a particular item belongs to, then you can check this in a dictionary. The word class is usually given in an abbreviated form (such as *n.* for noun) but there will be a key to these abbreviations, probably at the front of the dictionary. You need to bear in mind that it is possible for a word to belong to more than one word class – *access*, for example, can be both a noun and a verb – and you need to check which category you are dealing with by considering the word in its grammatical context.

2.4 NOUNS

Sometimes, speakers know a simplistic and traditional definition of a noun, which is that it is a naming word. In one sense, this is an appropriate way to define a noun. In fact, *noun* derives from the Latin word for a name, which is *nomen*. Nouns make up one of the most central categories of all word classes (the other being verbs). What we mean by 'central' is that nouns and verbs are the most useful elements in constructing a very basic sentence such as

noun	verb	noun
cats	*like*	*cream*

It is significant that children normally learn several nouns before they learn any other words, and that about 75 per cent of a child's first 50 or so words will be nouns.

The simplest way to test whether a word is a noun (and far more reliable than asking yourself if the item in question is a naming word) is to isolate it and then see if it is possible to place *the* (the **definite article**) in front of it. For instance you might want to test your judgement that the underlined words in the following sentences are nouns, particularly because they are both naming something (an animal and a place respectively):

much to my amazement a large fat <u>cat</u> was sleeping in our <u>garden</u>

You can isolate *cat* and *garden* to see if the definite article test works. It is perfectly possible to say *the cat* and *the garden*, so this tells us that they are indeed nouns. However, it's easy to overlook other nouns which name things less concrete than *cat* and *garden*. In the above example, *amazement* is also a noun (*the amazement* is again perfectly possible as in *the amazement I felt at that moment was obvious*), although it refers to something intangible and rather more abstract than *cat* or *garden*. Even though *cat* and *garden* are concrete and *amazement* is abstract, all nouns of this kind which can be preceded by *the* are known as **common nouns**. Sometimes, though, it can be useful to subdivide common nouns into **concrete nouns,** which refer to measurable or tangible objects, and **abstract nouns,** which refer to concepts and things which have no material existence.

In contrast to common nouns there is a group of nouns known as **proper nouns**. The difference between common and proper nouns is that proper nouns name something or someone unique. They are the nouns which in writing we would write with a capital letter and which are the names of places, people, pets, rivers, months, days of the week and so on. Examples of proper nouns might include *London* (the name of a unique place), *Jane* (the name of a specific person – although of course there will be more than one person called Jane), and *Monday* (the name of a particular day). The way in which proper nouns differ most obviously from common nouns is that the definite article test doesn't really work on them:

common noun	proper noun
the city	**the London*
the woman	**the Jane*
the day	**the Monday*

However, there is the possibility of *the* preceding these nouns in certain contexts. For example:

The Jane I know is the one with blonde hair
The London my father remembers was a much cleaner place
The Monday I mean is the one just before Christmas

(And in fact there are one or two proper nouns that have *the* as part of their name and do not occur without it. Examples include *The Thames* and *The Hague*.) More importantly, proper nouns such as these occur in the same positions in phrases and sentences in which common nouns occur:

The cat is my best friend
Jane is my best friend
The man was lost in London
The man was lost in the maze

The position in which members of a word class occur in a sentence is one of the key factors which characterises them. We will look more closely at the grammatical context in which nouns occur in Part III.

☐ **definite articles** ⇨ 2.9
☐ **meanings of common nouns** ⇨ 3.9
☐ **singular and plural nouns** ⇨ 4.3
☐ **noun phrases** ⇨ 5.2

2.5   LEXICAL VERBS

Verbs, like nouns, are of central importance as a class of words. You could in fact consider them as the most important aspect of language because of their central role in constructing sentences and the influence they exert over other elements in a sentence. 'Verb' derives from the Latin *verbum* which means 'word' and this is an appropriate indication of the importance of this word class.

Verbs are sometimes notionally defined as 'doing words' but this is not a very accurate way to approach identifying them. For one thing, verbs do not always refer to actions: they can also refer to states. Consider the verbs in the following sentence:

Jane strolls into the park where she relaxes and feels content

Whereas *strolls* clearly refers to a deliberate physical activity, *relaxes* is less obviously an action (although still a physical process) while *feels* refers not to an action of Jane's but to her state of mind. Verbs which refer to physical processes, such as *stroll* and *relax* are referred to as **dynamic verbs** in contrast to **stative verbs** which refer to states and conditions.

A more watertight (and grammatical) way to check if a word is a verb is to look for a property that only verbs possess (much as we did with nouns). This is the ability to make a contrast between **present tense** and **past tense**. If we isolate the verbs underlined in the above sentence, we see that it is possible to form them in both the present tense and the past:

present tense	past tense
walk(s) (I walk / she walks)	*walked (I walked / she walked)*
relax(es)	*relaxed*
feel(s)	*felt*

To reiterate an earlier point, many word forms exist as members of more than one word class, and this is particularly true of nouns and verbs. An example of this from the given sentence is *park*. In the example, *park* is clearly a noun – it is preceded by *the* (and it is naming something – in this case a place). However, it is also possible to use *park* as a verb where contrasts of tense can be employed:

Kathy <u>parks</u> the car	(present tense)
Kathy <u>parked</u> the car	(past tense)

It is easy to assign a word to the wrong word class if you do not pay attention to how the word is being used in context. You will find that your ability to identify word classes will become more secure as you learn more about the positions which the different word classes take up within the structure of a sentence: we will come to this more fully later but we will use this approach to some extent in our discussion of words in the remaining classes.

The heading at the top of this section refers to **lexical verbs** rather than simply 'verbs'. Lexical verb is a term which is sometimes used to distinguish verbs like *walk, relax, feel* and *park* from **auxiliaries** or **auxiliary verbs** which make up a very small closed class of words. Auxiliaries are added to the lexical verb for various purposes. For example, the following sentence uses the auxiliary *has* to indicate that the process the lexical verb *finished* refers to is complete and that this fact is still of some relevance:

Ian <u>has finished</u> the book (so I can borrow it next)

Although *has* provides a useful shade of meaning in this example, it is *finished* which denotes exactly what Ian has done (it might be contrasted with *Ian has <u>burnt</u> the book*, for example) and it is this specificity of meaning which is indicated when we say *finished* is a lexical verb (and of course it belongs to an open or lexical group of words). Lexical verbs are also sometimes known as **full verbs** or **main verbs** but it is perfectly acceptable simply to refer to them as verbs provided there is no need to distinguish between them and auxiliaries.

> ☐ **auxiliaries** ⇨ 2.10
> ☐ **verb meanings** ⇨ 3.9
> ☐ **tenses** ⇨ 5.3

2.6   ADJECTIVES

Adjectives, while not as central as nouns and verbs in the basic structure of sentences, are nevertheless an important and relatively distinctive open class.

Although they are traditionally defined as describing words, this is not the basis for accurate identification of adjectives since words of other classes also have descriptive properties. We can identify adjectives by reference to each of two features – first, the positions in which they appear in sentences and, second, their ability to be graded.

With regard to the positions in which adjectives occur, **central adjectives** are able to appear in two positions. First, they can occur before a noun, as in *the extraordinary boy* or *lucky Jim*. In this position their function is **attributive**. In other words, they give us information about an attribute of the noun. Secondly, they can occur after certain verbs like *be* and *appear* (what are known as **copular verbs**) as in *the boy is extraordinary* or *Jim appears lucky*. In this position their function is **predicative**. In other words, they occur in the **predicate** – the part of a clause which consists of the verb and the items which follow it. Central adjectives, then, are found in both attributive and predicative position. However, there are some adjectives which only appear in one of these two positions:

predicative only	
the child is afraid	**the afraid child*
attributive only	
the chief mourner	**the mourner is chief*

Adjectives such as *afraid* and *chief* are clearly less central than adjectives which occur in both attributive and predicative position. You need to be careful not to confuse adjectives with nouns since nouns can also occur in these positions. The difference, however, is that a noun is highly unlikely to be able to occur in both in a comparable way to an adjective:

position	adjective	noun
attributive	*the extraordinary boy*	*the newspaper boy*
predicative	*the boy is extraordinary*	**the boy is newspaper*
predicative	*Jim is lucky*	*Jim is boss*
attributive	*lucky Jim*	**boss Jim*

Although nouns are likely to be far less flexible than adjectives in their ability to appear in both these positions, it is helpful to have another characteristic to identify in adjectives in order to assign them to the correct class. This is the fact that most adjectives are **gradable**. In other words, we can indicate to what extent the quality referred to by an adjective applies. For example, a person may be *lucky*, or they may be *very lucky*, *fairly lucky*, *extremely lucky* and so on.

Intensifiers like v*ery*, *fairly* and *extremely* precede adjectives in this way but not nouns. (Be careful here though since some adverbs can also be graded in this way.) Combinations such as **very newspaper* and **fairly boss* are clearly not permissible. There are one or two adjectives like *perfect* and *unique* which it might be unusual to grade since their meaning is absolute. In actual fact, though, you may come across these 'ungradable' adjectives being graded as in *a most perfect day* and *an extremely unique gift*.

In conclusion, central adjectives can be identified by their ability not only to occur both attributively and predicatively but also to be preceded by intensifiers. A handful of adjectives don't meet all these criteria, but if you're uncertain whether a word is an adjective or a noun you can of course apply the definite article test which we used to identify nouns.

□ **meanings of adjectives** ⇨ 3.9
□ **other ways to grade adjectives** ⇨ 4.5
□ **position of adjectives** ⇨ 5.2, 5.4
□ **copular verbs** ⇨ 6.6

2.7 ADVERBS

Just as adjectives are less central than nouns and verbs, so adverbs are less central than the other three open classes. In fact, they are a very diverse group and this can make them difficult both to define and to identify. We have to identify adverbs by looking at several features which characterise them – although not all these features will apply to all adverbs. Like adjectives, many adverbs have a describing purpose in a sentence and adverbs have other features in common with adjectives too, but the differences are important and crucial to note if you are not to confuse these two classes. You can check whether a word is an adjective or adverb by seeing which position it can appear in. If the word can appear in **attributive** position then it is an adjective:

the <u>lovely</u> hotel	adjective
the <u>careful</u> person	adjective
* the <u>carefully</u> person	adverb

Adverbs have the ability not only to give information about, amongst other things, how, where and when, but also to allow you to comment on whole utterances. For instance:

<u>Fortunately,</u> <u>today</u> the dog has eaten his food <u>quietly</u> <u>outside.</u>
comment   when   how   where

You will see that two of the adverbs in this sentence – *fortunately* and *quietly* – end in *-ly*. This typifies many adverbs particularly of the 'comment' and 'how' types. This may help you to identify some adverbs but be careful not to confuse them with any adjectives that end in *-ly* such as *lovely* and *likely*.

In the example *Fortunately today the dog has eaten his food quietly outside*, you may notice that adverbs seem to be less central elements in a sentence. If you stripped the adverbs away from the example, the essence of the sentence – *the dog has eaten his food* – still remains. Only occasionally are adverbs crucial to the completion of a sentence's meaning.

Adverbs can be divided into three subclasses – **adjuncts, conjuncts** and **disjuncts.** (In Chapter 7 we will, however, extend the use of these terms to include units larger than single adverbs but which function like adverbs.) The first subclass, adjuncts, is by far the largest.

Adjuncts have a certain amount in common with adjectives and might be considered their first cousins:

> *The <u>careful</u> surgeon completed the operation*   adjective
> *The surgeon completed the operation <u>carefully</u>*   adverb (adjunct)

What *careful* and *carefully* have in common in these two examples is their ability to provide more information – about the surgeon in the first example and about how the surgeon performed the operation in the second example. The meanings of these two sentences are clearly closely linked (we would expect a *careful* surgeon to operate *carefully*) but not identical. Further, an important difference between the adjective in the first sentence and the adverb in the second is that the adjective *careful* can only appear in this sentence in its given position preceding *surgeon* whereas the adverb *carefully* could appear in any one of several positions:

> *The surgeon completed the operation <u>carefully</u>*
> *<u>Carefully</u>, the surgeon completed the operation*
> *The surgeon <u>carefully</u> completed the operation*
> *? The surgeon completed <u>carefully</u> the operation*

An adverb such as *carefully* is typical of many adverbs in the adjunct subclass in that it modifies information given by one or more of the other elements.

In terms of their meaning, adverbs which are adjuncts provide us with information about how, where, when and to what extent. Adverbs which tell us how are **adverbs of manner**:

> *The surgeon completed the operation <u>carefully</u>*
> *<u>Silently</u>, Arusha observed what Dave was doing*

Adverbs of place indicate location or direction:

Put the parcel <u>here</u>	location
She turned the key <u>clockwise</u>	direction

Adverbs of time denote when something happened, how long it lasted or how often it happened:

Someone saved my life <u>tonight</u>	when
The symphony lasted <u>forever</u>	how long
He telephoned her <u>nightly</u>	how often

Adverbs of degree indicate extent, including whether a piece of information applies to more than one item:

She found her job <u>particularly</u> difficult in the winter
She ignored him at the party <u>simply</u> to make a point
She loved him, and he loved her <u>too</u>

Some of the adverbs of degree form a further subset of **intensifiers**. The adverb *particularly* in the set of examples above is an intensifier: it indicates a point on an imagined scale and can therefore be contrasted with other intensifiers:

She found her job <u>particularly / somewhat / fairly / slightly</u> difficult ...

You can see from the examples of the different types of adjuncts that adverbs can appear both before and after items which they qualify, although there are restrictions on this. Conjuncts and disjuncts often have more flexibility of position than many adjuncts as their functions are essentially different.

Sometimes adjuncts are **wh-words**. A *wh*-word is – unsurprisingly – one which begins with *wh*- although *how* and *however* are also included in the *wh*-group. Examples of *wh*-adverbs include *how*, *when*, *where*, and *why*. They often take the place of a regular adverb in a question, although they can occur in other constructions. In addition to replacing simply another adverb, they can also take the place of a larger unit such as a phrase or a clause:

The surgeon performed the operation <u>carefully</u>	adverb
The surgeon performed the operation <u>with great care</u>	phrase
<u>How</u> did the surgeon perform the operation?	
He telephoned her <u>nightly</u>	adverb
He telephoned her <u>every night</u>	phrase

> *When* did he telephone her?
> *How often* did he telephone her?
> She fell asleep *outside*   adverb
> She fell asleep *on the sofa*   phrase
> > *Where* did she fall asleep?
> She went to France *to buy some champagne*   clause
> > *Why* did she go to France?

Further uses of *wh*-adverbs, as well as larger units such as phrases and clauses, are explored in Part III.

Adverbs which are adjuncts give additional information either about a particular element of a sentence or about the event referred to in a sentence. In this respect they contrast with disjuncts and conjuncts which relate only to complete sentences and do not give information as such. One function of disjuncts is to comment on what is being said:

> *Obviously*, I should have told her what happened
> *(It is obvious that I should have told her ...)*
> *Probably*, I should have told her what happened
> *(It is probable that I should have told her ...)*

A further function of disjuncts is to indicate the 'voice' in which something is said:

> *Frankly*, I should have told her what happened
> *(I am being frank when I say I should have told her what happened)*
> *Confidentially*, I think she will lose her job
> *(I am being confidential when I say I think she will lose her job)*

Whereas disjuncts relate to the sentence in which they occur (or possibly to just part of it if it is a complex sentence), conjuncts relate one sentence or one part of a sentence to another. They include adverbs such as *moreover, therefore, however* and *nevertheless*. If one of these conjuncts appeared in an isolated sentence it would seem slightly strange:

> *They decided to go for a picnic nevertheless*

The presence of *nevertheless* here implies the existence of a previous statement indicating that a picnic was not a good idea:

> *1. It looked as if it might rain*
> *2. They decided to go for a picnic nevertheless*

A conjunct therefore has the property of linking two sentences together. It could also link two parts of the same sentence:

> *She wasn't free to go to New York at Christmas and <u>besides</u> she couldn't afford it*

It is important to remember here that the adverbs are not central to the structure of the sentence. Only occasionally are adverbs crucial to the completion of a core sentence.

- ☐ *wh*-words ⇨ 2.13
- ☐ **formation of adverbs** ⇨ 3.4
- ☐ **adverb phrases** ⇨ 5.4
- ☐ **adverbs as obligatory elements** ⇨ 6.8
- ☐ **adjuncts, conjuncts, disjuncts** ⇨ 7.11
- ☐ **conjuncts** ⇨ 8.6

2.8   PRONOUNS

We move now to the closed class words and how to identify them. Since the closed classes form much smaller groups of words than nouns, verbs, adjectives and adverbs, it will be possible to list them fairly comprehensively. We will also consider what characterises the closed class words and the functions they perform.

We will begin our survey of closed class words by looking at pronouns. There is a close relationship between pronouns and determiners and we will look at this in section 2.9. When we were looking at the words of the open classes, notional definitions of word classes – such as 'a noun is a naming word' – were sometimes mentioned. We saw that these definitions were helpful in some respects but misleading in others. The same is true of the notional definition of a pronoun which is that it 'takes the place of a noun'. In reality, the picture is far more complex than this. It is certainly true that pronouns can function as substitutes for nouns. In the following example, the personal pronoun *she* acts as a substitute for the proper noun *Michelle*:

> <u>*Michelle*</u> *was offered an exciting new job and <u>she</u> decided to take it*

Here, the pronoun *she* is used to avoid a clumsy repetition of *Michelle*. In the following example, however, the pronoun – this time *them* – replaces not a single noun but a noun together with some other words which are dependent on it (namely, a **noun phrase**):

> *Annette left some fresh jam doughnuts on the table*
> *and Ashley came in and scoffed them*

Here, the pronoun *them* replaces not the plural noun *doughnuts* but the noun phrase *some fresh jam doughnuts*. It is also possible for a pronoun to replace part of a phrase:

> *Sarah chose a Kenyan safari but Martin preferred a South African one*

In this example, *a Kenyan safari* is a noun phrase. What Martin actually preferred was *a South African safari* (another noun phrase which parallels *a Kenyan safari*) but part of the phrase – the noun *safari* – has been replaced by the pronoun *one*.

As well as performing this substitution role to avoid unnecessary repetition of both single nouns and longer phrases, some pronouns are used not in a substitutional function but in order to refer to what is unknown:

> *Somebody has stolen my chocolate muffin*
> *I looked, but there was nothing in the cupboard*

In these two examples, we could not claim that *somebody* and *nothing* are replacing nouns or noun phrases.

Table 2.1   The primary pronouns of English

		Personal pronouns		Possessive pronouns		Reflexive pronouns
		subjective form	objective form	dependent form	independent form	
singular	1st person	I	me	my	mine	myself
	2nd person	you	you	your	yours	yourself
	3rd person	he	him	his	his	himself
		she	her	her	hers	herself
		it	it	its	(its)	itself
		they	them	their	theirs	themself
plural	1st person	we	us	our	ours	ourselves
	2nd person	you	you	your	yours	yourselves
	3rd person	they	them	their	theirs	themselves

So far, we have considered just a few examples of pronouns: *she, them, one, somebody* and *nothing*. Pronouns can be divided into several subclasses of which the most central are the **primary pronouns**. These are shown in Table 2.1. The most significant feature of the primary pronouns is that they are not a random group but a systematic one, as Table 2.1 shows. First, there is a basic distinction of **number**: primary pronouns, like most nouns, are either singular or plural. There is a further distinction of **person** – first, second or third. This distinction is closely linked with the form which verbs take although this is far more noticeable in many other languages than it is in English. However, we do make a distinction in English in the present tense between third person singular and, say, first person singular: in other words *she laughs* contrasts with *I laugh*. All the primary pronouns occur in several forms as **personal pronouns**, as **possessive pronouns** and as **reflexive pronouns**. The personal pronouns are subdivided again into the **subjective** form and the **objective** form. This distinction relates to the position in which the pronouns occur. The subjective form is used when the pronoun is in the subject position in a sentence – namely before the verb – whereas the objective form is used when it is in the object position after the verb:

> *They love football*
> * *Them love football*
> *Richard telephoned me*
> * *Richard telephoned I*

Some flexibility exists in the use of subjective and objective forms, however. In informal usage, for example, *me* might occur in subject position:

> *Me and Julian went to the cinema last night*

The possessive pronouns take either a **dependent** or an **independent** form. The independent form acts as a replacement for a complete noun phrase:

> *This house is <u>the doctor's and her husband's</u>*
> *This house is <u>theirs</u>*

By contrast, the dependent form precedes a noun which it qualifies:

> *This is <u>Janet's</u> house*
> *This is <u>her</u> house*

Dependent possessive pronouns may also be classified as determiners and in many respects they are more typical determiners than they are pronouns. However, for the sake of completeness they are included in the set of primary pronouns. **Reflexive pronouns** are used to refer back to someone or something mentioned previously:

> *Gregory went to Lambeth Palace by himself*
> *I fell down the stairs and (I) hurt myself*
> * *I fell down the stairs and the splinters hurt myself*

The ungrammaticality of the last example above shows that there are restrictions on the referential scope of reflexive pronouns.

Table 2.1 shows that the set of *they* pronouns occurs as both a plural and a singular set. We have already noted that changes to closed classes of words happen very slowly but the acceptance of the *they* set as singular pronouns is an example of a recent development. As users have become more and more conscious of gender issues in the language, they have looked for a way of avoiding references which are intended to be non-gender-specific but which actually suggest the male of the species. For example, in a sentence such as *A human being is unique among mammals in that he has a thumb* the pronoun *he* is, in theory, meant to refer to any human, male or female. However, when speakers encounter *he* in a context such as this, they often assume maleness. Sometimes speakers try to get round this difficulty by using *he or she*:

> *If any student would like a parking permit he or she should go to reception*

The frequent use of *he or she* can seem rather clumsy and what has happened increasingly is that speakers have started to use *they* (albeit with the plural form of the verb) when the gender of a single referent is unknown. Further evidence that speakers are starting to treat *they* as a singular pronoun is the use of the reflexive form *themself* (for example, *Someone fell off the roof and they hurt themself very badly*) which of course is in contrast to the plural *themselves*.

You will notice that the independent form of *it*, namely *its*, is bracketed in Table 2.1 This is because there is no actual reason why that form should not exist but in practice we don't really use it:

> *This is the dog's dinner*
> *This is its dinner*
> *? I will have my dinner while the dog has its*

Most speakers would probably say that this last example sounds clumsy but we could use it without being ungrammatical.

A further pronoun which could be included in the table of primary pronouns is the **generic pronoun** *one*. This is used in the third person singular (for example, *One needs to take care of oneself*) but is becoming increasingly rare particularly since it is considered very formal. The generic pronoun *one* is distinct from the **substitute pronoun** *one* which we saw in an earlier example (*Sarah chose a Kenyan safari and Martin chose a South African one*). Here, *one* is functioning as a substitute for *safari* and clearly not as a way of referring to an unspecified person.

We have looked at the primary pronouns of English in some detail and we will now look briefly at the other subclasses of pronoun. First, there are several **wh-pronouns** and these, like the primary pronouns, can be divided into subclasses:

interrogative pronouns
who, whom, whose, what, which

relative pronouns
who, whom, which, that

nominal relative pronouns
who, whoever, whosoever, whom, whomsoever
which, whichever, what, whatever, whatsoever

conditional pronouns
who(so)ever, whom(so)ever, which(so)ever, what(so)ever

Many of the forms listed above have more than one function. *Who*, for instance, can be an interrogative pronoun, a relative pronoun, and a nominal relative pronoun. **Interrogative pronouns** are used to ask questions:

Liz has a flat in Majorca
Who has a flat in Majorca?

Relative pronouns are used to introduce relative clauses. Similarly, **nominal relative pronouns** introduce nominal relative clauses while **conditional wh-pronouns** introduce *wh*-conditional clauses. These three types of *wh*-pronouns and their associated clauses are considered in detail in Part III but here are examples of each type within the context of a sentence:

relative *wh*-pronoun   *This is the car which I want to buy*
nominal relative *wh*-pronoun *Who to ask was something of a problem*
conditional *wh*-pronoun   *Whatever happens, I'm leaving*

You will notice that *wh*-pronouns such as *whoever* can also take the form *whosoever*. This is a slightly more formal usage but it can also be used for emphasis. The pronoun *whom* is the objective form of *who* but again it is rather formal and most speakers rarely use it now, if at all.

The next group of pronouns is the **indefinite pronouns**. The main ones are:

some	*any*	*none*	*all*
someone	*anyone*	*no one*	*everyone*
somebody	*anybody*	*nobody*	*everybody*
something	*anything*	*nothing*	*everything*

More often than not, these pronouns do not have an identifiable referent and are not therefore functioning as noun or noun phrase substitutes as such. The pronouns *either, neither, both* and *each* in addition to *enough, much, many, few, little, several* and *another* are also classified as indefinite pronouns although they may seem less clearly 'indefinite' than the other examples given here.

Finally, there are the four **demonstrative pronouns**. These are:

this	*that*
these	*those*

This and *that* are singular and have plural counterparts in *these* and *those*. The demonstrative pronouns, like the primary pronouns, are **deictic**. This means that their meaning is relative to the speaker or the context. In the sentence *I want these not those* where the speaker is referring to two boxes of chocolates, we would infer that the box of chocolates the speaker wants is whichever one is nearer to them. We will look more closely at **deixis** in Chapter 8.

To summarise, we have identified four subclasses of pronouns, some of which we have subdivided again:

primary pronouns
    personal pronouns
    possessive pronouns
    reflexive pronoun

wh-pronouns
    interrogative *wh*-pronouns
    relative *wh*-pronouns
    nominal relative *wh*-pronouns
    conditional *wh*-pronouns

indefinite pronouns

demonstrative pronouns

It would also have been possible to subdivide the indefinite pronouns into further subclasses. In any case, you can see that although pronouns make up a relatively small set of words, they fulfil a considerable range of functions.

One final subclass of pronouns which we need to mention briefly is the subclass of **numerals**. Numerals subdivide into cardinal numerals (*one, two three...*), ordinal numerals (*first, second, third...*) and fractions (*a quarter, two-thirds, five-eighths...*). We have already seen how the substitute pronoun *one*, which is a cardinal numeral, operates. Here is a further example containing this particular pronoun:

> *Terry wanted a new piano and Keith wanted <u>one</u> too*

Here, *one* is a substitute for *a new piano* and is a means of avoiding a clumsy repetition of this phrase. The other cardinal and ordinal numerals can function in a comparable way by making language more economical:

> *<u>Seven</u> turned up for the rehearsal*
> *Aidan made three wishes on his birthday: the <u>first</u> was for his brother*

In the first example above, *seven* stands for all the various individuals who turned up (making it unnecessary to list them) while in the second example *first* refers to one of the three wishes. It is arguable that cardinal numerals could also be classified as a subclass of nouns since in certain contexts they can be made plural – a central characteristic of nouns.

> *They arrived at the party in <u>twos</u> and <u>threes</u>*

Furthermore, they appear in comparable positions to head nouns:

> *They were an experienced and skilful <u>team</u>*   concrete noun
> *They were an experienced and skilful <u>eleven</u>*   numeral

Numerals are a slightly problematic group to classify. However, the fact that they share similarities in different contexts with nouns, pronouns and determiners is a reason to classify them within these classes rather than as a word class in their own right.

> ☐ **nouns** ⇨ 2.4
> ☐ **wh-words** ⇨ 2.13
> ☐ **subjective and objective forms** ⇨ 4.6
> ☐ **noun phrases** ⇨ 5.2

38 LEXICAL FRAMEWORKS

☐ **nominal relative clauses** ⇨ 6.12
☐ **relative clauses** ⇨ 6.13
☐ **interrogative sentences** ⇨ 7.4
☐ ***wh*-conditional clauses** ⇨ 7.11
☐ **deixis** ⇨ 8.4

2.9 DETERMINERS

Determiners are only found in noun phrases, although they are not an obligatory element of this structure. A noun phrase is a noun plus any other elements which belong to or depend on that **head noun**. Determiners only occur at the beginning of a noun phrase. Adjectives (and other nouns) can also occur before the head noun but they come after any determiners. They do not function in the same way as determiners and they possess different grammatical properties so there is no sound argument for treating determiners as a subclass of adjectives.

We will consider noun phrase structure in detail in section 5.2, but the following example shows the position of determiners in the context of a noun phrase:

determiners	premodification	head noun	postmodification
all these	*large sugary*	*doughnuts*	*filled with jam and cream*

In fact, determiners subdivide as a group into **predeterminers**, **central determiners** and **postdeterminers**. Table 2.2 illustrates the main types of determiner. One way in which determiners differ from adjectives is that there are restrictions on the number of determiners which can occur in any noun phrase whereas, in theory at least, there is no restriction on the number of adjectives. There may be a predeterminer, a central determiner and a postdeterminer but there can be no co-occurrence of any of these types. In other words, a noun phrase which included the central determiner *these* could not also contain the central determiner *some*:

* *some these delicious chocolates*

The restrictions on co-occurrence of determiners is the principle by which determiners are assigned to either the pre-, post- or central determiner groups. It is not the case, however, that any central determiner can occur with any pre- or postdeterminer. Central determiners are identified primarily on the basis

Table 2.2   Determiners

	Predeterminers	Central determiners	Postdeterminers
Articles	**definite article** **indefinite article**	the a/an	
Possessive determiners		my your his etc.	
***Wh*-determiners**	**interrogative**	*whose* *what* *which*	
	exclamative	what such		
	relative	*whose* *which*	
	nominal relative	*what* *what(so)ever* *which* *which(so)ever*	
	conditional	*what(so)ever* *which(so)ever*	
Indefinite determiners	*all* (of) *both* (of)	*some* *any* no *(n)either* *each* *every* *enough* *much* *another* *other*	*many/more/most* *few/-er/-est* *little/less/least* *several* *(every)*
Demonstrative determiners		*this* *these* *that* *those*	
Numerals	**cardinal** **ordinal**		*one, two, three ...* first, second, third ...
	fraction	*half (of)* *a third (of)* *a quarter (of) ...*	

that they cannot occur with each other. You will see from Table 2.2 that there are only a few predeterminers. The exclamatives *what* and *such* normally only occur before the central determiner *a/an* as in *What a lovely day it is*. By contrast, the indefinite predeterminers can occur with a much wider range of central determiners as in <u>*all (of)*</u> *these good ideas* or <u>*both (of)*</u> *your sisters*. Fractions are also included as predeterminers (<u>*one-third (of)*</u> *the price*) since they function in a similar way to *all* and *both*. The determiner *every* can be a central determiner preceding a postdeterminer such as a numeral – <u>*every*</u> *third day* – but *every* can also be used as a postdeterminer when its function is emphatic: *he ignored my* <u>*every*</u> *wish*.

Postdeterminers and predeterminers do not have to occur with a central determiner. However, whatever determiners do occur have a prescribed sequence. It is possible to have a predeterminer, a central determiner and a postdeterminer in one noun phrase although there are many restrictions on these combinations:

determiners			head noun	
pre-	central	post-		
all	*your*	*many*	*ideas*	*(were useless)*

Many of the determiners in Table 2.2 are italicised. These are the forms which are also pronouns. You need to be very careful to distinguish between determiners and pronouns. Determiners will always be followed by a head noun (although there may be some premodifying element such as an adjective between the determiner and the head noun):

<u>*Which*</u> *is the best way to London from here?*	pronoun
<u>*Which*</u> *route is the best way to London from here?*	determiner
I really have had <u>*enough*</u>	pronoun
I really have had <u>*enough*</u> *greasy chips*	determiner

In the above examples, the pronouns *which* and *enough* are in contrast to the determiners *which* and *enough* which occur with *route* and *greasy chips* respectively.

☐ **noun phrase structure** ⇨ 5.2
☐ **exclamative sentences** ⇨ 7.6

2.10   AUXILIARIES

Auxiliaries or **auxiliary verbs** are a very small group of verbs and they only occur in **verb phrases**. We saw in the preceding section that determiners are optional elements of a noun phrase but if they do occur they will introduce the noun phrase. Similarly, auxiliaries are optional elements of verb phrases although they are in fact used very extensively, as are determiners, due to their ability to further define the main element of the phrase in question. The term 'auxiliary' comes from the Latin *auxilium* which means 'help' or 'assistance'. **Modal auxiliaries** assist us in creating additional shades of meaning within the verb phrase while **primary auxiliaries** chiefly enable us to indicate different **aspects** of the verb phrase:

> primary auxiliaries
> *have, be, do*
>
> modal auxiliaries
> *can, could, shall, should, will, would, may, might, must*

It is the primary auxiliaries *have* and *be* which are used to create different aspects. Aspects are rather like tenses and indicate whether the action or state of a verb is complete or on-going. Here are two examples to show this:

> Phil *has composed* his first symphony
> Liz *is looking after* the children

In the first of these examples, the use of the primary auxiliary *have* (in the form *has*) indicates that the composition of the symphony is complete. In the second example, the use of *be* (in the form *is*) is a crucial part of the information that Liz's action is on-going. We will look at the construction of the full range of verb aspects in Chapter 5. The primary auxiliary *do* is used either for emphasis:

> Liz *does* enjoy looking after the children

or to ask a question:

> *Does* Liz enjoy looking after the children?

or in negation:

> Liz *does not* enjoy looking after the children

The primary auxiliary *do* therefore has a different role from the primary auxiliaries *be* and *have*.

The following examples illustrate the range of meanings which modal auxiliaries express:

example	expressing ...
Now I've left work, I <u>can/could</u> take a holiday	ability
I <u>can/could</u> take a holiday in June or July	possibility
My boss said I <u>can/could/may/might</u> take a holiday	permission
I <u>shall/will</u> take a holiday at Christmas	intention
If everything goes to plan I <u>will</u> take a holiday soon	prediction
I <u>should</u> take a holiday if I'm to get over my illness	obligation
I <u>should</u> take a holiday sometime next year	prediction
I <u>would</u> take a holiday if I had the money	qualified intention
I <u>may/might</u> take a holiday if I see a trip I fancy	possibility
I <u>must</u> take a holiday or I shall make myself ill	necessity

These are the main semantic functions of the modal auxiliaries, the differences between them sometimes being very subtle. There are also a few marginal auxiliaries such as *have to, need to* and *ought to* which express similar meanings to *must* and *should*: for example, *I ought to take a holiday* is comparable in meaning to *I should take a holiday*. The marginal auxiliary *used to* expresses something habitual or continuous in the past: *I used to like swimming but I'm not so keen now*.

The order of auxiliaries, like the order of determiners, is prescribed. Auxiliaries always precede the head verb. Modal auxiliaries precede primary ones and the primary auxiliary *have* will precede the primary auxiliary *be* if both occur. All these points are explored further in Chapter 5.

> ☐ **verb phrases** ⇨ 5.3
> ☐ **question structures** ⇨ 7.4

2.11   PREPOSITIONS

Prepositions are a moderately large group as far as grammatical words go. We will identify a considerable number here in order to have a representative sample of this word class. Prepositions are used to show the relationship between two elements, although again this is a notional definition which is not grammatically watertight. Consider these examples:

The dog ran <u>under</u> the table
The dog ran <u>round</u> the table
The dog ran <u>into</u> the table

In all three examples, a preposition is used to indicate the relationship between *the dog ran* and *the table*. Of course, prepositions are not the only word class which can express the relationship between one thing and another. For example, the verb *loves* expresses a relationship between *Debra* and *Sam* in the sentence *Debra loves Sam*. If we are to identify a feature of prepositions which is grammatical rather than semantic, then it is that prepositions are typically followed by noun phrases (such as *the table*) with which they form a **prepositional phrase**.

Prepositions most typically express relationships of time and place, although other relationships may be expressed too. Prepositions may be **simple** or **complex**. A simple preposition is a single word such as *under, round* and *into* while a complex preposition consists of two or three words. Examples include *according to, on behalf of* and *with regard to*. Here is a selection of both simple and complex prepositions. Those which express time or place have been listed separately. Others, which express a range of aspects such as cause and purpose, have been grouped together:

> prepositions of time
> *about, after, at, before, between, by, during, from, in, out of, past,*
> *post, prior to, since, towards, until*
>
> prepositions of place
> *about, above, across, against, along, among, at, away from, behind, below,*
> *beneath, beside, between, beyond, by, by way of, close to, down,*
> *from, in, inside, into, near, off, on, onto, outside, over, past, round,*
> *through, towards, under, within*
>
> prepositions of cause, purpose, association, attitude and so on
> *about, according to, anti, apart from, because of, besides, by,*
> *concerning, contrary to, despite, due to, except, for, in return for,*
> *instead of, of, regarding, with, with regard to, without*

Some prepositions have more than one semantic function. *About*, for example, can express time, place and association:

She arrived about noon	time
She walked about the shopping centre	place
She was concerned about her health	association

We saw earlier that there is a close relationship between pronouns and determiners and that many words of these classes take the same form. A comparable relationship exists between prepositions and adverbs:

She walked about the shopping centre	preposition
She walked about	adverb (of place)

- ☐ **noun phrases** ⇨ 5.2
- ☐ **prepositional phrases** ⇨ 5.5

2.12   CONJUNCTIONS

Conjunctions, as their name suggests, are used to join linguistic elements. They can be subdivided into **coordinating conjunctions** (or **coordinators**) and **subordinating conjunctions** (or **subordinators**). Essentially, there are only three coordinating conjunctions. These are *and*, *but* and *or*. More marginal coordinators are *nor*, which is the negative counterpart of *or*, and *for*. Coordinators join words, phrases and clauses of a similar status. Their role is explored in detail in section 7.9.

Subordinating conjunctions, by contrast, form a much larger group. Subordinating conjunctions mainly join clauses together although they do this in a rather different way from coordinating conjunctions. Like prepositions, they can be simple or complex. Here is a selection of subordinating conjunctions:

> *after, although, as, as far as, assuming that, because, before, if, in case, in order that, provided that, since, that, unless, until, when, whereas, while*

Subordinating conjunctions occur at the beginning of clauses: when a subordinating conjunction introduces a clause in this way it has the effect of making that clause **subordinate** to another clause in the same sentence (and the sentence will be **complex**).

We noted earlier that many prepositions share the same forms as adverbs. Similarly, some prepositions share the same forms as subordinating conjunctions. However, whereas prepositions normally introduce a noun phrase, a subordinating conjunction introduces a clause (a grammatical unit which contains a verb element). The following examples show how *since* can be either a preposition, an adverb or a subordinating conjunction:

I haven't eaten <u>since lunchtime</u>	preposition
I ate at lunchtime and haven't eaten <u>since</u>	adverb
I haven't eaten <u>since Sue arrived</u>	subordinating conjunction
<u>*Since the cupboard is bare*</u>*, I haven't eaten*	subordinating conjunction

- ☐ **coordination of phrases** ⇨ 5.7
- ☐ **clauses** ⇨ 6.1
- ☐ **compound sentences** ⇨ 7.9
- ☐ **complex sentences** ⇨ 7.10

2.13   *WH*-WORDS

There are three word classes which include a subset of items beginning with *wh-*, namely adverbs, pronouns and determiners. Items which begin with *wh-* are *wh*-words, although *how* and *however* are also included in this group. Collectively, *wh*-adverbs, *wh*-pronouns and *wh*-determiners perform similar grammatical functions. Table 2.3 shows you the complete set of *wh*-words and indicates the different functions they perform.

Table 2.3   *Wh*-words

Function	Type		
	Wh-adverb	**Wh-pronoun**	**Wh-determiner**
introducing an interrogative clause or sentence	how when where why	what which who whom whose	what which whose
examples	*When did he telephone her?*	*Who has a flat in Majorca?*	*Which book did you choose?*
introducing an exclamative clause or sentence	how		what
examples	*How irritating that person is*		*What a nuisance this person is*
introducing a relative clause	when where why	which who whom	which whose
examples	*This is a place where everyone has fun*	*This is the car which I want to buy*	*This is the person whose car I'm buying*

continued

Table 2.3   *continued*

Function	Type		
	Wh-adverb	*Wh*-pronoun	*Wh*-determiner
introducing a nominal relative clause	how when where why	what, what(so)ever which, which(so)ever who, who(so)ever whom, whom(so)ever	what which
examples	*Where to go was quite a problem*	*Who to ask was quite a problem*	*Which option to select was quite a problem*
introducing a *wh*-conditional clause	whenever wherever however	whatever whichever who(so)ever whom(so)ever	whatever whichever
examples	*Wherever you go, be careful*	*Whatever happens, I'm leaving*	*Whichever choice you make, think about it carefully*

Table 2.3 also gives examples of each of the *wh*-word types in the context of a clause or sentence. (Some of the examples are repeated from earlier sections in this chapter.) While it is helpful to understand how *wh*-words work as a group, at the same time it is important to maintain the distinction between those of the adverb class, those of the pronoun class and those of the determiner class.

- ☐ *wh*-adverbs ⇨ 2.7
- ☐ *wh*-pronouns ⇨ 2.8
- ☐ *wh*-determiners ⇨ 2.9
- ☐ **clauses** ⇨ 6.1
- ☐ **relative clauses** ⇨ 6.13
- ☐ **sentences** ⇨ 7.1
- ☐ **interrogative sentence** ⇨ 7.4
- ☐ **interrogative clauses** ⇨ 7.10
- ☐ **nominal relative clauses** ⇨ 7.10
- ☐ *wh*-**conditional clauses** ⇨ 7.11

3 Word Formation

3.1 SIMPLE AND COMPLEX WORDS

In this chapter, we will be looking closely at the internal structures of the words in the English language. The area of linguistics which is concerned with the internal structure of words is **morphology**. Morphology is normally divided into two branches – **lexical morphology** (sometimes known as **derivational morphology**) and **inflectional morphology**. Inflectional morphology deals with the way words are adapted in different grammatical contexts (such as making a noun plural), an aspect which is examined in Chapter 4. In this chapter we will be concerned with lexical morphology. In other words, we will be exploring the means by which existing words have been constructed and by which new words might be constructed.

When considering word formation, we can divide words into two broad categories – **simple words** and **complex words**. Simple words are those which cannot be analysed into smaller units of meaning. Examples might include *cat*, *paper*, *fear* and *rubbish*. Complex words, on the other hand, can be subdivided into smaller units of meaning. Here are some examples:

printer	*print + er*
unfortunately	*un + fortun(e) + ate + ly*
dispel	*dis + pel*

We know intuitively that the above examples are made up of smaller units because we have so many other words in our mental lexicons that follow similar patterns. For instance, there are many nouns which end in *-er* where this ending denotes the performer of the action to which it is attached. So a *print-er* is someone who prints, a *teach-er* is someone who teaches, a *sing-er* is someone who sings and so on. Similarly, we know of many instances where *un-* at the beginning of a word has the effect of oppositeness (as in *happy* / *unhappy* or *successful* / *unsuccessful*) and we can form new words by using the same pattern: *funny* has now given rise to *unfunny*. The *-ate* element in *unfortunately* is found on the end of several adjectives – *temperate*, *immaculate*, *delicate* and so on – and many adverbs are formed by adding *-ly* to an existing adjective. We are able to subdivide *dispel* into *dis* + *pel* not because we necessarily know that *-pel* comes from the Latin root meaning 'to drive' or 'to force' (consider *compel*, *expel* and *repel*) but because we know that *dis-* occurs at the start of many words with the meaning of 'away from' or 'the reverse of' as in *dismiss, disconnect, disagree* and *displease*.

Sometimes, however, it will not be clear to us whether a word is simple or complex. If we are unaware of a word's origins in another language such as Latin or Greek, then we would not necessarily identify it as a complex word. Examples of such words might indeed include *repel* or words such as *magic* or *usual*. This is not a difficulty here because we are not concerned with the historical origins (or **etymology**) of words. The focus of this chapter is an identification of the strategies which are used in English to form words partly with the aim of identifying how new words are likely to be formed.

Words which belong to open classes (nouns, verbs, adjectives and adverbs) form a huge group of words which it is impossible to count. In exploring word-formation strategies, we will only consider the open classes of words. There are two reasons for this. The first is that members of the closed classes are largely simple words – consider determiners such as *the, a/an, each, both, every* and so on – with relatively few being divisible into smaller units (examples include the conjunction *because* and the pronouns *myself, everyone*). The second reason is that our interest in word formation is very much in identifying how new words are formed and may be formed and of course the closed classes of words very rarely admit new members.

☐ **open and closed classes of words** ⇨ 2.3

3.2 SOME TERMS AND CONCEPTS

There are several important and useful terms for discussing the morphology of words. One of the aspects of word construction which we will frequently be considering is the position of particular units of construction. This is important because some units only occur at the beginning of a word (for example, the *un-* of *unfortunately*) and others only at the end (such as the *-ly* of *unfortunately*). When discussing the beginning of a word, we can say that an element is **word-initial** and, by contrast, an element at the end of a word is **word-final**. Very occasionally, we may wish to refer to an element positioned within the word and we would refer to this as **word-medial**.

Many words are complex in their construction and can therefore be broken down into smaller units of meaning. The smallest unit of meaning in a word is a **morpheme**. Therefore a word like *printer* given above which is made up of *print* + *er* is constructed from two morphemes while *un* + *fortun(e)* +*ate* + *ly* consists of four morphemes. Words which are indivisible into smaller elements of meaning such as *cat* and *rubbish* comprise a single morpheme only. Morphemes themselves can be subdivided into two types: **free morphemes** and **bound morphemes**. A free morpheme is one that can stand alone as a word in its own right. Thus *cat* and *rubbish* are free morphemes and so too are the *print* and *fortun(e)* elements of *printer* and *unfortunately*. Any morpheme which cannot stand alone is a bound morpheme. The *-er* of *printer*, and the *un-*, *-ate* and *-ly* of *unfortunately* are all bound morphemes.

In section 3.1 we divided words in terms of their structure into simple and complex words. Sometimes, however, it is helpful to make a three-way distinction between simple words, **compound words** and complex words, with a compound word being constructed from two free morphemes while a complex word is constructed from a root morpheme (free or bound) plus at least one bound morpheme. Here are examples of the three types:

simple word	*sketch*	
compound word	*sketchpad*	*sketch + pad*
complex word	*sketchy*	*sketch + -y*

The beauty of this three-way distinction is that it mirrors the three basic structural possibilities for sentences, which can also be simple, compound or complex. This is not just a matter of terminology, however: there is a genuine similarity between the internal structures of words and those of sentences.

We considered in Chapter 2 how all words might be said to have a kind of abstract existence – a form which is known as a lexeme. Morphemes are similarly abstract. Consider the word-initial bound morphemes in the following examples:

inelegant	*in + elegant*
impolite	*im + polite*
illegal	*il + legal*
irregular	*ir + regular*

These four examples (*in-*, *im- il-* and *ir-*) are used to express the opposite of what follows – *inelegant* is the opposite of *elegant* and so on. If we had a much fuller range of examples, we would see that *il-* only occurs when the following morpheme begins with /l/ (*illicit, illegible*) and *ir-* only occurs when the following morpheme begins with /r/ (*irreverend, irresponsible*), while *im-* only occurs before /b/ (*imbalance*), /m/ (*immature*) and /p/ (*impolite*), the reason being that /m/, /b/ and /p/ are all sounds made with the lips. All other comparable opposites are formed using *in-*. What this shows is that *in-*, *im- il-* and *ir-* are not four distinct morphemes but different forms of the same bound morpheme, the actual form used depending on the phonological (or pronunciation) environment in which it occurs. This is a sound argument for the existence of abstract forms or morphemes which are then realised by different **allomorphs**.

Two further terms which are useful when studying morphology are **root** and **base**. The **root** or **root morpheme** is the part of a complex word which is at the heart of the word's construction and its meaning. Roots can often be used to identify families of words. For example, we saw above that *impel*, *expel*, *compel* and *repel* all share the root *-pel*. The morpheme *-pel* is the root because it is at the heart of the construction of all these examples and its original meaning from Latin of 'drive' or 'force' is also central in semantic terms. Similarly, *original*, *originality*, *originate* and *originally* all share the root *origin*, although there is a contrast here with the *-pel* root in that *origin* is a word in itself (and a free morpheme) whereas *-pel* clearly is not (and is therefore a bound morpheme). A **base** is a unit to which other morphemes may be added to create a new word or words. In the example just given, the root *origin* provides the base for the adjective *original*. This in turn provides the base for both the noun *originality* and the adverb *originally*.

□ **lexemes** ⇨ 2.1
□ **simple sentences** ⇨ 7.8
□ **compound sentences** ⇨ 7.9
□ **complex sentences** ⇨ 7.10

3.3   WORD-FORMATION STRATEGIES

It is clear from our discussion so far that many words of the open classes have complex structures. In the following sections, we will look at the full range of strategies which are used in modern English to construct lexemes. So far we have seen that many words are constructed by the addition of bound morphemes either word-initially or word-finally. This process is known as **affixation** and is the most **productive** of the strategies used to form words. We will look at affixation in section 3.4. Two further strategies which are also very productive are **compounding** and **conversion** and we will consider these in sections 3.5 and 3.7. Section 3.8 will deal with the range of other strategies which are employed.

The term **word formation** is being used here as a useful blanket term. As we have already seen, some words are not really 'formed' in that they cannot be further divided into morphemes. Nevertheless, we may need to consider the origin or source of such words in order to provide a contrast with 'forming' processes such as affixation and compounding, and to provide an overview of the full range of strategies used in contemporary English to create open class words.

3.4   AFFIXATION

Affixation is the process by which bound morphemes (other than roots) are added to bases, either word-initially or word-finally, to form new words. A bound morpheme which is added in this way is an **affix**. An affix which occurs word-initially is more specifically termed a **prefix**, while one which is added word-finally is a **suffix**. In some languages, the word formation process may employ an **infix** – a bound morpheme which is inserted within the word. This is not a strategy used in English word formation although speakers occasionally infix a taboo word into another word as in *hoo-bloody-ray*. This is clearly done for effect – the effect being achieved by the fact that English words are not normally interrupted in this way.

It is important to make a distinction between prefixes and suffixes because these two types of bound morphemes behave rather differently in forming words. One particular difference is that a prefix will not normally change the class of a word. So, for example, when the prefix *dis-* is added to the verb *agree*, the resulting word – *disagree* – is still a verb. A prefix, then, is normally **class-preserving**. By contrast, a suffix may be class-preserving (both *king* and *king+dom* are nouns) but is equally likely to be **class-changing**. For instance, the addition of the suffix *-ly* to the adjective *sad* results in an adverb *sadly*. A further difference between prefixes and suffixes is that there are many prefixes which can be added to at least two word classes whereas suffixes tend to be word-class specific. For example, the prefix *dis-* is found in nouns (*distaste, disservice*), verbs (*disagree, disappear*), adjectives (*dissimilar, disreputable*) and obviously the adverbs derived from these adjectives (*dissimilarly, disreputably*). By contrast, most suffixes occur with a specific class of words only. Furthermore, no morpheme which functions as a prefix can also function as a suffix. Table 3.1 shows some common prefixes of English while Table 3.2 shows some common suffixes.

Table 3.2 shows that the majority of suffixes are used to form either nouns or adjectives. There is a particularly large number of noun suffixes. By contrast, there are only a handful of verb and adverb suffixes. A general observation which we can make about both prefixes and suffixes is that some are far more productive than others. In other words, some affixes are used in the creation of words much more than others. The verb and adverb suffixes

Table 3.1   Some common English prefixes

Prefix	Approximate meaning	Examples
anti-	against	antiseptic, anti-social
de-	reverse	destabilise, devaluation
dis-	reverse	disconnect, dismount
dis-	negative and opposite	disapprove, disloyal
in/im/il/ir-	opposite (and negative)	impatient, illogical
inter-	between	international, interplanetary
intra-	within, inside	intravenous, intrapersonal
mega-	very large	megalith, megastore
mini-	small	minicab, minibar
mis-	incorrect, wrong	misinformation, mismatch
mono-	one	monosyllabic, monotone
neo-	new	neologism, neo-classical
non-	not	non-standard, non-entity
poly-	many	polygon, polymath
post-	after	postcolonial, postnatal
pre-	before	precaution, preparation
pro-	in favour of, for	pro-Europe, pro-life
pro-	forward	progress, proceed
re-	again	reconsider, revision
trans-	across	transfer, translate
un-	reverse	undo, unpick
un-	remove	uncover, unsaddle
un-	not	unhappy, unnecessary

illustrate this. Of the four verb suffixes given in Table 3.2, -ise/-ize is used far more extensively to create new words than the other examples given. In recent years we have had *computerise, hospitalise, windowise* (meaning 'to find time for an appointment'), *anonymise* and many others. With regard to adverbs, *-ly* is a very common suffix as it occurs with many adjectives to form adverbs of manner – *happy/happily, quick/quickly* and so on. The other suffixes are less productive although it has become very common for speakers to coin adverbs with *-wise* as a more economical way of expressing *as far as x is concerned.* For example, *I'm feeling much better healthwise* or *Things haven't been going very well jobwise.*

Of the noun and adjective suffixes, again some are more productive than others. A suffix such as *-ment* occurs on many words but is rarely used now to form new words. Others, such as *-ee* and *-ism* are currently very productive. Table 3.2 includes established words (such as *government*) as well as more recent words (such as *ageism*) to illustrate this point. Some suffixes are themselves recently coined: *-oholic/-aholic* is an example of this. It is clipped from

Table 3.2   Some common English suffixes

Noun suffixes		Adjective suffixes		Verb suffixes		Adverb suffixes	
-age	dotage	-able ⎫	eligible	-ate	nominate	-fold	tenfold
-al	recital	-ible ⎭		-en	quicken	-free	scotfree
-ance ⎫	permanence	-al/-ial	practical	-ify	falsify	-ly	sadly
-ence ⎭		-ant ⎫	diligent	-ise ⎫	criticise	-wise	healthwise
-ancy ⎫	tenancy	-ent ⎭		-ize ⎭			
-ency ⎭		-ar	regular				
-ant ⎫	defendant	-ary	examplary				
-ent ⎭		-ate	delicate				
-ar/-er	registrar	-ed	redhanded				
-ate	delegate	-en	craven				
-ation ⎫	formation	-ful	truthful				
-tion ⎭		-ic	economic				
-dom	kingdom	-ing	swinging				
-ee	employee	-ish	childish				
-ery ⎫	snobbery	-ive	productive				
-ry ⎭		-less	feckless				
-ess	hostess	-like	childlike				
-ette	kitchenette	-ly	friendly				
-ful	spoonful	-ous	cavernous				
-ing	stitching	-some	troublesome				
-ism	ageism	-y	picky				
-ite	Blairite						
-ity	brutality						
-ive	collective						
-let	piglet						
-ling	fledgling						
-ment	government						
-ness	kindness						
-oholic ⎫	shopaholic						
-aholic ⎭							
-ship	leadership						
-some	twosome						

alcoholic (interestingly taking *-ohol-* from the base of the word as well as *-ic*, the suffix) and has the meaning of 'addicted to' as in *shopaholic, chocoholic*.

In recent years, some users of the language have objected to the suffixes *-ess* and *-ette* to denote female roles on the grounds that they imply women are in a disadvantageous position in comparison with men. This is because the suffix for the female form (such as *hostess, stewardess, usherette*) is an addition to a base, suggesting that the female form is an afterthought or is secondary to the male form. Also, there is an arguable imbalance between the male form being a free morpheme and the female form requiring a bound morpheme which is unable to stand alone and therefore suggestive of weakness. The suffix -*ette* is particularly objectionable to some users in that it is a **diminutive**. This means it indicates a smaller version of something: a *kitchenette*, for instance, is a small kitchen. The use of -*ette* to indicate a female form (*ladette* being a recent coinage) is therefore objected to on the grounds that the use of the diminutive ending implies the female is less important. Given these objections, it would not be surprising if the -*ess* suffix were eventually dropped from the language, in addition to -*ette* in some formulations.

It was noted above that most suffixes belong to one particular word class only. However, a handful of suffixes do occur on words of more than one class. If you look again at Table 3.2, for example, you will see that -*al* occurs in both nouns and adjectives, as do -*ate*, -*ful*, -*ing*, -*ive* and -*some*. You will also remember that while almost all prefixes are class-preserving, suffixes may be class-preserving or class-changing. So whereas -*ism*, for example, is added to a noun such as *age* to produce another noun, *ageism*, and is therefore class-preserving, a suffix such as -*ous* is added to the noun *cavern* to form the adjective *cavernous* and is therefore class-changing.

Another feature of affixes is that any one word may include more than one prefix and more than one suffix. However, prefixes and suffixes do not combine freely (for example, it would be impossible to have both -*ness* and -*ity* suffixing a word) and the order of occurrence of prefixes and suffixes is fixed, often due to the word class of the base. Here is a breakdown of possible and impossible combinations linked to the noun *disorganisation*:

dis -	*organ* -	*is(e)* -	*ation*
* *dis* -	*organ*		
	organ -	*ise*	
dis -	*organ* -	*ise*	
	organ -	*is(e)* -	*ation*
	* *organ*	-	*ation*

You can see here that although the prefix *dis*- does occur with some nouns (we had the examples *distaste* and *disservice* above) there is a semantic restriction which prevents **dis*organ*. This is because the prefix *dis*- is used to turn a positive meaning into a negative one. *Organ* has a more neutral meaning (when it refers to an institution used for a particular purpose) and this makes the addition of a prefix such as *dis*- inappropriate. With regard to the suffix -*ation*, we see that the combination **organation* is also impossible. Here, however, the restriction is a morphological, not a semantic one: this suffix only occurs on verbs and since *organ* is a noun, it is impossible to add *-ation* to it. These examples show us then that there can be both semantic and morphological restrictions on word formation.

Two suffixes which sometimes cause confusion are *-ed* and *-ing*. This is because both these forms also occur as grammatical endings (or inflections) on verbs. This is illustrated in:

> *The girl is walking to school*
> *The girl has walked to school*

However, both nouns and adjectives can be formed by the addition of the suffix *-ing* and adjectives can also be formed by the addition of *-ed*. When a new word is formed by adding *-ed* to a noun, the resulting word is always an adjective (as in *manner* and *mannered*). However, when *-ed* and *-ing* are added to verbs, a new noun or adjective may result, or an inflectional form of the verb may be produced. So, in *The girl enjoyed the dancing*, clearly *dancing* is a noun since it occurs after the definite article *the*. This form is sometimes referred to as a **deverbal noun** as it derives from a verb. In *The girl is walking to school*, the element *walking* is a verb since it occurs in a verb phrase after the primary auxiliary *is*. Similarly, in the following example the *-ed* form is a verb as it occurs in contrast to a present tense form in the first example and after a primary auxiliary in the second example:

> *The girl walked to school* (not *walks*)
> *The girl has walked to school*

In the following examples, however, the *-ed* forms occur attributively (in other words, they precede the nouns they modify) and so in this context we are dealing with adjectives:

> *The confused girl had not reached school*   (compare *The lazy girl...*)
> *The confusing question had everyone foxed* (compare *The tricky question...*)

These adjectives can be referred to as **deverbal adjectives**, again to indicate that they derive from verbs. Some linguists prefer, however, to treat them and deverbal nouns as verb forms so you will sometimes find them referred to as verbs or more specifically as **participles**.

☐ **verb inflections** ⇨ 4.4

3.5   COMPOUNDING

If you compare the following two examples you will see that they each consist of three morphemes:

unfriendly	*un + friend + ly*
child-friendly	*child + friend + ly*

The difference between them is that whereas *unfriendly* consists of the root *friend* plus two affixes, *child-friendly* consists of the root *child* combined with the root *friend* suffixed by *-ly*. This construction, which consists of two roots and in fact two pre-existing words – *child* and *friendly* – is a **compound** or **compound word**. In Chapter 2, we discussed what exactly a word might be. We observed that a word is not necessarily the same as a separate written element although the correlation between the two is a strong one. Compound words are often written as one element as in *lipstick* (a compound noun) or hyphenated as in *child-friendly* (a compound adjective) but they can be written as two separate elements such as *world war* or *Down's syndrome*. As we discussed in Chapter 2, there is a good argument for treating all compounds (whatever their written form) as one word or lexeme due to the virtual inseparability of the bases which form them. There is also the possibility of substituting compound words with alternative lexical items which are not compounds.

Compounding, like affixation, is a very productive way of forming words in English, and this process is particularly productive in relation to nouns and adjectives. Table 3.3 illustrates this.

As you can see from Table 3.3, compounding is typically the result of joining nouns, adjectives and verbs. Compound verbs are relatively rare and those which do exist are likely to be the result of **back-formation** or **conversion** (which we will cover in section 3.7). However, there is a very large group of **multi-word verbs**, formed by the combination of the verb with an adverb or preposition, which behave differently from compound verbs. We will examine these in section 3.6. Some examples of compound verbs are given in Table 3.4.

A final matter we need to address before moving on from compounding is illustrated in the following examples:

psychology	*technophobe*	*telegram*

At first glance, it doesn't seem particularly difficult to analyse these examples in terms of their morphemes. However, a problem exists in trying to decide which of the morphemes might be roots and which are affixes. In *technophobe*

Table 3.3 The formation of compound nouns and compound adjectives

Compound nouns

most productive combination	noun + noun	bookcase crash landing smokescreen
other possible structures	verb + noun adjective + noun noun + and + noun phrase	pickpocket mobile phone gin and tonic sell-by date mother-in-law
compound adjectives		
most productive combinations	noun + adjective	war-torn world-weary
other possible combinations	verb + adverb/preposition adjective + adjective adjective + noun phrase	throwaway ready-cooked long-life in-house ready-to-wear

('someone who is afraid of new technology'), for instance, is *techno-* a root to which the suffix *-phobe* has been added or is *-phobe* a root to which the prefix *techno-* has been added? It seems impossible to decide. If we argued that they were both roots then we would be dealing with a compound word but the elements which make up compound words like *answerphone* (*answer + phone*) can stand alone, whereas neither *techno* nor *phobe* are individual words. If, on the other hand, we explored the possibility of *techno-* and *-phobe* both being affixes we would have a further problem in that a prefix and a suffix alone cannot combine to form a word (for example, **disity* or **preness*). Also, these

Table 3.4 Some compound verbs

Type	Example of compound verbs	Make-up
back-formation (a suffix is removed from an existing word)	baby-sit fine-tune	from the noun baby-sitter from the noun fine-tuning
conversion (change of word class but the form remains the same)	cold-shoulder mastermind	was a noun was a noun
other examples	make do blackball	verb + verb adjective + noun

morphemes seem to have a more specific meaning than many affixes. The given examples, then, are neither **derived** words (those formed by adding affixes to a root) nor compound words but something in between. We call the morphemes which make up these in-between words **combining forms**.

3.6   MULTI-WORD VERBS

Whereas compound verbs are relatively rare (in contrast to compound nouns and compound adjectives), **multi-word verbs** (sometimes also known as **phrasal verbs**) are very common in contemporary English. A multi-word verb is a combination of two or three elements:

> verb + preposition
> verb + adverb
> verb + adverb + preposition

One key feature of multi-word verbs is that their meaning is partly or wholly **idiomatic**. This means that the meaning cannot be fully deduced from the individual meanings of the elements which constitute the multi-word verb. For example, in *Fred ran up some heavy debts*, *ran* has nothing to do with fast physical movement and *up* has nothing to do with direction (although in the example *Fred ran up a steep hill* these are the meanings which would come into play). As a multi-word verb, *run up* has the equivalent meaning of *accumulate*. It is a feature of multi-word verbs that they can often be replaced by a single-word lexical verb.

One other feature of multi-word verbs, and a crucial way in which they differ from compound verbs, is that the adverb or preposition can sometimes be separated from the verb:

verb + preposition	*The doctor <u>relied</u> <u>on</u> her assistant*
	This is the assistant <u>on</u> whom the doctor <u>relied</u>
verb + adverb	*Sue <u>gave</u> <u>away</u> the secret*
	Sue gave the secret <u>away</u>
verb + adverb + preposition	*This is a matter I shall <u>take</u> <u>up</u> <u>with</u> my colleague*
	I shall <u>take</u> this matter <u>up</u> <u>with</u> my colleague

Multi-word combinations of the kind illustrated above are a highly productive way of forming verbs in English. Consider, for instance, how many combinations there are with *up*. Here are just a few examples:

multi-word verb	meaning	example
to listen up	*to pay attention*	*Now listen up!*
to put up	*to provide a bed*	*Can you put me up tonight?*
to take up	*to respond or discuss*	*Jane took up the subject at once*
	to begin learning	*Jane took up archery*
	to fill time	*The walk took up the whole day*
to talk up	*to praise*	*The manager talked up the firm*
to speak up	*to speak loudly*	*She spoke up amid the din*

3.7 CONVERSION AND BACK-FORMATION

Conversion is another productive method for creating new words by a change of word class without any alteration to the form of the word itself. For example, *access* is a noun in *The police gained access to the premises* but in recent years *access* has also come to be used as a verb as in *The programmer accessed the files on her PC*. Conversion is a particularly productive way of creating verbs from nouns and, to a slightly lesser extent, nouns from verbs. Here are some more examples:

verbs from nouns
Julia Roberts co-starred with Hugh Grant in 'Notting Hill '
The critic rubbished the actor's performance
I've programmed your video to come on at eight
Jeanne had to elbow her way through the crowd

nouns from verbs
The thief made a quick lunge at the handbag
Keith took his old furniture to the dump

However, it is not unusual for adjectives to be converted to nouns as in *There was no doubt she was his equal* or for adjectives to be converted to verbs as in *The athlete tried to better his previous performance*. Occasionally words of other classes may be the source for a conversion: *The opposition tried to out the president* uses the adverb *out* as a verb.

Of course, it is not always possible, when dealing with forms which belong to more than one word class and which have existed for a long time, to tell which word came first. Sometimes we can make an educated guess. For example, *bottle* the noun must have come before *bottle* the verb since the meaning of this verb is 'to put something in a bottle' – an impossibility if bottles do not exist! Conversion is a process which happens frequently in contemporary English and speakers will convert words fairly freely if needed.

Back-formation usually results in a change of word class, and in this respect it is like conversion. However, back-formation is the less productive of the two strategies. It involves the modification of a word, usually through the removal of a suffix (or suffix-like ending) but occasionally a prefix. Most typically, suffixes are removed from nouns to create new verbs:

noun	*television*	verb derived	*to televise*
noun	*emotion*	verb derived	*to emote*
noun	*reminiscence*	verb derived	*to reminisce*

If a prefix is removed, however, the word class will not change since prefixes are class-preserving:

| adjective | *uncouth* | adjective derived | *couth* |

3.8 OTHER WORD-FORMATION STRATEGIES

Affixation, compounding and conversion are the most productive of the word-formation strategies in English. However, there are a range of other strategies employed in modern English to form new words. Here is a brief survey of them.

An **acronym** is an economical way of expressing a phrase since the first letter (or letters) usually of each word in the phrase is placed in sequence to form a new word. *Scuba*, for example, stands for *self-contained underwater breathing apparatus* and *AIDS* stands for *acquired immune deficiency syndrome*. Sometimes, when the initial letters do not form a new word, they are named individually as in *CID* (*Criminal Investigation Department*) or *BBC* (*British Broadcasting Corporation*). This type of acronym is known more specifically as an **initialism**. Sometimes a word can be a combination of an acronym and an initialism as in *CD-ROM*, where *CD* is an initialism (for *compact disk*) but *ROM* (*read only memory*) is an acronym.

Clipping involves shortening a word, usually by removing some of the latter part, as in *cred* (from *credibility*), *mash* (from *mashed potato*) *telly* (from *television*) and *mobile* (from *mobile phone*). Two examples of clippings where the opening part of the word has been removed are *phone* from *telephone* and *bus* from *omnibus*. One feature of clippings is that they nearly always refer to everyday objects. Purists might regard this as a kind of laziness in using the language but it is perfectly natural to clip a word in this way when it is in frequent use. Most clippings are monosyllabic words. Some will have two syllables as in *telly* and *mobile*.

A **blend** is a kind of compound although the base words are not joined in their entirety. Instead, part of one word is merged with part of another as in *brunch* (*breakfast* and *lunch*) and *smog* (*smoke* and *fog*). Sometimes it is possible to deduce the meaning of a blended word. However, some blends are not this transparent. For example, the computer term *bit* is a blend of *binary* and *digit*. Blends are most typically nouns although *ginormous* is an example of an adjective. Blends are also sometimes termed **portmanteau words**.

Eponymy is the use of a proper name to refer to an object or action. The resulting word is an **eponym**. Often, the object in question is an invention of the person after whom it is named. Speakers may be unaware that words such as *sandwich* and *wellington* are eponyms, although they may be more familiar with examples such as *hoover* and *boycott*.

Every language contains a handful of words which are **onomatopoeic**. **Onomatopoeia** is when a noun or verb refers to a sound (such as *miaow* or *crash*) and supposedly imitates that sound. However, onomatopoeic words vary from language to language which indicates that the imitation is only approximate. Onomatopoeic words are, though, the only words in any language where there is a strong correlation between the sound of a word and its meaning, although there may be a partial correlation in some words (such as the examples of *gruff*, *grumble* and *grumpy* discussed in section 1.2).

A handful of words are formed by the process of **reduplication**, which involves the doubling of the first element of the word. Occasionally, this repetition will be identical (for example, *no-no* as in *That dress is a real no-no*) but more typically there will be a consonant or vowel variation in the second element as in *willy-nilly*, *helter-skelter* or *flip-flop*. Reduplicative words are often playful and are quite frequently used when speaking to very young children but speakers will sometimes use reduplication when being patronising or sarcastic.

Loanwords or **borrowings** are words which are adopted into English from another language. Of course, a very large proportion of English words have their origin in French, Latin or Greek – to such an extent that we are rarely conscious of these words as borrowings. In any case, most of these words have been **anglicised**. This means that they no longer take the form they would take in their language of origin but have been adapted to sound or look English. However, wholesale borrowing is relatively common. Some fairly recent borrowings include food words such as *sushi* from Japanese or *tortilla* from Spanish. Non-culinary examples include *anorak* (from Eskimo), *feng-shui* (from Japanese) and *glasnost* from Russian.

3.9 MEANING RELATIONS

We will conclude our exploration of the English lexicon by taking a brief look at the meanings of the words in our language and the relationships between those meanings. In our discussion, you will notice that several of the technical terms we will use contain the bound morpheme *-onym*. This element comes from the Greek word (*onyma*) for 'name': it is useful to know this as it can make the terms a little easier to understand and learn.

We saw in Chapter 2 that all English words belong to either an open class or a closed class. In discussing the meanings and the meaning relationships of words we will be concentrating on the open classes of words although some of the observations will also apply to some members of the closed classes. Also in Chapter 2, we briefly discussed the question of how large the English lexicon actually is. Although it is impossible, for the reasons we outlined, to be precise about the size of the lexicon one thing we do know about English is that the lexicon is much larger than many other languages, probably larger than most other languages. The reason for this is an historical one. Various invasions and other social and historical changes have had a far-reaching impact on English which is why our language now consists not only of Germanic words (English comes from the Germanic family of languages) but also words from Old Norse (the language of the Vikings), French, Latin, and Greek as well as many other languages which have contributed just a handful of lexical items. Consequently, there are many words in our language which have very similar meanings but come from different sources. Here is an example:

Germanic *ask*   French *question*   Latin *interrogate*

In some contexts, these words could be used interchangeably:

> The police <u>asked</u> the woman about the robbery
> The police <u>questioned</u> the woman about the robbery
> The police <u>interrogated</u> the woman about the robbery

However, although *ask*, *question* and *interrogate* have very similar meanings in these three sentences, *interrogate* suggests a rather sterner style of questioning than *question* and certainly much sterner than *ask*. When words are deemed to have the same meaning, we say they are **synonyms**, or that they are **synony-mous** with each other. However, we would probably be doubtful about saying that *ask*, *question* and *interrogate* were true synonyms, for the reason already given.

Let us consider another example of possible synonyms, this time the nouns *sight* and *vision*. Again, in certain contexts, they appear interchangeable:

> *The optician told Liz she had very good <u>sight</u>*
> *The optician told Liz she had very good <u>vision</u>*

Here, we might be tempted to think that *sight* and *vision* are synonyms. However, looking at the rest of the semantic territory which these two nouns cover we can see some problems with this:

1 *She looked quite a <u>sight</u> when I saw her yesterday*
2 *That was a <u>sight</u> for sore eyes*
3 *She was a <u>vision</u> of loveliness on her wedding day*

Example 1 above probably suggests to most speakers that something unpleas-ant has been seen whereas example 2 suggests liking or approval. This illus-trates that *sight* in the sense of 'something seen' can be used both positively and negatively. By contrast, *vision* as used in example 3 has only a positive meaning and can even be used in the context of a religious or supernatural experience. These examples show then that *vision* and *sight*, which we at first considered to have identical meanings, have other aspects of meaning which prevent us from saying they are actually synonymous. This is true of almost all possible synonyms in the language. Logically, if two words really were identi-cal in meaning, it is likely that one of them would fall from use (as has already happened with many words). Many linguists consider English, despite its very large lexicon, to have no true synonyms.

We have noticed in our discussion of the nouns *sight* and *vision*, that each of these words has more than one meaning. We considered two possible meanings – 'ability to see' as well as 'something seen' – although both these words have further meanings. Many words function semantically in this way. In other words, they are **polysemous**. If you look up words such as *sight* and *vision* in a dictionary you would find that the different meanings are separately numbered. However, we would not normally wish to argue that a noun such as *sight* should be treated as several distinct words or lexemes simply because it has several definitions. Another example might be the noun *mouse,* which we discussed in section 2.1. The primary meaning of this word is in reference to a small rodent but a mouse can also be a timid female and, more recently, an item of IT equipment. Nevertheless, we would be unlikely to say that there are three separate words or lexemes all having the citation form <mouse>. This is because the meanings are clearly related to each other. Sometimes, however, two unrelated meanings may share the same citation form or word form and we would therefore wish to posit the existence of two separate lexemes to reflect this. An example of such a form is *rent*. There is a lexeme *rent* which means 'a payment for renting something' and there is a separate lexeme *rent* which means 'a rip or tear'. There is clearly no relationship between these two meanings (unlike the *mouse* meanings) and that is why we accept that we are dealing here with two separate lexemes. In fact, separate lexemes which share the same citation form often have differing etymologies, whereas the multiple meanings of single lexemes are often the result of metaphor (a person referred to as a mouse is timid like a mouse, and a computer mouse looks like a mouse). Words such as *rent* (*payment*) and *rent* (*rip*), which are separate lexemes but take the same citation form, are **homonyms.** You may also come across **homophones** which are words that share neither meaning nor citation form but sound the same as in *site/cite/sight* or *pier/peer*.

To return to the matter of synonyms, another feature which often distinguishes words of very similar meaning (apart from the fact that they might not cover precisely the same semantic territory) is that, whereas one word might be used informally, another will be reserved for more formal usage. This is a matter of **register,** and the appropriate context in which to use a word is embedded in its meaning. Dictionaries often indicate that a word is **slang** (such as *shagged out* meaning 'very tired') or **informal** (such as *hog* in the sense of 'keep to oneself') or rather **formal** (such as *pleasantry*, meaning 'an amusing remark'). Of course, many, if not the majority of open class words can be used in all kinds of situations but even so there is a likelihood that we might prefer one word to another depending on context. For example, you may be more likely to use the first example below to a friend whereas you would choose the second example to talk to someone you knew less well:

> *My younger sister bunked off school yesterday*
> *My younger sister played truant from school yesterday*

Speakers make subtle choices of this kind all the time. The fact that we rarely make linguistic blunders in our choice of words is evidence of the sophistication of our knowledge about not only the meanings but also the uses of the many items in our mental lexicon.

Another aspect of word meanings which has some relevance to what we have already discussed both in terms of range of meanings and in terms of context and formality is the contrast between **denotation** and **connotation.**

A word's **denotative** meaning is normally the person, object, quality, idea, action or state to which a word refers. This is known as its **referent**. So the referent or denotative meaning of *pig* is a particular farm animal. This is also the meaning you would expect to find first and foremost in a dictionary. However, many words also have **connotative** meanings and these refer to the emotions or attitudes which a particular word may evoke. In this sense, *pig* can be a term of abuse either for a greedy person or a male who behaves badly or a police officer. These uses of *pig* all have negative connotations. Depending on the context in which a word is used, positive or negative connotations may come into play:

1 *We were finding it hard to see the path because* <u>darkness</u> *had fallen*
2 *Count Dracula was a lover of* <u>darkness</u>
3 *The prince was struck by the* <u>darkness</u> *of Cinderella's eyes*

In example 1, *darkness* is used in a fairly neutral way to mean 'absence of light', whereas example 2 brings into play the negative connotations of *darkness* through its association with evil. By contrast, the darkness of Cinderella's eyes in example 3 is seen to be an attractive feature to the prince. Connotations, then, are often determined or brought out by context. Dictionaries will not always indicate all the connotations of a word but they will always indicate its denotation.

A further way of looking at the relationships between words relates to the fact that many words of the open classes seem to belong to sets. For example, *wine* belongs in a set with *sherry*, *port*, *cider*, *beer* and so on. These nouns in turn belong in a blanket set of *alcohol*. *Wine*, however, as well as being a subcategory of *alcohol*, can also be subdivided into types such as *Chardonnay* and *Merlot*. Sometimes it is helpful to represent these relationships in a **tree diagram** as shown in Figure 3.1. Here, *wine* is the group to which *Chardonnay*, *Merlot* and so on belong. In this use, *wine* is a **hypernym** – a name for an overarching category. Under the hypernym *wine*, we see various kinds of wine which all belong to that category. Each of these names is a **hyponym** or member of a category. (*Hyper-* incidentally means 'above' while *hypo-* means 'below'). However, although *wine* is a hypernym in relation to, say *Chardonnay*, *wine* is itself a hyponym of *alcohol*. Identifying **hypernyms** and **hyponyms** can be a useful way of looking at how words are related in terms of more general or more specific meanings, and provide a way of organising words into sets. This does not mean, though, that all open class words will fit comfortably into this type of classification.

In contrast to the sets we can identify using hypernymic and hyponymic relations, many words fit comfortably into pairs. Typical examples

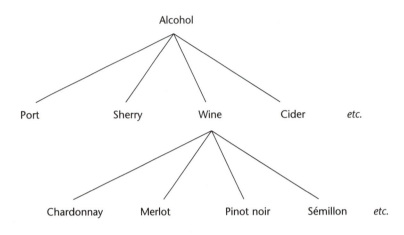

Figure 3.1 Some **hypernymic** and **hyponymic** relations

include *black* and *white* (although these also belong in a set of hyponyms of colour), *happy* and *sad*, *dead* and *alive*. Pairs which express opposites are known as **antonyms**. These usually express extremes of something gradable. For instance, *white* is at one end of a shade spectrum and *black* is at the other. Similarly, *hot* is at one end of a heat spectrum and *cold* is at the other. Many words are thought of in pairs but are not strictly antonyms. One such example is *dead/alive*. If something is not black, that doesn't mean it is white. On the other hand, if something animate is not dead then it must be alive. So whereas *black* and *white* are strictly opposites and therefore antonyms, pairs such as *dead/alive* which are mutually exclusive are **complementary** to each other. Another type of pair is *lend/borrow*. Here, if one person is lending, another person must be borrowing. *Learn* and *teach* are similar pairs. These examples are said to be in a **converse** relationship.

So far, we have looked at the meaning relationships of words with each other and of words in context. We will briefly look now at meaning relationships within derived words (those which are formed through affixation) and compound words. We have already considered some of the meanings which prefixes and suffixes attach to bases and how they indicate aspects such as reversal (*connect/disconnect*) or incorrectness (*information/misinformation*). A further point to note about affixes, however, is that their function will not always be the same. A salient example is the suffix *-ee*. In most cases, *-ee* indicates someone who is having something done to them: an employee is someone who is employed, a detainee is someone who is detained and so on. However, there are a good number of examples where this relationship doesn't hold:

1	y is an _employee_	x employed y
2	y is a _detainee_	x detained y
3	y is a _tutee_	x tutored y
4	y is an _absentee_	*x absented y
5	y is an _devotee_	*x devoted y
6	y is an _amputee_	*x amputated y

You can see here that whereas the x/y relationship is the same in examples 1 to 3, this is not true of 4 to 6. Furthermore, although _absentee_ and _devotee_ are comparable (an _absent_ person, a _devoted_ person), _amputee_ is different again. This variation in meaning relationships between morphemes is also found in compound words. Consider some of the examples from Table 3.3 of compound nouns formed by the joining of two nouns:

1	_bookcase_	a 'case' which is for books	x is for y
2	_crash landing_	a landing which is also a crash	x is also y
3	_smokescreen_	a screen which is made of smoke	x is made of y
4	_smokescreen_	a means of hiding one's intentions	?

The first three analyses show the relationship between the two bases of the compound word. However, although it is possible to express an x/y relationship between the bases, the relationship between x and y differs in each case. In addition, _smokescreen_ has a metaphorical meaning (example 4) and since this meaning is not transparent, it is hard to claim that there is a semantic relationship between _smoke_ and _screen_.

Finally, we will consider a slightly different relationship which can exist between certain words as illustrated in the following examples:

rancid butter	* _rancid wine_
make a will	* _make a letter_
propose marriage	* _offer marriage_

The above examples show that some words typically occur together and that there are restrictions on these occurrences. For instance we _make a will_ but do not _make a letter_; we _write a letter_ and may _write a will_ but _make a will_ sounds more natural. A typical or habitual combination of lexemes is known as a **collocation**. Collocations differ from compounds in that the combinations do not result in new lexemes. Nevertheless, our awareness of these typical combinations is further evidence of the sophistication of our lexical knowledge which was referred to above.

Part III
GRAMMATICAL FRAMEWORKS

4 INFLECTIONS

4.1 INFLECTIONS AS AN ASPECT OF GRAMMAR

Grammar is the set of rules of any given language that enable us to construct any sentence in that language which we recognise to be well-formed. In other words and to reiterate a point made in section 1.1, the grammar of English would enable us to construct a correct sentence such as *once upon a time three ugly frogs turned into handsome princes* but would prevent us from forming a sentence such as **ugly three frog once turn into princes upon a time handsome*. From this example, you can see that the rules of grammar essentially deal with two aspects of language construction. On the one hand, they deal with the principles of stringing words together to form larger units of construction such as phrases, clauses and sentences. This aspect of grammar which is concerned with word order is called **syntax**. (Chapters 5, 6 and 7 are about syntax.) In addition to there being a range of **syntactic rules** in our grammatical knowledge, there is another set of rules which tell us how to adapt words according to the grammatical context in which they occur. For instance, in the well-formed sentence above you can see that, because there is more than one frog and therefore more than one prince, *frog* and *prince* are both in the **plural form** and this is indicated in writing by adding <-s> to the spelling. One of the things which we recognise to be wrong in the ill-formed sentence is that the noun *frog* is not in the plural form. Similarly, the well-formed sentence uses the form *turned* to indicate the past tense of the verb whereas the *-ed* ending of *turned* has been omitted in the ill-formed sentence. Again this strikes us as odd because we expect the past tense in the context of *once upon a time*. Endings such as the plural marking on *frog* and *prince* and the past tense ending on *turn* are known as **inflections**.

Grammar is subdivided into syntax and inflections. Because inflections are part of the internal structure of a word, they can also be classified as a branch of morphology. In Chapter 3 we looked closely at lexical morphology – the aspect which deals with the formation of new words or lexemes. In this chapter we will be looking at **inflectional morphology**. Figure 4.1 shows the relationship between grammar and morphology. You need to be aware that the term 'grammar' is occasionally misapplied. Sometimes speakers believe

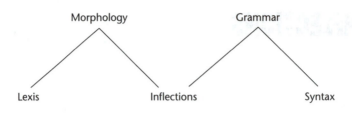

Figure 4.1   The relationship between morphology and grammar

that 'their grammar isn't very good' or 'English doesn't have any grammar'. The truth is that all languages have grammar as it would be impossible to construct any sentences in any language without it. It is true to say though that the grammar of each language is different even though languages share grammatical similarities to some degree or another. Similarly, if a speaker genuinely wasn't very good at grammar then their sentences would be muddled as in the earlier example of *ugly three frog once turn into princes upon a time handsome*. No one with normal development actually speaks like this. In fact, phenomenally, all speakers of a language are subconsciously in possession of all the grammatical rules they need to know in order to speak that language naturally. Speakers of different dialects will have some variations of course but all dialects are governed by grammatical principles.

☐ **lexical morphology** ⇨ 3.1

4.2   INFLECTIONS IN CONTEMPORARY ENGLISH

We saw above that inflections are a branch of grammar and that by inflections we mean endings which we add to a word to indicate aspects such as past tense or plural. One of the most important things about inflections is that they are not used to create a new word or lexeme. In Chapter 3 we looked at how suffixes such as *-ism* or *-ment* can be added to existing bases to form new words. So, for example, speakers have recently added *-ism* to *age* and so now we have both the noun *age* and the noun *ageism* in our lexicon. To the verb *manage* we have added *-ment* to give us both *manage* and *management*. When we add an inflection to a base, however, it does not create a new word. For example, no one would suggest that *mountain* and *mountains* in the following two sentences are separate lexical items:

> *The brave man climbed the dangerous mountain*
> *The brave man climbed three dangerous mountains*

In the second of these two examples, the inflection represented by <-s> has been added to *mountain* to indicate plurality. In Standard English it is obligatory to indicate when a noun is plural even though this might be inferred from the context since here there are *three* mountains. Inflections are used then to give us more grammatical information about words. They can be used to indicate singular or plural – what is sometimes known as **number** – and to indicate tense. They can also be used to indicate other features, as we shall see shortly. In Chapter 2 we considered how every word has some kind of abstract existence which can be realised in either speech or writing. This abstract form is a **lexeme**. When considering inflections, it can also be helpful to use the notion of a **stem**. A stem is what remains of a word when any inflections are removed from it. In other words, inflections are added to the stem of a word. So *frogs* is made up of the stem *frog* and the inflection -*s*, while *turned* is made up of the stem *turn* and the inflection -*ed*. (A stem is not quite the same as the root we discussed in Chapter 3 since the root can be less than the stem.)

If this book were about **Old English** (the English spoken from about AD 450 to about AD 1100) rather than contemporary English then the content of this chapter would be rather different and more extensive. This is because English used to have far more inflections than it has now, and these inflections were largely different in form. The reason why English lost the majority of its inflections is not of relevance here but you might like to consider English in the light of any other languages you speak or are learning and compare the range of inflections in each language. If you are studying historical English then you will almost certainly come across some of the lost inflections.

In contemporary English there are only a handful of regular inflections in addition to quite a number of irregular ones. Inflections can be found on nouns and verbs, on some adjectives and adverbs, and – in a manner of speaking – on some pronouns. Inflections, then, occur on all open classes of words but only on pronouns as far as the closed classes are concerned.

> ☐ **lexemes** ⇨ 2.1
> ☐ **suffixes** ⇨ 3.4

4.3 NOUN INFLECTIONS

Nouns can be inflected to show plurality and also to indicate possession. One interesting feature of common nouns, however, is that they do not all have a plural form. Consider the following examples:

An exciting <u>game</u> was taking place on the beach

> *Some exciting <u>games</u> were taking place on the beach*
> *In schools, <u>hockey</u> takes place in the autumn term*
> *In schools, *<u>hockeys</u> take place in the autumn term*

The noun *hockey* does not have a plural form which is why **hockeys* sounds strange. There is quite a considerable number of nouns (both abstract – such as *misery, hatred* and *amazement* – and concrete – such as *hockey, music,* and *furniture*) which have no plural form. Because these nouns cannot be made plural and therefore their referents cannot be counted, they are known as **non-count nouns**. By contrast, nouns which have a plural form are **count nouns**. (Also there are one or two nouns which look plural because they end in <-s> but are in fact non-count nouns. These include *billiards, physics* and *politics*.)

There are also some nouns which don't fit comfortably into either of these categories. First, there are those which exist in the plural only. Examples of these include *trousers* and *scissors*:

> *The trousers are ready to wear*
> * *The trouser is in need of repair*
> *The scissors are blunt*
> * *The scissor is blunt*

A second group of nouns which are neither clearly count nor non-count nouns is the group of **aggregate nouns**. These are nouns which refer to entities made up of several parts. Some of these, like *trousers* and *scissors*, have no singular form, as with *goods* and *dregs* in the following examples:

> *The goods are ready for collection*
> *The *good is ready for collection*
> *The dregs in a bottle of wine taste unpleasant*
> *The *dreg in a bottle of wine tastes unpleasant.*

There are also some aggregate nouns which look singular but take a plural form of the verb:

> *The police have surrounded the building*
> * *The police has surrounded the building*
> *The cattle are lowing*
> * *The cattle is lowing*

Aggregate nouns such as these should not be confused with **collective nouns**. 'Collective' is a semantic term for nouns which refer to groups (usually of people or animals) but grammatically they are count nouns since they have both singular and plural forms. *Family* and *herd* are examples of collective nouns:

The family is (are) spending Christmas at home
Three families are going on holiday together
The herd is (are) grazing in the field by the river
The herds are doing very well this year

Both *family* and *herd* have plural forms. Interestingly, we sometimes use the plural form of the verb (*are*, in this case) with a singular collective noun as a concession to our notion that the noun refers to several units.

Some nouns have both a count form and a non-count one. This depends on the particular meaning of the noun which is being employed. *Wine* is a good example of this. When we talk of wine in the generic sense of a drink made from grapes then *wine* is a non-count noun:

Wine is an alcoholic drink made from grapes
* *Wines are alcoholic drinks made from grapes*

However, when we talk of different varieties of wine, then *wine* is a count noun: *Australian wines are as enjoyable as French ones.*

When they take the plural form, count nouns have either a regular or an irregular ending. Here are some examples of nouns which take the regular plural ending, sometimes known as the *-s* **plural**:

singular form	plural form
cake	*cakes*
bun	*buns*
gas	*gases*

All three examples here take a regular and predictable ending although this ending shows itself in different forms. In writing, some nouns add not <-s> word-finally but <-es>. This is driven by the fact that when they are pronounced in the plural, they actually add an extra syllable. It is impossible to say *gas-s*, so the noun becomes *gas-es* with two syllables rather than one. A vowel has been added to make the plural form pronounceable and distinct from the singular form. In speech we sometimes add the sound /s/ to make a noun plural (as in *cakes*) and sometimes /z/ (as in *buns*, which is pronounced 'bunz'). Whether we pronounce /s/ or /z/ depends on the consonant which precedes the inflectional ending, a process known as **assimilation**. In effect, though, these are all variant forms of the -*s* plural. (This form is actually a bound morpheme.)

There are a number of nouns which form plurals in other ways. Table 4.1 illustrates the range of irregular endings and gives some examples.

We now turn our attention to the **possessive form** of nouns. In English, possession can be denoted by an inflectional ending, and in written English this is most typically indicated by <-'s>. In the following example two nouns – the proper noun *Susan* and the common noun *dog* – have possessive inflections: *Susan's brother was preparing the dog's dinner.* Here, both *Susan* and *dog* take the possessive form. When we talk about the possessive form or possessive inflection, however, we are not always referring strictly to the ownership of one person or thing by another person or thing. For instance, in a phrase such as *a hard day's work* the day doesn't possess the work: instead, the implication is that the work lasted a day. We need to make a distinction therefore

Table 4.1 Irregular plural forms

Irregular inflection type	Explanation	Singular / plural examples
zero inflection	the singular form is the same as the plural form	sheep / sheep
vowel mutation	the vowel within the word changes	tooth / teeth mouse / mice man / men
voicing of final consonant	a regular -s plural is added but also the last consonant in the stem is pronounced with a vibration of the vocal cords, changing the quality of the sound	sheaf / sheaves hoof / hooves bath / baths
irregular plural inflection	a handful of nouns retain an Old English inflectional form	child / children ox / oxen brother / brethren
foreign plurals	nouns which have come to English from other languages sometimes retain the regular plural form of their original language – although the regular plural form of English may also be used	Latin: stimulus / stimuli antenna / antennae matrix / matrices Greek: phenomenon / phenomena Hebrew: cherub / cherubim French: gateau / gateaux

between the possessive inflection and a possessive meaning. Sometimes in English we use an **of-construction** rather than a possessive inflection, so we might talk about either *the journey's end* or *the end of the journey*. Sometimes, we wouldn't use the possessive inflection at all, so we might refer to *the window of the kitchen* or to *the kitchen window* but never to *the kitchen's window*.

Possessive inflections can be added to both singular and plural nouns. Above, the examples are all of singular nouns. Plural nouns can also take this form although in practice the possessive form is often not discernible because its spoken form is identical to the plural form. However, nouns with irregular plural endings can take overt possessive inflections as in for example *the children's playground* or *the teeth's whiteness*. In writing we indicate a plural which has a possessive quality by using an apostrophe: *the dogs' dinners*.

Another term which is sometimes used when discussing noun inflections is **case**. This is a traditional grammatical term used particularly in languages where there is a fuller range of noun inflections than there is now in English. These inflections indicate aspects such as whether the noun is the subject of the sentence (the **nominative** case), the object of the sentence (the **accusative** case), or the possessor of something (the **genitive** case) to give just three examples. In modern English 'case' is a less appropriate term for talking about noun inflections. However, some linguists do refer to the possessive inflection in English as the genitive or genitive case. You might also come across the term **common case** which refers to any noun not in the possessive form, be it singular or plural.

☐ **nouns as a word class** ⇨ 2.4
☐ **morphemes** ⇨ 3.2
☐ **assimilation** ⇨ 10.6

4.4 VERB INFLECTIONS

We saw in section 4.3 that there are two types of inflection that can be added to nouns: plural inflections and possessive inflections. Verbs are subject to a wider range of inflections although this range is still very limited in comparison with languages such as French and German. When we were looking at the plural forms of nouns we saw that there were both regular and irregular inflectional forms, and this is also true of verbs. We will begin with the regular forms.

The uninflected stem of the verb is known as the **base form** of the verb. This form is also referred to as the **infinitive** and we make a distinction between the **to-infinitive** (as in *to write*) and the **bare infinitive,** which does not contain the particle *to*. The base form of the verb may be varied by the addition of four regular inflections. These regular inflections are found only with lexical verbs. (The primary auxiliary verbs have irregular inflectional forms while the modal auxiliaries do not inflect at all and this of course sets them apart from lexical verbs.)

The first of these verb inflections is the *-s* inflection which marks the third person singular of the present tense as the following **paradigm** (or inflectional set) shows:

singular	first person	*I walk*
	second person	*you walk*
	third person	*he/she/it walks*
plural	first person	*we walk*
	second person	*you walk*
	third person	*they walk*

If this **conjugation** (namely, this set of verb forms) were translated into French, for example, the verb would have a different inflectional ending for every person. In Standard English, however, the base form is used in the present tense for every person except the third person in the singular. (Like some of the irregular plural noun inflections, this is an historical hangover.) This inflection is used for all verbs, even those which have irregular forms elsewhere.

The relationship between the verb form and the subject which precedes it is one of **concord**. In other words, the person and number of the subject controls the form the verb takes. In most lexical verbs in English, this is apparent only in the present tense, where the use of the third person singular requires the *-s* inflection. Otherwise the base form is used:

first person singular subject	*I like listening to Mozart*
third person singular subject	* *Miriam/she like listening to Mozart*
	Miriam/she likes listening to Mozart

The second verb inflection found in English is again found on all verbs, whether or not they also have irregular inflectional forms. This is the inflection *-ing*: the base form of the verb plus the *-ing* inflection is known as the **-*ing* participle**. It occurs in various grammatical contexts which we will return to in later chapters but examples include:

Fred was walking to the shops
I am hoping to go to Australia soon

Following in his father's footsteps was important to Bob
He was sorry for *keeping* them *waiting*

The third regular verb inflection is the *-ed* inflection which is used to construct the past tense. Examples of regular verbs using this inflection include: *they walked, I gazed, she hoped* and *we admired*. The *-ed* inflection is sometimes realised in pronunciation as a /t/ and sometimes as a /d/ depending on the sound which precedes it.

The fourth regular verb inflection is the *-ed* **participle** inflection. It takes the same form as the regular past tense inflection but we make a distinction between these two inflections because their functions are different and also because irregular verbs may have different forms for the past tense and the *-ed* participle. Examples of the *-ed* participle might include

They have *walked* three miles today
Jane's painting was much *admired* by her friends
Considered carefully, it wasn't a very good idea

To summarise then, regular lexical verbs have five forms. They either occur in the base form without any inflectional ending – and this is sometimes described as **zero inflection** – or they take one of four inflectional endings as Table 4.2 shows. As we observed earlier, all lexical verbs can take a regular *-ing* participle inflection. Similarly, all lexical verbs (with the exception of *be, have* and *do*) take the regular *-s* inflection to denote the third person singular in the present tense, even though the pronunciation of this inflection varies depending on the sound which precedes it. Either the regular *-ed* past tense inflection or the regular *-ed* participle ending, however, may occur in irregular verbs, although often both these inflections will be irregular. We will look next at how irregular verbs form the past tense and the *-ed* participle.

Let us begin by comparing an irregular verb, such as *take,* with the regular verb *walk* which we used above. Table 4.3 shows that the irregular verb *take* has a different form for the *-ed* participle from the form it has for the *-ed*

Table 4.2   Regular verb inflections

Form	Grammatical function	Example
-s	third person singular present tense	she walks
-ing	-ing participle	she is walking
-ed	simple past tense	she walked
-ed	-ed participle	she has walked

Table 4.3   A comparison of the inflections of *walk* and *take*

base form	walk	take
-s	walks	takes
-ing participle	walking	taking
-ed past tense	walked	took
-ed participle	walked	taken

past tense. Neither of these forms could have been predicted from the base form, hence the irregularity. Not all irregular verbs are irregular in the same way, however. *Take* has three different forms – one for the base form, one for the past tense, and one for the *-ed* participle but other combinations are possible, as Table 4.4 illustrates.

Irregular verbs, then, take various patterns. Some, like *show*, retain the regular past tense form but have an irregular *-ed* participle form. Others have either an irregular past tense which is identical to the irregular *-ed* participle form or an irregular past tense and a different *-ed* participle form. Some verbs have the base form for both. Some verbs change their vowel in their irregular forms (a feature known as **vowel mutation**) while others take an *-en* instead of an *-ed* inflection for the *-ed* participle.

In section 2.10 we saw that English has three primary auxiliary verbs: *be*, *have*, and *do*. These are used to construct different aspects and voices in the verb phrase, although they can also occur as the lexical verb in a verb phrase. All three verbs are irregular but *be* is the most irregular verb in English. Table 4.5 compares the different forms of these three verbs. As you can see from the table, *be* is highly irregular in that it has three different present tense forms (all other verbs have only two) and two different past tense forms (all other verbs have only one) according to person. When looking at the various types of irregular verb in Table 4.4, you may have observed that despite the unpredictable forms of some verbs, a similarity between their different forms was

Table 4.4   Patterns of irregular verbs

Base form	-ed Past tense		-ed Participle
	Regular	Irregular	
show	showed		shown
make		made	made
lose		lost	lost
speak		spoke	spoken
swim		swam	swum
hurt		hurt	hurt

Table 4.5 The irregular primary verbs *be, have* and *do*

		Be	Have	Do
base form		be	have	do
present tense				
singular	1st person	am	have	do
	2nd person	are	have	do
	3rd person	is	has	does
plural	1st/2nd/3rd person	are	have	do
past tense				
singular	1st person	was	had	did
	2nd person	were	had	did
	3rd person	was	had	did
plural	1st/2nd/3rd person	were	had	did
-ing participle		being	having	doing
-ed participle		been	had	done

still identifiable (particularly when you consider pronunciation in preference to spelling in the case of forms like *buy* and *bought*). However, with the highly irregular verb *be* it is not possible to discern any family likeness between some of its forms: *be, are, am, is, was* and *were* appear fundamentally different and it would certainly not be accurate to claim that *am*, for example, is an inflectional form of *be*. When a particular form of a word, in this case a verb, is supplied by a completely unrelated form rather than by an inflectional ending, this is known as **suppletion**.

☐ **lexical verbs** ⇨ 2.5
☐ **auxiliary verbs** ⇨ 2.10
☐ **verb phrases** ⇨ 5.3

4.5 ADJECTIVE AND ADVERB INFLECTIONS

We saw in Chaper 2 that one of the qualities which both adjectives and adverbs share is their ability to be graded. What this means is that we can indicate to what extent a particular quality exists. For instance, we might say that a person is *tall*, or *extremely tall*. We might say someone ran *quickly* or that they ran *incredibly quickly*. Gradability, then, is a typical feature of adjectives and also of a lot of adverbs, particularly adverbs of manner. As well as grading adjectives and adverbs in this way, we can also use them to compare one person or thing with another. This is often done using the inflections *-er* and *-est* as the following examples show:

adjective *tall*	*Rosie is tall*
	Esther and Jenni are taller
	Laura is tallest
adverb *fast*	*Rosie ran fast*
	Esther and Jenni ran faster
	Laura ran fastest

The forms of adjectives and adverbs which have no inflectional endings are known as **absolute** forms. The *-er* inflection on an adjective or adverb gives the **comparative** form, and the *-est* inflection gives the **superlative** form.

Not all adjectives take the comparative and superlative inflections. If the word in question consists of three syllables or more, then it will probably construct the comparative by using the premodifying adverb *more* and the superlative by using the premodifying adverb *most*. Adverbs (as distinct from adjectives) which end in *-ly* all use *more* and *most*:

	absolute	comparative	superlative
adjectives	*tall*	*taller*	*tallest*
	beautiful	* *beautifuller*	* *beautifullest*
	beautiful	*more beautiful*	*most beautiful*
adverbs	*fast*	*faster*	*fastest*
	quickly	* *quicklier*	* *quickliest*
	quickly	*more quickly*	*most quickly*

We have seen in our discussion of the inflections of nouns and verbs that there are always some irregular forms. This is also true of adverbs and

Table 4.6   Irregular forms of adjectives and adverbs

	Adjectives			Adverbs		
Absolute	Comparative	Superlative		Absolute	Comparative	Superlative
good	better	best		well	better	best
bad	worse	worst		badly	worse	worst
				much	more	most
				little	less	least

adjectives where suppletive forms often occur for the comparative and superlative. Table 4.6 shows the irregular forms of some key adjectives and adverbs.

> ☐ **adjectives** ⇨ 2.6
> ☐ **adverbs** ⇨ 2.7

4.6 PRONOUN INFLECTIONS

So far, all the inflections we have identified and discussed have occurred on lexical words – namely, nouns, verbs, adjectives and adverbs. Inflections in the truest sense of the term do not occur on function words, but the discussion of inflections would be incomplete without mentioning the occurrence of suppletion in some personal pronouns. In Chapter 2 we saw how the personal pronouns take different forms which we refer to as subjective and objective forms. They are reproduced below:

		subjective	objective
singular	first person	*I*	*me*
	second person	*you*	*you*
	third person	*he*	*him*
		she	*her*
		it	*it*
plural	first person	*we*	*us*
	second person	*you*	*you*
	third person	*they*	*them*

The terms subjective and objective are derived from the position in which the pronouns typically appear: the subjective form normally appears in the subject position before the verb and the objective form normally occurs in the object position after the verb. So, the first person singular personal pronoun would normally be *I* before the verb and *me* after it:

I saw Pedro
Pedro saw *I
Pedro saw me

However, in informal English we sometimes use the objective form in subject position, usually when it is joined with another noun or pronoun:

<u>Me</u> and Jane are great friends
Jane and <u>her</u> went to Wimbledon together.

We discussed in section 4.3 the question of case in contemporary English and why it is not an especially appropriate term to use in relation to nouns. In Old English and in some other modern languages case can be applied to personal pronouns. In contemporary English it would be inappropriate to talk about subject and object cases for pronouns since the use of the different forms is not dictated strictly by position or function. It is more appropriate to refer to subjective and objective forms since these terms refer to typical rather than invariable occurrence.

Finally, in section 2.8 we noted that there are several different types of pronouns, including demonstrative pronouns. Demonstrative pronouns might also be said to have inflected forms for the plural, although their irregularity is evident:

singular	plural
this	*these*
that	*those*

- ☐ **pronouns** ⇨ 2.8
- ☐ **contemporary English** ⇨ 4.2
- ☐ **case** ⇨ 4.3

5 PHRASES

5.1 WHAT IS A PHRASE?

At the beginning of the previous chapter we established that grammar can be subdivided into two areas: **syntax** and **inflections**. Inflections are the grammatical endings which occur on open class words (and on some pronouns) and which give information about, for example, tense and number. An inflection is part of the internal structure of a word. Syntax, on the other hand, operates on a level higher than the word since it is concerned with the rules by which words are combined into larger units. It is possible to identify three larger units of construction, beginning with the smallest:

> **phrases**
> **clauses**
> **sentences**

This chapter and the following two chapters deal with these units of construction and therefore cover the range of syntactic rules which enable us to construct any well-formed sentence in the language. Chapter 8 shows you some of the strategies used to combine sentences into texts – what is known as **discourse**.

To illustrate what we mean by a phrase, take a look at the following example:

> *The black labrador was chewing a juicy bone very noisily*

One way of looking at this sentence is to regard it as a linear sequence of words: *the* precedes *black*, *black* precedes *labrador*, *labrador* precedes *was* and so on. Although mental syntactic rules enable us to place words in an appropriate order the rules do not operate simply in this linear fashion. Initially, the rules operate on a phrase level, then on a clause level and then on a sentence level. So we need to approach our example not as a sequence of individual words but as a sequence of word groups or **phrases**.

In Chapter 1, we noted that if speakers are asked to divide the words in a sentence into groups, we can predict that they will all do it in the same way:

> *the black labrador + was chewing + a juicy bone + very noisily*

We would not expect anyone to group the words like this, for example:

> *the black + labrador was + chewing a juicy + bone very noisily*

The reason for this phenomenon is that we instinctively know that words are grouped into phrases and that these are the basic building blocks for larger syntactic constructions. Our instinctive ability to identify phrases is linked with an awareness of how clauses are structured. Confronted with an example such as:

> *was chewing a juicy bone very noisily*

we recognise that information is missing about who was chewing. In other words, the **subject** slot is empty, and it can be filled by a phrase. Phrases are the building blocks of clauses because they fill clause slots in this way.

The example of *The black labrador was chewing a juicy bone very noisily* consists of four phrases. If, having asked speakers to identify the phrases in this example, you asked them to select what they considered to be the key word in each phrase, there would be general agreement on this:

> *the black <u>labrador</u>*
> *was <u>chewing</u>*
> *a juicy <u>bone</u>*
> *very <u>noisily</u>*

The key words have been underlined. These key words are known as **head words** or **heads**. They are the lexical items which are central to the phrase in the sense that some crucial information would be missing without the head word and the phrase would seem structurally incomplete. This is illustrated by the fact that the head words themselves, placed alone in sequence, normally result in a skeleton sentence which still makes a certain amount of sense and which captures the essence of the full example:

> *labrador chewing bone noisily*

In the four examples above, the head word occurs at the end of the phrase.

This is often, but not always, the case as we will see when we look at the full range of possibilities for structuring phrases.

There are five types of phrase:

noun phrase   abbreviated as NP
verb phrase   abbreviated as VP
adjective phrase   abbreviated as AdjP
adverb phrase   abbreviated as AdvP
prepositional phrase abbreviated as PP

You will notice that each of the four open word classes (noun, verb, adjective and adverb) has an associated phrase type. Prepositions are the only closed class which has an associated phrase type, and prepositional phrases differ in kind from the other four types.

Normally, in order to identify a phrase type, you need to begin by identifying the head word. If the head word is a noun, then the phrase is a noun phrase; if it's a verb, then the phrase is a verb phrase and so on. However, this approach doesn't operate in quite the same way for a prepositional phrase, although a preposition will still be the head word.

Another important point to make about phrases is that, with the exception of prepositional phrases, they may actually consist of a single lexical item. They do not have to consist of at least two words. It is particularly important to remember this given that the term 'phrase' suggests to most people 'more than one word'. There are two main reasons why we should treat individual words as phrases. The first is that, given the basic principle that words group together to form phrases, then we would not wish to have any words unaccounted for on that level of a clause's structure. This would not make for a very watertight or cohesive set of syntactic rules. Secondly, all phrases have the potential to be expanded: the head word may stand alone, or it may be **premodified** or **postmodified** by other elements. Consider this example:

Snakes appear dangerous

Here, it is impossible really to divide the words into groups. What we have in fact are three single-word phrases. *Snakes* is a noun, so it is the head of a noun phrase, *appear* is a verb so it is the head of a verb phrase, *dangerous* is an adjective so it is the head of an adjective phrase. What this means is that the structure of this clause in phrasal terms is:

NP + VP + AdjP

It is possible to expand each of these phrases so that they become more than a single word:

NP	VP	AdjP
British grass snakes	*may appear*	*rather dangerous*

As mentioned above, a prepositional phrase differs from the other four types in that a preposition cannot stand alone as a phrase. This is linked to its status as a grammatical word rather than a lexical word.

In section 1.5 we noted how linguists use different types of bracket to enclose various linguistic features or units. If you wish to mark off the phrases in a clause or sentence then you can use square brackets, so that the above example will look like this:

[British grass snakes$_{NP}$]   [may appear$_{VP}$]   [rather dangerous$_{AdjP}$]

You will also see that each bracket has been labelled to show what type of phrase it is. Bracketing isn't the only way of breaking down an example for analysis. Some linguists prefer to use tree diagrams and we will be looking at this method in Chapter 7.

In the following sections, we will examine each phrase type in turn. We will be spending rather more time on noun phrases and verb phrases since they are typically more central and more complex than the other types. This is partly to do with their function in clause structures. All phrases – whatever their form – fulfil a function within a clause. This is something we will consider in Chapter 6.

5.2   NOUN PHRASES

A noun phrase may consist of a single lexical item. On the other hand, noun phrases have the capacity to be long and complex – more so than other phrase types. The following two examples illustrate this contrast:

NP	VP	AdjP
<u>Doughnuts</u>	*are*	*really fattening*
These large sugary <u>doughnuts</u> filled with jam and cream	*are*	*really fattening*

The second noun phrase is much longer, with additional elements occurring both before and after the head noun. Elsewhere in our discussions we have seen that the internal order of elements in a linguistic unit is fixed rather than random. For example, we noted in section 3.4 that there is a restriction on the occurrence of affixes within the structure of a derived word. Similarly, noun phrases have an internal structure which dictates where additional elements occur in relation to the head noun. There are three possible positions for these elements. All four positions (the fourth being the head noun itself) are illustrated in the complex example given above and repeated below:

determiner	premodification	head noun	postmodification
these	*large sugary*	*doughnuts*	*filled with jam and cream*

Determiners are discussed in some detail in section 2.9. They can be subdivided into three categories: predeterminers, central determiners and postdeterminers. Determiners are not obligatory but if they do occur they will be at the beginning of the noun phrase. Furthermore, determiners only occur in noun phrases.

There are a range of elements which can occur in a premodifying position. Most typically, premodifiers will be adjectives (including deverbal adjectives or participles). It is possible to premodify a head noun with more than one adjective as in *large sugary doughnuts*. In theory there is no limit as to how many adjectives could premodify a head noun provided their meanings do not contradict each other, but in reality it is unlikely that there will be more than two or three at most:

It was a foolish, dangerous, expensive idea
? It was a foolish, dangerous, expensive, pointless, inopportune idea

When more than one adjective appears in premodifying position, an ordering process may come into play. For example, adjectives relating to size, age and colour are likely to occur in a set order. For instance, if *an old suitcase* was *large* and *blue*, speakers are likely to refer to it as *a large old blue suitcase*, placing the adjectives in the order of size, then age, then colour. Other combinations seem unnatural: **a blue old large suitcase*, **an old large blue suitcase*, **a large blue old suitcase*. Another example of a set order of adjectives is that a gradable adjective will occur before a non-gradable one. So an adjective such as *woollen* which is non-gradable would be preceded by an adjective such as *pretty* which is gradable: *a pretty woollen dress* not **a woollen pretty dress*.

Nouns as well as adjectives can precede head nouns. The noun may be either a common or a proper noun. Here are some examples:

determiner	premodifying noun	head noun
a	*leather*	*suitcase*

several	party	guests
	printer	cartridges
the	London	experience
	Gucci	fashion

Additionally, nouns in the possessive form – again, both proper and common nouns – can also premodify head nouns:

	possessive noun	head noun
(the)	children's	playground
(a)	composer's	music
	plovers'	eggs
	London's	churches

One point to note here though is that the indefinite article which occurs in *a composer's music* belongs not to *music* but to *composer's*. We can demonstrate this by rewriting the phrase as an *of*-construction:

   the music of a composer
 * *a music of a composer*

Because *music* is a non-count noun (and has no plural form) it is impossible to precede it with an indefinite article. Whereas it is not possible to tell whether *the* in *the children's playground* belongs to *children's* or *playground*, in *a composer's music*, the *a* must belong to *composer* because it is syntactically impossible for it to belong to *music*.

So far we have looked at the premodification of head nouns by adjectives, by other nouns and by nouns in the possessive form. We have seen that, when more than one premodifying adjective occurs, there is likely to be a prescribed sequence for these adjectives. Further, when the head noun is premodified by more than one type of premodifier, again there is a given order in which these elements will occur. For example, suppose a head noun *music* were to be premodified by the adjective *difficult*, by the noun *piano* and by the possessive noun plus definite article *the composer's*, then the elements would take the following order:

   the composer's   difficult   piano   music

Any other combination would not seem natural. The existence of a definite article with *composer's* would seem to dictate that this element occur at the start of the noun phrase since this is the natural position for determiners.

Premodifying nouns occur closer to the head noun than any adjectives because they typically categorise rather than qualify the head noun: in other words, *piano music* is a specific type of music but *difficult music* can be of any type.

Occasionally, elements other than adjectives or nouns may premodify a head noun. An adverb, for example, could occur in this position as in *the then headteacher*, and so could a short sentence such as *do as you please* in *their do-as-you-please attitude*. These are exceptions, though, and it is far more likely that any premodifying elements will be adjectives or nouns.

Finally, a word needs to be said about the premodification of premodifying elements. In the following noun phrase, the head noun *invitation* is premodified by the adjective *nice*: *a nice invitation*. It is possible to qualify the adjective *nice* with the adverb *rather* as in *a rather nice invitation*. It is clear that *rather* is attached to *nice* and not to *invitation* as it is not possible to remove *nice*: **a rather invitation*. This is not dissimilar to the observation we made earlier regarding *a composer's music* where we noted that *a* was attached not to the head noun *music* but to the premodifying possessive noun *composer's*. In addition, the fact that *nice* can be premodified in this way leads us to conclude that *nice* is itself a phrase (it can be expanded to *rather nice*) and that we are dealing here with a phrase within a phrase. We will return to this point later.

Let us now move on to the postmodification of head nouns. This is a more complex matter than the premodification of head nouns since there is again a range of items which can fulfil this function and, in addition, the postmodification has the potential to be more complex, as in this example where the head noun is underlined:

the <u>proposal</u> *for a new building which the committee put forward last week*

Here, the head noun *proposal* is postmodified by a prepositional phrase *for a new building* and by a **relative clause** *which the committee put forward last week*.

Head nouns can be postmodified by both phrases and clauses. It is very common for prepositional phrases to postmodify head nouns but adverb phrases occasionally occur **postnominally** (after the noun) when referring to time or place as in *the meeting yesterday* or *the trip abroad*. Only a handful of adjectives occur postnominally and in a limited range of contexts. Two examples are *apparent* in *heir apparent* and *elect* in *president elect*. The adjective *proper* also occurs after a noun when it is used emphatically as in *the meeting proper*.

A variety of clauses occur in postmodifying position. The clause may be a relative clause:

> the proposal <u>which the committee put forward last week</u>

or a **that**-clause:

> the belief <u>that God exists</u>

or a **comparative clause**:

> Rachael gave a louder cry <u>than Miriam did</u>

or one of a range of **non-finite** clauses. These are all covered in detail in section 6.3. Prepositional phrases and relative clauses are the most frequent types of postmodifers in noun phrases. Head nouns may be postmodified by more than one item although there are constraints on what may occur.

To conclude our discussion of noun phrase structure, a few further points need to be made about the head word of a noun phrase. We noted earlier that phrase type can be identified from the class of the head word. Normally, then, a noun is the head of a noun phrase. However, there are some exceptions to this. First, a pronoun can also be the head of a noun phrase. The pronoun may occur singly as a phrase or, like a head noun, it may be pre- or postmodified. Here are some examples:

NP	VP	
She	*has arrived*	personal pronoun only
Absolutely <u>anyone</u>	*may come*	pronoun + premodification
<u>Someone</u> who knows	*should be consulted*	pronoun + postmodification

Although pronouns can function as the head of a phrase in this way, there would be no real virtue in positing a pronoun phrase as a distinct phrase type. The reason for this is that the degree of overlap which would exist between noun phrases and pronoun phrases, in terms of both their internal structure and their typical function within a clause, would make for an uneconomical description of syntactic rules.

Cardinal numerals might also be the head of a noun phrase. They are classified in section 2.8 as a subset of pronouns but with the qualification that they sometimes function more like nouns. Examples might include *the magnificent seven* or *the Guildford four*. Finally, some adjectives can occur **pronominally** (in the position of the noun). An example would be *innocent* in *The innocent were allowed to leave*. There is no likelihood here that *innocent* is a noun because, if it were, it would have a plural inflection since the verb *were* is plural. Adjectives are often used this way when the noun *people* might be understood:

the innocent	*were allowed to leave*
the innocent people	*were allowed to leave*
the charity workers were concerned about	*the homeless*
the charity workers were concerned about	*the homeless people*

However, adjectives can also be used pronominally to refer to a concept as in *She had a strong sense of the divine*.

This section has shown you something of the complexities of noun phrase structure. When a noun phrase is very long and complex you will need to take care to identify the head word correctly as the noun phrase may well contain more than one noun, as we have already seen. One way to identify the head word is to decide which word is most central to the meaning. Another method, when the noun phrase is in subject position (namely it is succeeded by a verb phrase) is to identify which element is controlling the verb phrase in terms of it being singular or plural:

NP	VP
The beautiful house admired by architects	*has burnt down*

In the noun phrase above, there are two nouns – *house* and *architects*. *House* is singular, whereas *architects* is plural. The first element of the verb phrase *has* is also singular. There is **concord** between a head noun in subject position and the following verb phrase so this shows that the head of the noun phrase is *house* rather than *architects*. We can double-check this by making *house* plural and *architects* singular:

NP	VP
The beautiful houses admired by the architect	*have burnt down*

Now *has* has become *have* in concord with the plural *houses*. This small test shows us then that *house* is the head word in this complex noun phrase.

☐ determiners ⇨ 2.9
☐ phrases within phrases ⇨ 5.6

5.3   VERB PHRASES

Noun phrases and verb phrases are the most central in the construction of clauses. One major contrast between noun phrases and verb phrases, however, is the much greater restriction on the number of elements which can occur in a verb phrase. Like noun phrases (and adjective and adverb phrases), verb phrases may consist merely of the head word. This single item will be a lexical as opposed to an auxiliary verb. Whereas a noun phrase has the potential to be extremely long, especially when it contains both pre- and postmodification, a verb phrase will be no longer than the following example:

NP	VP
Those naughty children	*might have been being told off*

A verb phrase of this kind, which has six elements, is rare. The first four elements – *might have been being* – are auxiliary verbs, while the lexical verb *told off* is a multi-word verb. Some speakers might question whether this example is natural, although it could occur in a sentence such as *I heard a lot of shouting so I thought those naughty children <u>might have been being told off</u> by their mother.*

A verb phrase, then, may be simple and consist of just a lexical verb (which may be a multi-word verb) or it may include one or more auxiliaries up to a maximum of four. Auxiliaries subdivide into primary auxiliaries and modal auxiliaries:

primary auxiliaries	*be, have, do*
modal auxiliaries	*can, could, shall, should, will, would, may, must, might*

The modal auxiliaries are used to add shades of meaning, such as obligation (*must*) or possibility (*might*) to the verb phrase. The primary auxiliaries *be* and *have* are used to construct different **aspects** and **voices**. The primary auxiliary *do* is used in question forms, in negative constructions, and for emphasis.

One of the features which verb phrases may possess is **tense**, and this is where we will begin our exploration of the many facets of verb phrases. We noted in section 2.5 that all lexical verbs can exhibit a contrast of tense. There are only two tenses in English: the **past** and the **present**. The present tense is indicated either by the base form or by an *-s* inflection (in the third person singular), and the past tense is indicated by an *-ed* inflection on regular verbs or an equivalent form in irregular verbs. Sometimes speakers are under the misapprehension that the present tense only refers to the present time and that the past tense only refers to past time, but this is not necessarily the case. In an example such as *Wine appeals to many people* the verb *appeals* is in the present tense but the time reference is broader than the present moment since the sentence is stating a general truth. In *I said I would give him dinner when he arrived* the verb *arrived* is in the past tense, but in the context of the sentence it refers to a moment in the future. We must be careful not to make assumptions about time and tense. We need to distinguish between the meaning of a sentence and the grammatical form of the verb phrase. Tense is a grammatical ending on a verb stem not a semantic reference to a particular time. In English, there exists only the past tense and the present tense in terms of inflectional endings. There is no future tense in English. If we want to make a future reference we need to use a structure such as *Fred will help* or *Fred is going to help*. Here are some examples of present and past tense contrasts in English in both regular and irregular verbs:

present tense	past tense
Jane likes music	*Jane liked music*
We admire her painting	*We admired her painting*
Phil buys a lot of wine	*Phil bought a lot of wine*
You take some liberties	*You took some liberties*

The above examples all contain simple verb phrases consisting of the lexical verb only. In each instance, the verb is marked for either present or past tense. When a verb or verb phrase is marked for tense it is **finite**. By contrast, when a verb is not marked for tense it is **non-finite**. If a finite verb phrase consists of a lexical verb only, then tense will, of necessity, be marked on that element. Otherwise, tense is marked on the first element of the verb phrase.

We will move on now to consider the role and position of auxiliary verbs in verb phrases. Not only must auxiliary verbs (like *might* and *have*) precede lexical verbs but there is also a fixed order in which auxiliary verbs occur, with modal auxiliaries (like *might*) preceding primary ones (like *have*). So *Fred might have arrived by now* can be contrasted with the ill-formed example **Fred have might arrived by now*. We noted above that finite verb phrases are those which are marked for tense and that tense is always marked on the first element of the verb phrase. What this means is that if the verb phrase contains a modal auxiliary, then tense will be marked on the modal. Modals are unusual in that they do not have contrasting forms for tense in the way that lexical (and primary) verbs do. Nevertheless, if a modal is present, you need to assume it carries tense marking. The reason for this is that modal auxiliaries do not occur in non-finite verb phrases.

One important feature of verb phrases which consist of more than one element is that each auxiliary dictates the form which the following element takes. If there is a modal auxiliary present, the element which follows it will be in the base form. Consider the following examples:

	NP	VP	NP
1	Jane	likes	music
2	Jane	*might likes	music
3	Jane	*might liked	music
4	Jane	might like	music

Example 1 contains a verb phrase which consists of a finite lexical verb in the present tense – *likes*. Examples 2 and 3 illustrate how, when a modal is introduced, it is no longer necessary to mark the next element (in this case the lexical verb *like*) for tense. Example 4 shows how the element which follows the modal needs to take the base form if it is to be grammatical.

Although a verb phrase can only contain one modal auxiliary, it can contain up to three primary auxiliaries. The main purpose of primary auxiliaries is to indicate **aspect**. Aspect, like modality, gives us more information about the verb but from a rather different angle. Aspect indicates whether the action or state referred to by the lexical verb is in progress or is complete. This basic contrast is a contrast between the **progressive aspect** and the **perfect aspect**. These aspects are indicated using the primary auxiliaries *be* and *have*.

There are two progressive aspects: the **present progressive** and the **past progressive**. Here are examples of them:

present progressive   Sara *is helping* her sister
                       They *are approaching* the motorway

past progressive   Sara *was helping* her sister
                       They *were approaching* the motorway

All four examples indicate that the actions in question (*helping* and *approaching*) were still in progress at the point of utterance. You can see that there is a distinction between present and past progressive. Present and past are indicated on the first element in the verb phrase which, as we have already noted, is the element marked for tense in finite verb phrases. In the present progressive examples, the present tense is indicated by *is* and *are*. In the past progressive examples, the past tense is indicated by *was* and *were*. You will see therefore that in order to construct the progressive aspect we use the primary auxiliary *be*. When *be* is used in this way, the following element will take the

-ing inflection (in a similar way to the modal auxiliary triggering the base form). The resulting verb form in a lexical verb is known as the **-*ing* form** (or the **-*ing* participle**).

In contrast to the progressive aspect, we construct the perfect aspect using the primary auxiliary *have*. The perfect aspect denotes that the action or state referred to by the lexical verb is complete. There are two perfect aspects: the **present perfect** and the **past perfect**:

present perfect	*Sara <u>has helped</u> her sister*
	They <u>have approached</u> the motorway
past perfect	*Sara <u>had helped</u> her sister*
	They <u>had approached</u> the motorway

Again, the first element in the verb phrase indicates present or past, so that the primary auxiliary takes the form *has* or *have* in the present perfect and the form *had* in the past perfect. The presence of the primary auxiliary *have* for the perfect aspect triggers the **-*ed* form** (or **-*ed* participle**) in the following element (or its equivalent if the verb is irregular). This is in contrast to the -*ing* form triggered by the primary auxiliary *be* for the progressive aspect.

Both the progressive aspect and the perfect aspect may occur with a modal auxiliary as the following examples show:

progressive aspect	progressive aspect + modal auxiliary
1a *Sara <u>is helping</u> her sister*	1b *Sara <u>might be helping</u> her sister*
perfect aspect	perfect aspect + modal auxiliary
2a *Sara <u>has helped</u> her sister*	2b *Sara <u>might have helped</u> her sister*

You will notice in examples 1b and 2b how the presence of the modal *might* triggers the base forms of *be* and *have*. Since tense is now marked on the modal auxiliary, the distinction between past and present aspect disappears. *Have*, however, as the primary auxiliary for the perfect aspect, continues to trigger the -*ed* form for the element which follows it – in this case the lexical verb – while *be* continues to trigger the -*ing* form.

It is also possible for the verb aspect to be both perfect and progressive, and again there is a contrast of past and present. This means that both a **present perfect progressive** and a **past perfect progressive** aspect exist. The primary auxiliary *have* precedes the primary auxiliary *be* when this aspect is constructed:

present perfect progressive	*Debra <u>has been skating</u>*
	They <u>have been dancing</u>

past perfect progressive   *Debra <u>had been skating</u>*

                                   They <u>had been dancing</u>

We noted above that the primary auxiliary *have* triggers the *-ed* form in the following element. Here, the following element is the primary auxiliary *be* which is an irregular verb. The equivalent *-ed* form is *been*. In turn, the primary auxiliary *be* will trigger the *-ing* form as you can see in *dancing* and *skating*. Again, it is possible to include a modal auxiliary in these verb phrases, and again this modal auxiliary will have a knock-on effect on the form of the following element:

perfect progressive, no modal	perfect progressive with modal
Debra has been skating	*Debra could have been skating*
They have been dancing	*They could have been dancing*

From the preceding discussion, then, we can see the range of tenses and aspects which it is possible to express in the verb phrase as well as the roles which auxiliary verbs play. In addition we can identify the relationship between the various elements of a verb phrase in terms of the form they take. This information is summarised in Table 5.1.

So far we have seen a considerable amount which demonstrates the complex, multi-faceted nature of verb phrases. We have seen in earlier sections how verbs and verb phrases are marked to some extent for person and for singular or plural, and in this section we have seen how they can be marked for both tense and aspect. We now need to consider a further dimension and this is the feature of **voice**. Compare the following two examples:

NP	VP	
The singer	*was performing*	*(the song)*
The song	*was being performed*	*(by the singer)*

If you contrast the examples in terms of the relationship between the verb phrase and the noun phrase subject which precedes it, you will notice that in the first example the subject is actually doing the *performing* denoted by the verb. In other words, the singer is active in carrying out the performing. By contrast, the *song* of the second example is inactive and is, as it were, having the performing done to it. The contrast between these two examples is a contrast of voice. The verb phrase in the first example is **active** (or in the **active voice**) while the verb phrase in the second example is **passive** (or in the **passive voice**). This in turn means that the clauses in which they occur are also active or passive. We will look more closely at active and passive clauses

Table 5.1   Verb tenses and aspects

	Verb phrase			
	Auxiliary verbs		Lexical verb (head)	
modal (e.g. *might*)	primary HAVE	primary BE		
	(marks for perfect aspect)	(marks for progressive aspect)		
triggers base form	triggers -ed form	triggers -ing form		
			ask	present tense
			asked	past tense
	have		*asked*	present perfect aspect
	had		*asked*	past perfect aspect
		am	*asking*	present progressive aspect
		was	*asking*	past progressive aspect
	have	*been*	*asking*	present perfect progressive aspect
	had	*been*	*asking*	past perfect progressive aspect
				with MODAL:
might	*have*		*asked*	perfect aspect
might		*be*	*asking*	progressive aspect
might	*have*	*been*	*asking*	perfect progressive aspect

in Chapter 6, but here we are simply concerned with the form of the verb phrase in these constructions.

There is a contrast then between the active verb phrase *was performing* and the passive verb phrase *was being performed*. The passive phrase contains an additional auxiliary from the primary verb *be*. In this example, the additional element is *being*. When a clause is made passive, certain changes take place within the clause. However, a change is also evident within the verb phrase. We have already seen that *be* is used as a primary auxiliary to indicate the progressive aspect. In addition, *be* is used to indicate the passive voice. The difference is that when *be* marks the progressive aspect it triggers the *-ing* form in the following element (as in *was performing*) but when it marks the passive voice it triggers the *-ed* form, hence *was being performed*. All the tenses and aspects which were summarised in Table 5.1 were in the active voice. Table 5.2

shows the same range of tenses and aspects but in the passive voice. You will also see that modal auxiliaries can occur in passive verb phrases.

At the beginning of this section we noted that the longest well-formed verb phrase in English could consist of up to four auxiliaries plus the lexical verb, and we had the example of *those naughty children <u>might have been being told off</u>*. We can see now that this verb phrase comprises the elements shown in Table 5.3. Although it is unlikely you will come across – or use yourself – many verb phrases which contain four auxiliary elements, it is important to know the manner in which a verb phrase can be extended, particularly as there is a clear contrast between strategies used for expanding noun phrases and those used for expanding verb phrases.

The final dimension of verb phrases which we need to consider is another contrast, this time in terms of **finite** and **non-finite** verb phrases. As

Table 5.2   Verb tenses and aspects in the passive voice

	Verb phrase					
	Auxiliary verbs			Lexical verb (head)		
modal (e.g. *might*)	primary HAVE	primary BE	primary BE			
	(marks for perfect aspect)	(marks for progressive aspect)	(marks for passive voice)			
triggers base form	triggers -ed form	triggers -ing form	triggers -ed form			
			am	*asked*	present tense	
			was	*asked*	past tense	
	have		*been*	*asked*	present perfect aspect	
	had		*been*	*asked*	past perfect aspect	
		am	*being*	*asked*	present progressive aspect	
		was	*being*	*asked*	past progressive aspect	
	have	*been*	*being*	*asked*	present perfect progressive aspect	
	had	*been*	*being*	*asked*	past perfect progressive aspect	
					with MODAL:	
might	*have*		*been*	*asked*	perfect aspect	
might		*be*	*being*	*asked*	progressive aspect	
might	*have*	*been*	*being*	*asked*	perfect progressive aspect	

Table 5.3   Analysis of a complex VP *might have been being told off*

modal auxiliary	primary auxiliary <u>have</u> (perfect aspect)	primary auxiliary <u>be</u> (progressive aspect)	primary auxiliary <u>be</u> (passive voice)	lexical verb
triggers base form	triggers -*ed* form	triggers -*ing* form	triggers -*ed* form	
might	*have*	*been*	*being*	*told off*

we have already seen, a verb or verb phrase which is marked for tense is finite. The tense will be marked on the first element or only element of the verb phrase. All the following examples of verb phrases are finite:

	NP	VP
1	*John*	*tried*
2	*John*	*has tried*
3	*John*	*is trying*
4	*John*	*might have tried*

In the first example, the verb phrase consists solely of the lexical verb *tried*. As we can contrast *tried* which is past tense and *tries* which is present tense, this tells us the verb is marked for tense and the verb phrase is therefore finite. In examples 2 and 3, as well as the head verb there is a primary auxiliary verb and any tense will be marked on this first element. Again, we can establish a contrast between *has* and *had* and between *is* and *was,* and this tells us that *has tried* and *is trying* are also finite verb phrases. In example 4, the presence of the modal auxiliary *might* is evidence of tense marking so this last verb phrase is also finite. By contrast, here are some sentences which contain non-finite verb phrases:

> <u>To arrive</u> on time was their objective
> <u>To have arrived</u> on time was their objective

In the first example, the verb phrase consists of the base or infinitive form with the **infinitive particle** *to*. It is impossible to make a past/present contrast between *arrive* and *arrived* since we cannot say *to arrived. (Tense marking is not possible on the infinitive particle, of course.) This shows us that *to arrive* is a non-finite verb phrase. The second example also has the verb in the infinitive form which here exhibits the perfect aspect. However, *have* must be in the base form not the present tense form since *to had arrived* is not possible. Non-finite verb phrases can also take the base form of the verb but without the *to* particle:

> *Susan has helped <u>wash up</u>*

In this example the finite verb phrase <u>has helped</u> is complemented by the non-finite verb phrase <u>wash up</u>. This is a multi-word verb in the base form: no contrast with *washed up* would be acceptable in this context.

Verb phrases which begin with *-ed* or *-ing* participles are also non-finite:

> 1 <u>*Summoned*</u> *to an urgent meeting, Philip left at once*
> 2 *Philip went out for a walk, <u>hoping</u> to see a rainbow*
> 3 <u>*Having been caught*</u> *asleep at work, Philip was fired*

Examples 1 and 2 contain the single-word verb phrases *summoned* and *hoping* which are non-finite. So too is example 3 *having been caught* which contains two auxiliaries – *having* which indicates perfect aspect and *been* which indicates passive voice. The verb phrase is non-finite because the first element *having* is not marked for tense. You will notice, however, that examples 1, 2 and 3 also contain finite verb phrases (*left*, *went out* and *was fired*). This is because non-finite verbs lack the grammatical completeness which a finite verb gives to a sentence. To summarise, non-finite verb phrases have no marking for tense. They will take one of the following forms:

> base or infinitive form of the verb with or without *to*
> *-ing* form as the first or only element
> *-ed* form as the first or only element

It is difficult to discuss verb phrases as being finite or non-finite without referring to their role in the structure of clauses and sentences but we will be dealing with this shortly.

In this section we have seen how verb phrases can carry a complex load of grammatical information regarding features such as tense, aspect, voice and finiteness. One final point needs to be made before we move on to look at the three remaining phrase types. We noted at the start of this chapter that phrases are identifiable groups of words (and even single-word phrases have the potential to be expanded into multi-word phrases). We have seen that the internal structure of phrases is rule-governed and this means that phrases cannot include elements other than those allowed by the phrase structure rules. What this essentially means is that a verb phrase will comprise a lexical verb plus any auxiliaries (or possibly the infinitive particle *to* if it is a non-finite verb phrase) but nothing else. However, there is an exception to this principle and that is when an adverb, which is a more mobile class of word, interrupts the verb phrase as in the third and fourth examples below:

1   *have been told off*
2   * *have mother been told off*
3   *have <u>certainly</u> been told off*
4   *have been <u>severely</u> told off*

Disjuncts such as *certainly* tend to occur after the first auxiliary whereas adverbs of manner are more likely to occur immediately before the lexical verb to modify its meaning: here the children have not just been told off but *severely* told off. It would not be especially helpful to retrace our steps and reconsider adverbs as a central part of the verb phrase structure but it is important to be aware that they can appear in the positions shown.

- adverbs ⇨ 2.7
- auxiliaries ⇨ 2.10
- verb inflections ⇨ 4.4
- active and passive clauses ⇨ 6.9

5.4   ADJECTIVE AND ADVERB PHRASES

In contrast to noun phrases and verb phrases, we will be able to deal with adjective phrases and adverb phrases fairly briefly. Adjective phrases and adverb phrases are not dissimilar in their range of possibilities for pre- and postmodification which is why we will deal with them in the same section. In accordance with the construction principles we have already noted for noun phrases and verb phrases, an adjective or adverb phrase may consist merely of the head word or it may be expanded into a longer phrase with pre- or post-modifying elements. To begin with, here are some examples of adjective and adverb phrases which contain only a head word:

NP	VP	AdjP
The hungry cat	*was feeling*	*aggressive*
My new shoes	*felt*	*uncomfortable*

NP	VP	AdvP
The hungry cat	*snarled*	*aggressively*

NP	VP	NP	AdvP
My new shoes	*pinched*	*me*	*uncomfortably*

In the above examples, the adjective and adverb phrases occur in the same position at the end of the sentence. This is not, however, a restriction on where they can occur: we will resume a discussion of the position the various phrases take when we move on to clause structure in Chapter 6.

We saw earlier that there exists the potential to expand noun phrases by adding quite a number of premodifying elements. Head words in adjective and adverb phrases are most typically premodified by a single adverb, normally an intensifier:

> *The hungry cat was feeling <u>extremely aggressive</u>*
> *My new shoes felt <u>incredibly uncomfortable</u>*
> *The hungry cat snarled <u>really aggressively</u>*
> *My new shoes pinched me <u>so uncomfortably</u>*

Very occasionally, a head adjective or head adverb is postmodified by an adverb such as *enough* or *indeed* but this is fairly unusual and often sounds quite formal. More typically, head adjectives and head adverbs will be post-modified by a prepositional phrase or by one of a range of clauses (as we shall see later). In this respect, they resemble noun phrases.

> ☐ intensifiers ⇨ 2.7
> ☐ clauses as postmodifiers in adjective and adverb phrases ⇨ 6.13

5.5 PREPOSITIONAL PHRASES

Prepositional phrases differ from the other four types of phrase in that a preposition cannot stand alone as the head word of a phrase. Although a preposition is still the head word in a prepositional phrase, it has to be accompanied by another element – or **prepositional complement** – if the phrase is to be complete. Most typically, the prepositional complement will be a noun phrase. Consider this example:

NP	VP	PP
Jackie	*was searching*	*in the cupboard*

Here, the prepositional phrase consists of the preposition *in* complemented by the noun phrase *the cupboard*. We could represent this structure in either of the following ways:

> *[in the cupboard* ₚₚ *]*
> *[in [the cupboard* ₙₚ *]* ₚₚ *]*

The second example shows the structure of the prepositional phrase in rather more detail. You will see that the noun phrase in the example above is a simple one in that it consists only of a determiner plus the head noun. However, there is no restriction on the relative simplicity or complexity of a noun phrase which complements a preposition in this way. Here are a few more examples of prepositional phrases, with the noun phrase underlined:

> *around London*
> *under a stone*
> *for my closest friend*
> *to the best friend ever*

In addition to being complemented by noun phrases, prepositional phrases can also consist of the preposition followed by an adverb (or adverb phrase): *by tomorrow, above here, until now* are just three examples. In common with nouns, adjectives and adverbs as heads, prepositions can also be complemented by different types of clauses, a feature we will look at closely in Chapter 6.

We now return to the matter of prepositional phrases being able to postmodify head nouns, head adjectives and occasionally head adverbs. We will begin by taking a head noun as an example.

NP	VP	NP	NP
Clive	*gave*	*Kate*	*a large bouquet*

As you can see, there are three noun phrases in the above example. Two of them consist simply of proper nouns, *Clive* and *Kate*. The third noun phrase consists of the head noun *bouquet* plus a determiner and a premodifying adjective *large*. Supposing we now wished to specify what kind of flowers were in the bouquet, we could add the prepositional phrase *of roses*:

NP	VP	NP	NP
Clive	*gave*	*Kate*	*a large bouquet of roses*

In the new example *bouquet* is both premodified by *large* and postmodified by *of roses*. The head noun is still *bouquet* as we can see if we make this noun phrase the subject of a sentence. It is *bouquet* which will govern whether the verb is singular or plural, not *roses*:

> *A large <u>bouquet</u> of roses is very romantic*
> * *A large <u>bouquet</u> of roses are very romantic*

However, not all prepositional phrases in a sentence will necessarily be part of an extended noun phrase. Look at this example:

> *Heidi cycled fifty miles for charity*

You may at first consider whether the correct analysis of this example is

> [*Heidi* ~NP~] [*cycled* ~VP~] [*fifty miles for charity* ~NP~]

The difference, though, between *fifty miles for charity* and *a large bouquet of roses* is that *for charity* can occur in a different position in the sentence whereas *of roses* cannot:

> *For charity Heidi cycled fifty miles*
> *Heidi, for charity, cycled fifty miles*
> * *Of roses Clive gave Kate a large bouquet*
> * *Clive gave Kate of roses a large bouquet*

The fact that *of roses* cannot be removed from its position after *bouquet* indicates that it is an integral part of the noun phrase of which *bouquet* is the head. *For charity*, by contrast, is a separate phrase as shown by its mobility within the sentence. The correct phrasal analysis of this example is:

> [*Heidi* ~NP~] [*cycled* ~VP~] [*fifty miles* ~NP~] [*for charity* ~PP~]

We noted in section 5.4 that prepositional phrases can also postmodify head words in adjective and adverb phrases. Here are some examples:

adjective phrase	*Peter felt <u>ready for a beer</u>*
	Maureen appeared <u>aware of the danger</u>
adverb phrase	*<u>Unhappily for Sara</u>, she fell off her bike*
	Brian didn't win the race, <u>surprisingly in my opinion</u>

The range of adjectives taking prepositional phrase complements is much greater than the range of adverbs doing so. The adverb structures, as in the examples above, normally give a viewpoint or opinion.

☐ **clauses as postmodifying elements** ⇨ 6.13

5.6 EMBEDDING

We have seen in sections 5.2, 5.4 and 5.5 that phrases are expanded by adding words of other classes – for example by premodifying an adjective with an adverb – or by adding other phrases – for example postmodifying a head noun with a prepositional phrase. The occurrence of one linguistic unit within another is sometimes referred to as **embedding**. When we say that one linguistic item is embedded within another, we are also implying that the embedded item is in some way subordinate to or dependent on the item in which it is embedded. If we took our earlier noun phrase *a nice invitation* as an example, we might describe the adjective (or indeed adjective phrase) *nice* as being embedded within the noun phrase as the adjective is less central than the head noun *invitation*. It might also be helpful to think of an adjective phrase being embedded within the noun phrase when we consider how the adjective *nice* could be modified by the intensifier *rather* to give *a rather nice invitation*:

[*a* [*rather nice* $_{AdjP}$] *invitation* $_{NP}$]

Here we can see the relationship between *rather* and *nice* (there is no direct relationship between *rather* and *invitation*) and their combined relationship with the head noun *invitation*.

The concept of embedding is particularly useful in that it allows us to see the potential for repeated patterns in syntactic structure. For example, a prepositional phrase which postmodifies the head of a noun phrase may contain a noun which is itself postmodified. Consider the complex noun phrase in the following example:

NP	VP	NP
Jane	*told*	*an amusing story about her friend with measles*

The complex noun phrase in this sentence can be analysed as follows:

[*an amusing <u>story</u>* [*about* [*her friend* [*with* [*measles*$_{NP}$] $_{PP}$] $_{NP}$] $_{PP}$] $_{NP}$]

The head of the whole phrase is *story*. This head word is postmodified by the prepositional phrase *about her friend*. This prepositional phrase contains the noun phrase *her friend* and the head of this noun phrase, *friend*, is itself post-modified by the prepositional phrase *with measles*. There is no possibility that this last prepositional phrase modifies *story* rather than *friend* since **an amusing story with measles* would be distinctly odd. Instead, what we see is a kind of Russian doll effect with one phrase embedded within another and the resulting phrase in turn being embedded in a higher level phrase. The ability of patterns to repeat themselves in this way is known as **recursion**. To show you the full pattern of recursion in what may be a slightly clearer fashion, this example is presented in a tree diagram in Figure 5.1.

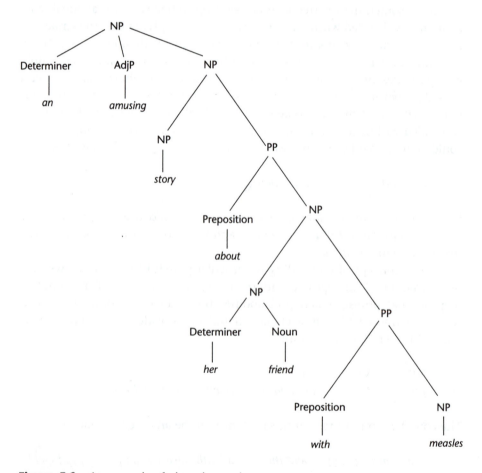

Figure 5.1   An example of phrasal recursion

5.7 COORDINATION AND APPOSITION OF PHRASES

Although we will look at the internal structure of clauses in the next chapter, we will consider briefly here the way phrases can be linked together in two specific ways within a clause or sentence. **Coordination** is the joining together of two linguistic units on an equal footing and most typically uses the conjunction *and* (although *but* and *or* are also found). Here is an example of noun phrase coordination:

PP	NP	VP	NP
For supper	*Lloyd*	*cooked*	*salmon fillets and new potatoes*

In this analysis *salmon fillets and new potatoes* has been treated as a single noun phrase but if we analyse it further we can see that it is actually a compound noun phrase in which two separate noun phrases are joined by the conjunction *and*:

[[*salmon fillets* $_{NP}$] *and* [*new potatoes* $_{NP}$] $_{NP}$]

Figure 5.2 also shows this construction in a diagrammatic form. If we take our analysis a step further then we see that this example is really a conflation of two separate statements:

For supper Lloyd cooked salmon fillets
For supper Lloyd cooked new potatoes

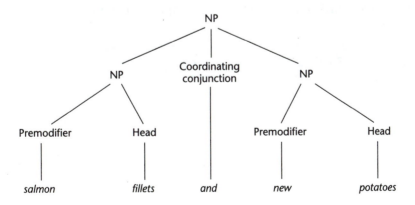

Figure 5.2   An example of a compound noun phrase

This shows how the coordination of phrases can be used as a very economical way of expressing meaning.

It is not just noun phrases which can be coordinated. Here are some examples of other phrases being joined in this way:

Daniel <u>*bathed and changed*</u> the baby	*VP coordination*
Helen was <u>*tired but happy*</u>	*AdjP coordination*
Rachael slept <u>*soundly and peacefully*</u>	*AdvP coordination*
Louise worked <u>*with speed and with diligence*</u>	*PP coordination*

We noted above that coordination involves the joining of elements on an equal basis. Not only are the elements in the above compounds equal in syntactic terms, they are the same in formal terms. What this means is that a noun phrase can only be coordinated with another noun phrase and so on. A combination of, say, an adjective phrase with an adverb phrase would be impossible: **Helen was tired but happily.*

Another way in which noun phrases co-occur is through **apposition**, as in the following example:

NP	VP	NP	NP	PP
Jo	*asked*	*her friend's sister*	*an English teacher*	*for some help*

In this sentence there are two adjacent noun phrases – *her friend's sister* and *an English teacher* – which actually refer to the same person. These are known as **noun phrases in apposition**. Apposition is another way of achieving economy in language: we can analyse the given example as a merging and reduction of something like *Jo asked her friend's sister for some help* and *Jo's friend's sister is an English teacher*. Economy is an aspect of language which we will consider further in the following chapters on sentences, clauses and discourse.

☐ **coordinating conjunctions** ⇨ 2.12

6 Clauses

6.1 WHAT IS A CLAUSE?

A **clause**, like a phrase, is a unit of syntactic construction. In Chapter 5, we saw how phrases are formed from words and that each phrase type has its own particular internal structure. As phrases are formed from words, so clauses are formed from phrases. This does not mean that a clause is a random group of phrases: a clause has a specific structure, as we shall see shortly. As a unit of construction, then, a clause is a larger unit than a phrase. The unit of construction larger than the clause is the sentence, which will consist of one or more clauses. We will look more closely at sentence structures and types in Chapter 7.

Although there are many different types of clause fulfilling a range of functions within sentences, it is possible to identify the features which typify a clause. We will therefore begin by looking at the most central clause types. Much of the rest of our discussion will then be about modifications to these basic types.

Most central to a clause is its **verb element**. We have already seen that verb phrases are multi-faceted in the way they provide information about tense, aspect, voice and so on. Typically, a clause contains a verb phrase which is finite (meaning it is marked for tense) and which is active rather than passive since this is the voice most frequently used by speakers. The verb phrase is normally preceded by a subject element and followed by any elements needed to make the clause grammatically complete. Consider the following example:

Catherine has gained ten GCSEs

This is an example of a typical clause. The verb *has gained* is both active and finite. The meaning of the verb is completed by the noun phrase *ten GCSEs*. The verb is preceded by the subject noun phrase *Catherine*. This structure is typical of clauses in that it is the structure we use to make a statement. This is known as a **declarative** structure.

At present, this clause only contains **obligatory** elements. What this means is that if we remove any of the phrases from the clause, it would be syntactically incomplete. It would be possible of course to add some optional items to this clause:

> *Fortunately, Catherine has gained ten GCSEs this summer*

However, in our discussion we will mainly be concentrating on the obligatory elements in clauses as these will enable us to identify the basic clause structures of English. The features, then, which most typify a clause are that the verb phrase will be finite and in the active voice and the structure of the clause will be declarative.

6.2   THE FIVE CLAUSE ELEMENTS

Clauses are made up of a combination of clause elements. There are five clause elements, each one having a different function within the clause:

subject
verb
object
complement
adverbial

(These may be abbreviated as S, V, O, C, A.) We saw above that clauses typically contain a verb and a subject. They also contain any items needed to complete the meaning of the verb, most typically objects or complements. Sometimes verbs will require an obligatory adverbial but normally adverbials are optional elements in a clause.

The verb element is always realised by a verb phrase. The other elements are likely to be realised by phrases but it is possible that another clause can fulfil the role of a clause element. It is important to make a clear distinction between phrase types and clause elements. Consider the following example:

function	S	V	O
	The black labrador	*has bitten*	*Mr Allington*
form	NP	VP	NP

If we analyse this clause in terms of phrase structure then we can see it consists of NP + VP + NP. In terms of clause elements, however, the structure is SVO. When we identify *the black labrador* as a noun phrase, we are analysing its

form. When we identify it as the subject of the clause, we are analysing its **function**. You will notice there are two noun phrases in the clause: although *the black labrador* and *Mr Allington* share the same form, they each have a different function within the clause. The next five sections will take you through the five clause elements, explaining their functions and looking at the positions in which they occur within a clause.

6.3   SUBJECT ELEMENT

The **subject** typically occurs before the verb element in what may be termed the **subject position**. Here are some examples:

	subject	verb + other elements
1	*Helen*	*has been tidying her CD collection*
2	*These friends*	*are looking for a new house*
3	*It*	*is going to rain shortly*
4	*There*	*will be a storm tonight*

The subject element is very likely to be a noun phrase, such as *Helen* in example 1 and *these friends* in example 2. Occasionally, you will come across *it* or *there* in the subject position as in examples 3 and 4. These are unusual subjects in that they refer to nothing in particular. When *it* or *there* are used in this way, the subject is termed a **dummy subject**. A clause can also occur in subject position. We will consider this in section 6.11.

A key feature of the subject function is that the subject dictates whether the verb will be singular or plural, as far as such a distinction is possible. Sometimes, it may also be possible to make a distinction between first, second or third person. This distinction will come into play most obviously when the verb *be* is employed, either as a lexical verb or as a primary auxiliary:

subject	verb		
I	<u>*am*</u> *considering*	*a career move*	1st person
you	<u>*are*</u> *making*	*a terrible mistake*	2nd person
She / Helen	<u>*is*</u> *having*	*another baby*	3rd person

In many instances, however, there will be no specific marking for person or number on the verb because there are so few verbal inflections in English.

☐ verb inflections ⇨ 4.4
☐ clauses as clause elements ⇨ 6.12

6.4   VERB ELEMENT

Whereas the subject element can take the form of a noun phrase, or a dummy subject, or even another clause, the verb element has to be a verb phrase. The verb element is the most central part of the clause, and the lexical verb present in the verb phrase will also dictate what obligatory elements will follow the verb. Consider these two examples:

subject	verb
Paul	*fell*
* *Paul*	*broke*

Whereas the first example is complete as it stands, the second example *Paul broke* is incomplete. (What is missing is an object element after the verb.) This shows us that there is a close relationship between the lexical verb and the rest of the clause. In other words, the choice of lexical verb will dictate what element or elements, if any, should follow the verb element in order to make the clause grammatically complete. This is known as **verb complementation**. (You need to be careful not to confuse the terms 'complement' and 'complementation' meaning the obligatory element(s) which follow verbs with 'complement' as a specific type of clause element.)

Due to the existence of this special bond between the verb and its following elements, a clause has traditionally been divided into two parts: the **subject** and the **predicate**. The predicate is the verb element plus any verb complementation. The subject is, if you like, the focus or topic of the sentence while the predicate is what we want to say about the subject. If we complete the example *Paul broke* by adding *his ankle* then the clause could be analysed like this:

subject	predicate
Paul	*broke his ankle*

Paul is our chosen topic or focus while *broke his ankle* is what we want to say about *Paul*. You may sometimes find the verb element of a clause referred to as a **predicator** which is indicative of its role within the predicate.

We have already looked in some detail in section 5.3 at the complexities of verb phrases. We saw that they can be marked for modality, tense, aspect and voice as well as to some extent for number and person. As we have just seen, though, the verb element does not function in isolation but exerts a semantic and grammatical influence over other elements. Of all the elements in a clause, the verb element is the most important and the most obligatory.

☐ verb phrases ⇨ 5.3

6.5   OBJECT ELEMENT

The incomplete clause in the previous section (*Paul broke*) was completed by adding an **object**:

subject	verb	object
Paul	*broke*	*his ankle*

The object element contrasts with the subject element in that its position is after the verb element. Whereas all verbs can be preceded by a subject, only some verbs need to be followed by an object element. Verbs which require an object are **transitive verbs**. You can see from the example above that *break* is a transitive verb. If you contrast this with the earlier example, *Paul fell*, which is grammatically complete as it stands, then you can see that some verbs do not require an object or any other complementation. These are **intransitive verbs**.

Like the subject element, the object is most typically a noun phrase, as in the example *Paul broke his ankle*. However, the object can also be a clause – an aspect which we will consider in section 6.12. There are many transitive verbs but there are also some verbs which are followed by two objects:

S	V	O	O
Jane	*gave*	*Phil*	*this book on wine*
Andrew	*bought*	*Kathy*	*a sports car*
Gill	*told*	*Imogen*	*a bedtime story*

Verbs which take two objects are **ditransitive**. Although there are two objects complementing each of these verbs, the two objects do not behave identically. The first object can be moved to the end of the clause if the noun phrase is converted to a prepositional phrase with *to* or *for*:

Jane gave this book on wine to Phil
Andrew bought a sports car for Kathy
Gill told a bedtime story to Imogen

This shows that the first object is rather less central than the second one. The people in our examples – *Phil, Kathy* and *Imogen* – are really recipients of the actual item which was given, bought or told. For this reason, the first, less central type of object is sometimes referred to as an **indirect object** (O_i) while the second is the **direct object** (O_d). So a new example might be analysed as:

S	V	O_i	O_d
Judith	*promised*	*Matthew*	*a present*

Some verbs, such as promise, can be both ditransitive as in the above examples or **monotransitive**, taking just one object. For example, *Judith promised many things* would be a grammatically complete clause with one object. Similarly, some verbs can be used both transitively and intransitively – *read* and *write* are examples.

☐ clauses as clause elements ⟹ 6.12

6.6   COMPLEMENT ELEMENT

We have seen so far that some verbs require no complementation, and that some verbs (namely, transitive verbs) require an object. There is also a small group of verbs which are followed by a **complement** as opposed to an object element. Consider these examples:

S	V	O
The committee	*have made*	*a decision*
S	V	C
Sue	*was feeling*	*very sleepy*

There is a significant difference in function between *a decision* in the first example and *very sleepy* in the second. Whereas *a decision* has a referent which is distinct from the subject referent *the committee*, *very sleepy* refers to *Sue*, the subject of the clause. Another difference is that the first example can be rearranged to give the passive clause *a decision has been made by the committee* whereas **very sleepy was being felt by Sue* is not grammatically possible. So, just as an object is needed to provide completeness in a clause that contains a transitive verb, a complement is needed to give completeness when there is a **copula** or **copular verb** in the clause. Copular verbs make up just a small set of verbs and include: *be, feel* (in the sense used above), *seem, appear, become*. The verb *be* is the most central of all the copular verbs and you may sometimes come across it referred to simply as **the copula**.

In our previous example, the complement was an adjective phrase *very sleepy*. However, it is equally likely to be a noun phrase as in *Andrew became a QC*. Prepositional phrases can be complements when they follow a copular verb: they describe someone's mood, position or state as in *Phil was in a daze*. Further, complements do not necessarily refer to the subject of the sentence. A distinction can be made between a **subject complement** (C_S) and an **object complement** (C_O). (These are sometimes referred to as the **subject predicative** and **object predicative** respectively and you can use these terms if you wish to avoid confusion with the term 'complement'.) The subject complement gives us more information about the subject of the clause, and the object complement gives us more information about the object element. Here are some examples of both types of complement:

S	V	C_S		complement type
Armstrong	*became*	*the first man on the moon*		NP
The weather	*has turned*	*very nasty*		AdjP
No one	*was*	*in danger*		PP

S	V	O	C_O	complement type
The judges	*pronounced*	*Jackie*	*the winner*	NP
Chris	*made*	*Sara*	*really angry*	AdjP
Exams	*were putting*	*her*	*in a spin*	PP

Verbs which take both an object and an object complement are **complex-transitive** verbs. Whereas the range of copular verbs which take a subject complement is limited, there is a wide range of verbs which take an object and an object complement. The relationship between the object and the object complement can be expressed using the copula *be*:

S	V	O	C_O	
The judges	*pronounced*	*Jackie*	*the winner*	(*Jackie was the winner*)
Chris	*made*	*Sara*	*really angry*	(*Sara was really angry*)
Exams	*were putting*	*her*	*in a spin*	(*She was in a spin*)

This relationship is fundamentally different from the relationship between an indirect and direct object:

> *Andrew bought Kathy a sports car*   **Kathy is a sports car*

This provides a useful way of distinguishing between verb types when dealing with verbs that take two complements.

6.7 ADVERBIAL ELEMENT

The adverbial element is so called because it functions like an adverb. This means that its position is less fixed than that of the other clause elements. Adverbials also have a wider range of functions in terms of meaning. An adverbial element is most likely to be an adverb phrase or a prepositional phrase, although a clause can also function as an adverbial. Here are some examples of adverbials in a variety of clause positions:

Julia speaks French <u>very fluently</u>	AdvP as adverbial
I would like <u>nevertheless</u> to go to America soon	AdvP as adverbial
Terry was digging up the weeds<u> in his garden</u>	PP as adverbial
<u>At a glance</u> she looked very poorly	PP as adverbial

The above examples show you how the adverbial element can occur in various positions. A further point to note about these particular adverbial examples, however, is that they are not obligatory. They could all be removed without any real loss of meaning and without causing grammatical incompleteness. This is another way in which adverbial elements differ from other clause elements. Only a small number of verbs require an adverbial for their complementation. Here are some examples:

S	V	A
A drunk	*was leaning*	*against the wall*
The opera	*lasted*	*nearly three hours*
My friends	*live*	*in Monmouth*

None of the above examples would be complete if the adverbial were removed. This is a contrast to the optional adverbials in the previous set of examples. The verb *put* is unusual in that it requires both an object and an adverbial:

S	V	O	A
Terry	*put*	*the rubbish*	*in the dustbin*

This is a commonly used verb. You can see that it would be grammatically incomplete without the adverbial element.

☐ meanings of adverbial elements ⇨ 7.11

6.8   CLAUSE STRUCTURES

We have now looked at the functions of the five elements which make up clauses and we have also seen which different forms those elements can take. We can therefore summarise what we have covered in terms of the range of basic clause structures possible. The examples given below have already been used in the preceding five sections.

clause structure		example		
S V	*Paul*	*fell*		
S V O	*Paul*	*broke*	*his ankle*	
S V O_i O_d	*Andrew*	*bought*	*Kathy*	*a sports car*
S V C_s	*Sue*	*was feeling*	*very sleepy*	
S V O C_o	*Chris*	*made*	*Sara*	*really angry*
S V A	*A drunk*	*was leaning*	*against the wall*	
S V O A	*Terry*	*put*	*the rubbish*	*in the dustbin*

All the clause elements in these structures are obligatory. If any element were removed then the clause would be incomplete. Of course, the above examples do not represent the full range of clause structures possible. They represent a syntactic starting point: any clause can therefore be analysed in terms of these basic structures. Here is an example which contains more than the obligatory elements:

S	V	A	Vocative
The taxi	*is waiting*	*outside,*	*Louise*

The first three elements here conform to the SVA clause structure. However, the adverbial element is not obligatory: *the taxi is waiting* is syntactically complete but some additional information is given by the adverbial *outside*. Also in this example, you can see that the remark is being addressed to *Louise*. In speech in particular we often name the person or persons we are speaking to. This method of address is a **vocative**. The vocative is an optional not an obligatory element, and is more peripheral than the adverbial in that vocatives do not enter into clause structures as such.

You will also notice that the basic structures given above all contain the subject followed by the verb as the minimum structural elements. Any verb complementation such as an object follows the verb element. For this reason English is sometimes referred to as an SVO language. This is in contrast to a language such as Japanese which has an SOV order or Welsh which is VSO. Interestingly, something like 75 per cent of the world's languages have an SVO clause structure in common with English.

6.9   ACTIVE AND PASSIVE CLAUSES

In section 5.3 we saw how a verb phrase could be either **active** or **passive** and how this in turn will make the clause active or passive. Here are examples of both types:

> active   *Everyone admired Gill's garden*
> passive   *Gill's garden was admired by everyone*

In an active clause, the subject is normally the **agent**. What this means is that the subject is carrying out the action referred to by the lexical verb. The object on the other hand is the **affected** – the person or thing to which the verb is being done as it were. Agent and affected refer to semantic as opposed to grammatical roles. We instinctively know that, if the verb is active, the grammatical subject is the agent.

Only a transitive verb – like *admire* – can be made passive. The passive is often seen as a transformation from the active rather than as a primary structure in its own right. This is because the active voice is far more typical and natural to language than the passive voice. In order to convert an active clause such as *Everyone admired Gill's garden* to a passive one, the object of the passive clause has to be moved into subject position. The verb phrase is then modified by using the auxiliary *be* so that *admired* becomes *was admired*. This transformation results in *Gill's garden was admired*. The presence in the verb phrase of the auxiliary *was* (followed by an *-ed* form) to mark the passive voice indicates that the grammatical subject is now the affected not the agent. Finally, there is an option with regard to the agent, *everyone*. This element can either be omitted since *Gill's garden was admired* is grammatically complete, or it can be added in a ***by*-phrase**: *Gill's garden was admired by everyone*. The *by*-phrase functions as an adverbial element in the passive clause:

S	V	A
Gill's garden	*was admired*	*by everyone*

Although only transitive verbs can become passive, not all transitive verbs can undergo this process. This is due to the semantic properties of the verbs in question. We had an example earlier of *Paul broke his ankle*. This clause could not be made passive because Paul is not the agent despite being the subject of an active clause: **Paul's ankle was broken by Paul*. On the other hand we could passivise *Paul broke a glass bowl* because *Paul* is the agent of this clause: *A glass bowl was broken by Paul*.

Although passives come less naturally to us as speakers than active clauses, they are very useful in a variety of contexts. For instance, if you didn't know who the agent was then a passive would be a useful construction:

| active | *? has murdered Mr Constable* |
| passive | *Mr Constable has been murdered* |

Similarly, you may wish to avoid indicating who the agent is either because it isn't especially important or because you don't wish to ascribe responsibility:

| active | *The headteacher has increased the homework for Year 11* |
| passive | *The homework for Year 11 has been increased* |

The passive is also an appropriate construction for focusing on the affected since it brings this element to the front of the clause:

| active | *the earth orbits the sun* |
| passive | *the sun is orbited by the earth* |

Finally, the passive often sounds more formal than its active counterpart. As already mentioned, the active voice is more instinctive for speakers and used far more extensively than the passive, and young children take quite a while to assimilate the passive construction. This supports our earlier point that clauses are typically active, although the passive has a range of valuable functions in our language.

6.10 NON-FINITE CLAUSES

We noted above that not only are clauses typically active, they are also typically finite, meaning the verb element is marked for tense. However, verbs, as we saw in section 5.3, may also be non-finite. If the verb element in any clause is not marked for tense then the clause itself will also be non-finite. When a clause is non-finite, then it does not sound grammatically complete on its own. Non-finite clauses therefore normally occur as part of a higher level clause which does contain a finite verb. In the following examples of sentences which contain a non-finite clause, the non-finite clause has been underlined and is labelled to show its clause elements:

to- infinitive	
without subject	*The aim was <u>to explore (V) the area (O)</u>*
with subject	*The captain wanted <u>the crew (S) to explore (V) the area (O)</u>*

bare infinitive

without subject   *Phil helped <u>cook (V) the dinner(O)</u>*

with subject   *She made <u>Julian (S) wash up (V)</u>*

    -ing participle

without subject   *<u>Loving (V) wine (O)</u> he moved to Bordeaux*

with subject   *<u>Norman (S) loving (V) wine (O)</u> they gave him some claret*

    -ed participle

without subject   *<u>Treated (V) kindly (A)</u> the labrador will be good*

with subject   *<u>Business (S) finished (V)</u> they all went home*

None of the underlined non-finite clauses could stand alone and still sound grammatically complete. They all occur instead with or within finite clauses. Another feature of non-finite clauses is that they may or may not have a subject element whereas finite clauses typically have a subject preceding the verb. When no subject element is present in the non-finite clause, the subject has to be inferred. For example, in *Loving wine he moved to Bordeaux* the subject of the verb *love* can be found in the subject of the finite clause *he*.

    ☐ non-finite verb phrases ⇨ 5.3
    ☐ clauses as clause elements ⇨ 6.12

6.11   MAIN AND SUBORDINATE CLAUSES

Within the structure of a sentence, a clause is either **main** or **subordinate**. Consider the following example:

    When Ruth arrives, I might open a bottle of wine.

You can see that this sentence contains two verb phrases: *arrives* and *might open*. The latter has a subject pronoun *I* and is complemented by the object *a bottle of wine*, making *I might open a bottle of wine* an SVO clause. The verb *arrive* is an intransitive verb so it has no complements but it does have a subject, namely *Ruth*. *Ruth arrives* is also a clause and its structure is SV. This clause, however, differs from the other one in that it is introduced by the subordinating conjunction *when*. If we separate these two clauses we will notice a crucial difference between them:

    * *When Ruth arrives*
    I might open a bottle of wine

Whereas the second clause can stand alone and still be grammatically complete, this is not true of *When Ruth arrives*. This clause needs to be attached to a free-standing clause as part of a complete sentence. Any clause which has the potential to stand alone is a **main clause**. A clause which does not have this capacity is a **subordinate clause**. Because a subordinate clause depends on a main clause for grammatical completeness, it is sometimes referred to as a **dependent clause**. Similarly, a main clause is sometimes referred to as an **independent clause**.

We noted at the beginning of this chapter that a sentence will consist of one or more clauses. If a sentence consists of one clause only then that clause has to be a main clause or the sentence will be grammatically incomplete. A main clause always contains a finite verb and typically contains an overt subject. It may of course be active or passive. We will look more closely at sentences containing more than one clause in Chapter 7.

We saw in the previous section that our examples of non-finite clauses were grammatically incomplete when taken in isolation. This demonstrates that any clause which is non-finite is subordinate. So too is any clause which is introduced by a subordinating conjunction. Many clauses which begin with a *wh*-word are also subordinate. There are many different types of subordinate clause and these can be analysed both in terms of their forms and their functions. We will look at some of these aspects in the following sections and in the next chapter.

> ☐ *wh*-words ⇨ 2.13
> ☐ main clauses as simple sentences ⇨ 7.8
> ☐ main clauses in compound sentences ⇨ 7.9
> ☐ main clauses in complex sentences ⇨ 7.10
> ☐ subordinate clauses ⇨ 7.10

6.12 CLAUSES AS CLAUSE ELEMENTS

In sections 6.3 to 6.7 we looked at the five clause elements and their functions, and we considered the phrase types which were likely to perform these roles. We noted that the verb element has to be a verb phrase but the other elements are less prescribed. For example, we saw that the subject complement could be a noun phrase (*Armstrong became the first man on the moon*), an adjective phrase (*The weather has turned very nasty*) or a prepositional phrase (*No one was in danger*). We will now move on to consider how clauses can fulfil the function of the subject, object, complement and adverbial elements. Any clause which functions as a clause element in this way will be a subordinate clause since it will be unable to stand alone.

We will begin by considering one of our earlier examples a little more closely, namely *The aim was to explore the area*. Here, there is a finite verb *was* and the subject of this verb is *the aim*. We know that *be* is a copular verb and therefore requires a complement to follow it. Here, though, the complement is not a noun phrase or adjective phrase but another clause *to explore the area*. We can represent this analysis as follows:

Alternatively, we can represent this example as a tree diagram as in Figure 6.1.

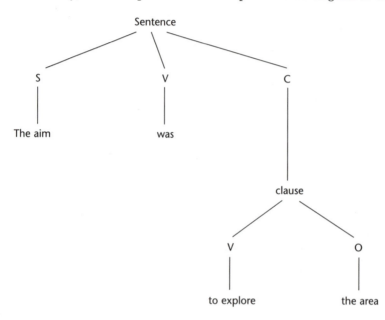

Figure 6.1   An example of an embedded clause functioning as a clause element

The tree diagram shows how the complement element of the finite clause is realised by a non-finite clause. Here we have another example of **embedding**, since the non-finite clause is embedded within the finite one. You will also notice that the label at the top of the tree diagram is 'sentence' not 'clause'. This is because we are dealing here with more than one clause. When a clause occurs in a position where we most typically expect to find a noun phrase then the clause is a **nominal clause**. A nominal clause may occur as either subject, object or complement (as we have just seen). Here are examples of nominal clauses in subject and object positions:

S		V	C	
Algebra		*is*	*difficult*	NP as subject
To study algebra		*is*	*difficult*	non-finite clause as subject

S	V	O	
Tim	*wants*	*a foreign holiday*	NP as object
Tim	*wants*	*to start a theatre company*	non-finite clause as object

We will now take a closer look at the example: *Treated kindly, the labrador will be good*. Here, we have a complete finite clause *the labrador will be good*, which has an adverbial element *treated kindly* added at the beginning. We saw in section 6.7 that the adverbial element is likely to be an adverb phrase or a prepositional phrase but could also be a clause. Here it is a non-finite clause. A clause which functions as an adverbial is termed an **adverbial clause**. The following examples show an adverb phrase, a prepositional phrase and a clause functioning as the adverbial element:

A	S	V	C	
Probably	*the labrador*	*will be*	*good*	AdvP as adverbial
In all likelihood	*the labrador*	*will be*	*good*	PP as adverbial
Treated kindly	*the labrador*	*will be*	*good*	clause as adverbial

We saw in Figure 6.1 that a clause may be embedded in another clause when it performs the function of a clause element such as the complement in *The aim was to explore the area*. In this example, the non-finite clause *to explore the area* is an obligatory element since the sentence would be incomplete without it. This is in contrast to the role of the non-finite clause *treated kindly* since here the function of the non-finite clause is as an optional adverbial element. Figure 6.2 gives a diagrammatic representation of the full example *Treated kindly, the labrador will be good*.

It isn't just non-finite clauses which function as clause elements. Compare the non-finite examples already given with finite clauses introduced by a subordinating conjunction:

clause as subject

	S	V	C
non-finite	*To study algebra*	*is*	*difficult*
finite	*That algebra is difficult*	*is*	*a well-known fact*

clause as object

	S	V	O
non-finite	*Tim*	*wants*	*to start a theatre company*
finite	*Tim*	*wonders*	*whether he can start a theatre company*

clause as complement

	S	V	C
non-finite	*The aim*	*was*	*to explore the area*
finite	*The aim*	*was*	*that they should explore the area*

clause as adverbial

	A	S	V	C
non-finite	*Treated kindly*	*the labrador*	*will be*	*good*
finite	*If he is treated kindly*	*the labrador*	*will be*	*good*

We can see then that clause elements can take the form of either phrases or clauses and that clauses which perform clause element functions can be either finite or non-finite. This should give you some idea of how complex syntactic structure can be. It is therefore an extraordinary phenomenon that we are able to operate our mental set of syntactic rules without having to think about it and that we are all able to construct sentences of considerable complexity without error.

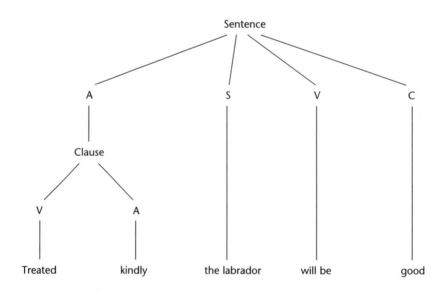

Figure 6.2   An example of a clause functioning as an adverbial element

6.13 CLAUSES WITHIN PHRASES

In Chapter 5 we saw how nouns (or pronouns) and adjectives could be post-modified by, for example, prepositional phrases and how prepositional phrases could take noun phrases and adverb phrases as the prepositional complement. We are returning to phrase structure in this section to see how head nouns and head adjectives can be postmodified by a range of clause types and how prepositional phrases can take clauses as their complements. We will begin with nouns and adjectives. Here is the full range of clauses which appear as postmodifiers in these phrase types:

noun phrases	adjective phrases
non-finite *to*-infinitive clause	non-finite *to*-infinitive clause
non-finite *-ing* clause	non-finite *-ing* clause
non-finite *-ed* clause	
that-clause	*that*-clause
relative clause	
	wh-clause
comparative clause	comparative clause

There is only a partial overlap between the sets of clauses which each phrase type allows for postmodification. We will look at each type in turn, beginning with the non-finite clauses. The head nouns and head adjectives have been underlined:

	noun phrase	adjective phrase
to-infinitive clause	*a <u>place</u> to stay*	*<u>happy</u> to help*
	a <u>place</u> for people to stay	*<u>happy</u> for you to help*
non-finite *-ing* clause	*the <u>storm</u> brewing at sea*	*<u>busy</u> getting ready*
non-finite *-ed* clause	*the <u>storm</u> weathered at sea*	

The *to*-infinitive clauses can appear with or without an overt subject. As we have seen before, if there is no subject present before the verb then the subject and consequently the agent has to be inferred from the context. So if, for example, the noun phrase *a place to stay* occurred in the context of *I am looking for a place to stay* then the inferred meaning is *I am looking for a place for me to stay*. When a subject is present in the non-finite clause then the clause is introduced by the subordinating conjunction *for*.

Both nouns and adjectives can be postmodified by **that-clauses**. These are subordinate clauses introduced by the subordinating conjunction *that*. The verb in the clause will be finite. Here are some examples. Again, the head noun or adjective has been underlined:

	noun phrase			adjective phrase
1	the <u>belief</u> that God exists		4	<u>glad</u> that you're feeling better
2	a faint <u>hope</u> that he will phone		5	<u>afraid</u> that she'll see a ghost
3	the <u>view</u> that plants have feelings		6	<u>anxious</u> that he be caught

One feature of these clauses is that speakers will often omit *that*, usually because this is less formal: *I'm glad Ø you're feeling better*. This isn't always possible, however: **the view plants have feelings* (rather than *the view that plants have feelings*) seems awkward.

If you look at example 6 in the previous paragraph you will see that the verb element is unusual: *be caught* rather than *is caught*. This use of the infinitive form of the *be* auxiliary as opposed to the third person singular present tense is sometimes used when the adjective expresses a wish or hope. This use is known as the **subjunctive mood** and it contrasts with all the other verbs we have looked at which are **indicative**. The subjunctive is rarely used in English and it is becoming rarer. You are just as likely to hear speakers say *anxious that he is caught* as *anxious that he be caught*.

We now move on to **relative clauses** which only postmodify nouns and pronouns. We have already seen that some syntactic structures are particularly economical. This is certainly true of relative clauses. Consider these two sentences:

> *That man bought his shirt in C&A*
> *I saw that man*

We can conflate these two sentences by using a relative clause. There are two options and the relative clause in each has been underlined:

> *That man <u>who/whom I saw</u> bought his shirt in C&A*
> *I saw that man <u>who bought his shirt in C&A</u>*

In each case, the relative clause postmodifies the head word *man*. The relative clause is so-called because it is normally introduced by a **relative pronoun** which has the function of referring us back ('relating' us if you like) to a preceding noun. The noun to which the relative pronoun refers – in these examples *man* – is the **antecedent**. As well as being introduced by a relative pronoun, the relative clause can be introduced by a handful of other items. Here is the full range:

relative pronouns	*which*	*(that)*	*the colour which I selected*
	who	*(that)*	*the man who shops at C&A*
	whom	*(that)*	*the man whom I saw*
relative determiner	*which*		*(he became) president which position suited him very well*
	whose		*the man whose wallet I found*
relative adverbs	*when*	*(that)*	*the moment when they knew*
	where	*(that)*	*the place where they met*
	why	*(that)*	*the reason why it happened*

The relative pronoun *whom* is used when the antecedent would be the object of the verb in the relative clause. *Whom* is becoming archaic, however, and speakers tend to use *who*. All three *wh-* relative pronouns and all three relative adverbs can be replaced by *that*, again usually to provide a more informal tone: *the colour that I selected* is less formal than *the colour which I selected*. Be careful not to confuse the relative pronoun *that* with the subordinating conjunction *that* at the start of *that*-clauses. If the clause is a relative clause you will probably be able to replace *that* with *who, whom* or *which*:

> *the man that shops at C&A*
> *the man who shops at C&A*
> *the belief that God exists*
> * *the belief who/whom/which God exists*

Sometimes it is possible to omit the relative pronoun at the start of the relative clause:

> *the man who/whom/that I saw*
> *the man Ø I saw*
> *the colour which/that I selected*
> *the colour Ø I selected*

This is because the relative pronoun will be understood from the context.

Where no relative pronoun occurs in a relative clause, we say that the clause has a **zero relative pronoun.**

Finally, relative clauses can be introduced by a preposition and relative pronoun. This can be seen in a sentence such as *Scope is the charity for which I did a sponsored walk* (example 1 below). Alternatively, the preposition can be placed at the end of the relative clause as example 2 shows:

1   *Scope is the charity for which I did a sponsored walk*
2   *Scope is the charity which I did a sponsored walk for*

The structure of example 1 is more formal than that of example 2.

Let us return briefly to the postmodifying *-ing* and *-ed* clauses we considered at the start of this section. Here again are the two noun phrase examples, this time incorporated into a sentence:

The lifeguards discussed the storm brewing at sea
The sailors described the storm weathered at sea

Some linguists interpret the postmodification in these noun phrases as a reduction of a fuller clause:

the storm which was brewing at sea
the storm which was weathered at sea

These forms are now relative clauses, the first one containing a verb in the progressive aspect and the second containing a verb in the passive voice. Because the postmodifying non-finite *-ing* and *-ed* clauses have this capacity to be expanded into full relative clauses, they are sometimes referred to as **reduced relative clauses.**

We will now return to adjectives to see how they can be postmodified by *wh*-clauses. *Wh*-clauses are introduced by a *wh*-word. Here is a selection of examples with the adjectives underlined:

1   *uncertain what he is doing*
2   *happy where they were living*
3   *doubtful what to do*
4   *confident which way to go*

As you can see from these examples, the *wh*-clause can be either finite (examples 1 and 2) or non-finite (examples 3 and 4).

The final type of clause which can occur in both adjective and noun phrases is a **comparative clause**. Since comparative clauses can also postmodify adverbs we will consider noun, adjective and adverb phrases together here. There are two types of comparative clause. The first type actually expresses comparison and uses *than* as a subordinator as illustrated below:

noun phrase
Victoria did <u>less homework than she intended</u>
Vanessa has got <u>a better suntan than I have</u>

adjective phrase
The patient felt <u>healthier than the doctor had expected</u>
Louise is <u>more talented than her friends are</u>

adverb phrase
Bill drove the car <u>more carefully than his wife did</u>
Andrew revised for his exams <u>much less thoroughly than he had intended</u>

The head word in each of these phrases is followed by a *than*-clause. All these clauses contain a finite verb. In noun phrases, as in adverb phrases, the head word will be premodified by *more* or *less* or, in a noun phrase, the head noun may be premodified by an adjective in the comparative form as in *a better suntan*. In adjective phrases, the adjective will either take the inflectional comparative form as in *healthier* or again will be premodified by *more* or *less*.

The second type of comparative clause expresses equivalence:

noun phrase
Victoria did not write <u>as good an essay as she had hoped</u>
The aid worker helped <u>as many as she could</u>

adjective phrase
Bill's reactions were not <u>as quick as Vanessa's were</u>

adverb phrase
At the interview Martin performed <u>as impressively as anyone performed</u>

The comparative constructions here involve the correlative subordinators *as...as*. The first *as* precedes the head word and the second *as* introduces the postmodifying clause. Noun phrases which take comparative clauses do so in a different way from adjective and adverb phrases. One possibility is that the first *as* will be attached to an adjective which premodifies the head noun: *as good an essay as she had hoped*. This process affects the order of elements in the noun phrase since the adjective is moved into a position in front of the determiner. The second possibility is that the head word in the noun phrase will be a pronoun: *as many as she could*.

To complete this section, we will briefly look at clauses as prepositional complements. These will be either *wh*-clauses or *-ing* clauses as you can see in the following examples where both the preposition and its complement have been underlined:

1   *This is an event for whoever wants to get involved*
2   *They discussed the problem of how they would raise some money*
3   *In trying to help, she actually made matters worse*
4   *Why don't you go out for a walk instead of watching the television*
5   *It was really a question of finding the right person for the job*

Examples 1 and 2 show prepositional phrases where the prepositional complement is a *wh*-clause. Here, the prepositional phrases are embedded in noun phrases postmodifying the nouns *event* and *problem*. In examples 3 and 4, the preposition is complemented by an *-ing* participle clause. The prepositional phrase here is not embedded in a noun phrase but functions as an adverbial element to the main clause. In example 5, the complement is again an *-ing* clause but here the prepositional phrase is postmodifying the noun *question*.

☐ *wh*-words ⇨ 2.13
☐ noun phrases ⇨ 5.2
☐ adjective phrases ⇨ 5.4
☐ prepositional phrases ⇨ 5.5
☐ non-finite clause ⇨ 6.10

6.14   NOMINAL RELATIVE CLAUSES

A **nominal relative clause**, as the name suggests, shares features of both nominal clauses and relative clauses. All nominal relative clauses begin with a *wh*-word. Here are some examples which were originally given in Chapter 2:

Where to go was quite a problem
Who to ask was quite a problem
Which option to select was quite a problem

The feature these clauses share with other nominal clauses is that they occur where a noun phrase might occur. In the above examples they are all in subject position although it is equally possible for them to occur as objects or complements:

> *He asked <u>what had happened</u>*   object
> *The impersonator became <u>whoever they wanted him to be</u>*   complement

These clauses resemble relative clauses insofar as they begin with a *wh*-word but, in contrast to relative clauses, the antecedent is implied rather than overt. So the nominal relative clause *what had happened* could be reformulated as a noun phrase with the head noun postmodified by a full relative clause: *the event which had happened*. Similarly, *whoever they wanted him to be* could be expanded into *the characters which they wanted him to be*.

> ☐ *wh*-words ⇨ 2.13
> ☐ nominal clauses ⇨ 6.11
> ☐ relative clauses ⇨ 6.13

6.15 NEGATIVE CLAUSES

So far virtually all our examples have been in the **affirmative**. This means that the proposition expressed by a sentence is taken to be true. If we wish to deny the truth of a statement, then we need to make it grammatically **negative**. This is normally done using the negative particle *not*:

	affirmative		negative
1a	*Ravin <u>is</u> a good manager*	1b	*Ravin <u>is not</u> a good manager*
2a	*Emma <u>might come</u> home*	2b	*Emma <u>might not come</u> home*
3a	*Emma <u>might have come</u> home*	3b	*Emma <u>might not have come</u> home*
4a	*Louise <u>liked</u> the film*	4b	*Louise <u>did not like</u> the film*

The verb phrases in the examples have been underlined. You can see that the negative particle is added to the verb phrase. There are rules which govern where the negative particle is positioned. If the lexical verb is *be* and the verb phrase contains only the lexical verb then the negative particle will occur after the verb. You can see this in examples 1a and 1b. Examples 2a, 2b and 3a, 3b show that when the verb phrase contains auxiliaries, the negative particle is added after the first auxiliary. In examples 4a and 4b you can see that a single-word verb phrase requires the primary auxiliary *do* to be added to the verb phrase so that the negative particle can be positioned after this auxiliary. When *do* is used in this way it is referred to as an **operator**.

Very often when we make a verb phrase negative, we form a **contraction**. This is when a word is shortened in the process of being joined to a preceding word. Thus *is not* becomes *isn't*, *did not* becomes *didn't* and so on.

Contractions are used a great deal in speech since they sound less formal than uncontracted forms.

Clauses and sentences can also include negative items other than the negative particle, although they do not negate the truth of a clause or sentence in the way 'not' does. Here are some examples:

> *He told me <u>never</u> to do it again*   (adverb)
> *It really is <u>no</u> use*   (determiner)
> *She said <u>nothing</u> about a trip to America*   (pronoun)
> *<u>Nobody</u> came to answer the door*   (pronoun)

The position of *never* in the first example is crucial to the meaning of the sentence. There is a contrast in meaning between *He told me never to do it again* and *He never told me to do it again*. This is because a negative element does not affect any preceding phrases or clauses, but only those which follow it.

☐ auxiliary verbs ⇨ 2.10

6.16 VERBLESS CLAUSES

So far, we have considered finite clauses as most typical of clause type and structure and non-finite clauses as a less central type. To complete the picture we need to consider clauses which do not contain a verb element at all – **verbless clauses**. Here are some examples:

> *<u>Although unhappy with the decision</u>, Debra agreed to help*
> *Paul would like some champagne and caviar, <u>if available</u>*

The verbless clauses in the above examples are underlined. The reason these examples could be considered clauses is because they both begin with a subordinating conjunction, which normally introduces a full subordinate clause. Further, both these examples have the potential to be expanded into full clauses:

scj	S	V	C
although	Ø	Ø	*unhappy with the decision*
although	*she*	*was*	*unhappy with the decision*
if	Ø	Ø	*available*
if	*they*	*are*	*available*

It is possible then to analyse these examples as verbless clauses functioning as adverbial elements of the main clauses in which they occur. Here are some further examples of verbless clauses:

Without any money, Sara couldn't go on holiday
Angry at her sister, Sara stomped out of the room

It is a little more difficult to argue that these are clauses, however. *Without any money* is a prepositional phrase while *angry at her sister* is an adjective phrase. Both examples are functioning as adverbial elements to the main clauses. If we were to treat these examples as verbless clauses it would have to be on the basis that they could be expanded into full clauses either by adding a non-finite verb element or by adding a subordinating conjunction, a subject element and a verb element:

V	C			
being	*without any money*			*Sara couldn't go on holiday*
scj	S	V	C	
since	*she*	*was*	*without any money*	*Sara couldn't go on holiday*
V	C			
feeling	*angry at her sister*			*Sara stomped out of the room*
scj	S	V	C	
because	*she*	*was*	*angry at her sister*	*Sara stomped out of the room*

The adverbial elements in the examples are now subordinate clauses rather than phrases. It may seem something of a contradiction in terms to have a verbless clause since a verb element is a prerequisite of a clause. On the other hand, this approach allows for a more comprehensive analysis in terms of clause structures. You need to decide for yourself which approach to take. The argument for treating those examples which begin with a subordinating conjunction as a verbless clause is perhaps stronger than the argument for treating phrases functioning as adverbial elements in this way.

Of course, in speech in particular we often omit clause elements because we rely a lot on context for interpretation of meaning. For example, if someone goes into a pub and says *pint of bitter* to the bar attendant then this will be interpreted as *I would like a pint of bitter*. The other clause elements are unnecessary. These kinds of fragments are sometimes termed **minor sentences**. Writers often make use of minor sentences, especially to achieve a more immediate, abrupt effect. This is the opening voiceover of a well known television science fiction series:

Space. The final frontier. These are the voyages of the Starship Enterprise...

The first and second sentences here are minor sentences, both noun phrases. There is a directness about these two minor sentences which would be lost if the opening were re-worded as something like *Space is the final frontier*, particularly since these minor sentences describe the visual image of outer space which we see on our television screens.

7 Sentences

7.1 WHAT IS A SENTENCE?

A sentence is the largest unit of syntactic structure. In the previous chapter we looked at the structure of clauses. A sentence must consist of at least one clause but it may consist of several. If a sentence contains just one clause then that clause needs to be a main clause for the sentence to be grammatically complete. If the sentence consists of more than one clause, then for the same reason there will need to be at least one main clause.

It is important to emphasise here that when we talk about sentences we are talking about structural principles rather than written conventions. When we write we indicate sentence divisions by beginning a sentence with a capital letter and concluding it with a full stop. However, a writer may punctuate in a way which doesn't entirely correspond with grammatical sentence boundaries. For example, suppose a writer had written this:

I agreed to go with them. Although I wasn't really happy with the idea.

A teacher may well correct this punctuation on the grounds that the second sentence cannot stand alone and should therefore be connected to the first sentence. The writer, on the other hand, might argue that they had deliberately separated off the second written sentence because they wanted to make it seem like an afterthought. They may also have wanted their writing to be informal. In other words, a writer may adapt punctuation conventions to suit their own purposes. Consider the following example from a novel by Susan Hill:

It will be all right, I shan't have to stay here, even now.

In terms of written conventions we are dealing here with one sentence. The writer is trying to give the impression of a character's flow of panicky thoughts which is presumably why the sentence has been punctuated in this way. Grammatically, however, there are two sentences here:

S	V	C		
It	*will be*	*all right*		

S	V		A	A
I	*shan't have to stay*		*here*	*even now*

As you can see, there are two main clauses and since there is no conjunction joining them together we should treat them as two distinct sentences grammatically. These examples show you how grammatical sentences may not equate with written punctuated sentences. That is why you should think of a sentence primarily in terms of grammatical rules, not as something you see written on the page.

Another consideration is that when we speak we do not speak in neat grammatical sentences. Sometimes speakers leave what they are saying unfinished. Sometimes they make a false start and have to restructure what they are saying. Equally, they might lose the thread of what they are saying so that the end of the 'sentence' doesn't fully correspond with the start. Often speakers join the units of their speech together with items like *and, but* and *so*, which can make it difficult to decide where sentences might begin or end. This is another reason why we should think of a sentence as part of our mental set of syntactic rules. Neither spoken nor written language will necessarily divide neatly into sentences. Nevertheless, when we speak or write we are still using the implicit notion of the sentence to guide the way we structure our language. If we had no mental sense of clauses and sentences, we would have no awareness of grammatical incompleteness and yet all speakers have the ability to judge whether a given string of words is grammatically complete or incomplete.

In this chapter we will be looking at sentences from several angles. We will begin by looking at structural variations to clauses which give rise to different types of sentence and at how structural variations can change the focus of a sentence. We will then go on to look at how clauses join together to form sentences larger than one clause. Finally we will look more closely at the adverbial element in a clause or sentence since this element has a much wider range of functions than the other four clause elements.

□ conjunctions ⇨ 2.12
□ clause structures ⇨ 6.8

7.2 SENTENCE TYPES

We saw in Chapter 6 that a declarative clause consists of a subject and predicate (where the predicate is the verb element plus any verb complementation) and is the most typical clause structure. It therefore follows that this is also the most representative type of sentence structure. We will now move on to look at the other possibilities for sentence structure and we will be looking at them in terms of variations on the declarative structure. There are four **sentence types**:

type	typical use	example
declarative	**statement**	*You're wearing a new dress*
interrogative	**question**	*Are you wearing a new dress?*
imperative	**directive**	*Buy yourself a new dress*
exclamative	**exclamation**	*What a lovely new dress you're wearing*

Here again we are dealing with the distinction between form and function. The labels in the left-hand column indicate the syntactic form the sentence will take while those in the second column indicate the functions that these forms normally perform. Significantly, though, these forms and functions do not always correlate. Consider this sentence, which takes the declarative form:

>   *That coffee's very hot*

If this were uttered by a speaker who had just put the palm of their hand against a coffee pot to test the temperature, then the sentence could reasonably be interpreted as a statement. If, however, they said it having gulped down a mouthful of the coffee and burnt themselves then it is probably functioning as an exclamation. If it were spoken urgently to a child about to touch the coffee pot then it could be functioning as a command, telling the child not to touch. These examples show us that in various contexts the function of a particular type of sentence may vary. Sometimes, the selection of sentence type is linked to appropriateness of use. A parent might tell their noisy child *Be quiet*, which is an imperative form, but they might use an interrogative form *Would you mind turning down your radio?* to noisy neighbours since it sounds more polite even though a command or request is implicit in the utterance.

It is very important to keep the distinction between the form and the function of sentence types clear in your mind. In the next four sections we will examine the four types and look at the syntactic rules which underlie their construction.

7.3   DECLARATIVE SENTENCES

We looked in some detail at declarative structures in Chapter 6 where we saw that they typically have an overt subject, a verb element and any necessary verb complementation. The declarative sentence may also contain one or more adverbial elements. Here is an example:

S	V	O	A	A
Philip	*will visit*	*his dentist*	*in Streatham*	*today*

The obligatory elements here are the subject, verb and object, while the adverbial elements are optional extras which provide additional information. The SVO structure tells us that this clause is declarative.

We noticed above that a declarative sentence is normally used to make a statement. This statement may of course have a more specific purpose. For instance, the statement *I'd like you to come shopping with me* could express an invitation as well as stating a fact about the speaker. There are some verbs which have a very precise purpose in that the actual uttering of those verbs performs the function to which they refer. For example

> I <u>promise</u> that I won't tell anyone your secret
> I <u>swear</u> I will tell the truth
> I <u>name</u> this ship Titanic
> I now <u>pronounce</u> you husband and wife

By uttering these verbs the speaker actually performs the act of promising, swearing, naming or pronouncing. That is why these verbs are referred to as **performative** verbs. However, they are only performative when used by the speaker in the first person, in the simple present tense and in a declarative context. *Will you swear to tell the truth?* is a question, not an actual commitment.

Declarative sentences are by far the most common structures we use in language and may be regarded as typifying the order of elements in English. However, many of the sentences we utter will be variations on this basic order as we shall see in the following sections.

☐ declarative structure in clauses ⇨ 6.1

7.4   INTERROGATIVE SENTENCES

Interrogative sentences are normally used to ask a question. Here are some examples:

1 *Are you very rich?*
2 *Does he speak Russian?*

3 *Could they have reached the summit?*
4 *What is the capital of Peru?*
5 *What did the thief take?*
6 *When will we finish this job?*

The first three questions differ in kind from the other three in the type of answers they elicit. The straightforward answer to questions 1, 2 and 3 would be *yes* or *no* (although of course in reality speakers often give fuller answers than this). Questions which expect the answer *yes* or *no* are **yes-no questions**. These contrast with examples 4, 5 and 6 where more specific information is required even if that only involves one word. You will notice that these three examples all begin with a *wh*-word. Questions of this kind which require a specific response are **wh-questions**.

Questions normally require an interrogative structure. Most characteristic of interrogative structure as a departure from declarative structure is a change of position between the subject and the verb:

declarative			interrogative		
S	V	C	V	S	C
You	*are*	*very rich*	*Are*	*you*	*very rich?*

In this example, the subject *you* and the verb *are* have changed positions. This is the simple signal that the sentence has become interrogative. However, this simple exchange only takes place with the verb *be*. Consider this example:

declarative			interrogative			
S	V	O	V_{op}	S	V	O
He	*speaks*	*Russian*	*Does*	*he*	*speak*	*Russian?*

We observed a similar process to this when we were looking at negative clauses in section 6.13. If we follow the same principle we used for *You are very rich* to make *He speaks Russian* an interrogative then our outcome would be **Speaks he Russian?* Instead of merely inverting the subject and verb we need to use the primary auxiliary *do* as the **operator**. It is the operator which changes places with the subject while the rest of the verb phrase retains its position after the subject. If the verb phrase already contains an operator, in other words if there is already an auxiliary in the verb phrase, then there is no need to add the auxiliary *do*. If the verb phrase contains more than one auxiliary, then it is the first auxiliary which is the operator. (You may also remember that this is the auxiliary which carries tense.) In our third *yes-no* example, then, there is no need of the auxiliary *do*:

declarative

S	V		O
They	*could have reached*		*the summit*

interrogative

V_{op}	S	V	O
Could	*they*	*have reached*	*the summit?*

Here, the first auxiliary in the declarative verb phrase *could* is the operator and changes places with the subject. The process by which declarative structures are made interrogative is known as **subject–operator inversion**. Remember though that the operator rule does not apply when the lexical verb *be* constitutes a single word verb phrase where **subject–verb inversion** is sufficient.

The formation of *wh*-questions also usually requires subject–operator inversion but two additional processes are involved, namely the substitution of one sentence element with a *wh*-word and, often, the bringing of this element to the front:

declarative			interrogative ·			
S	V	O	$O_{Wh\text{-}}$	V_{op}	S	V
The thief	*took*	*my wallet*	*What*	*did*	*the thief*	*take?*

In this example, three processes have taken place to form the question. The object element about which the question is being asked, namely *my wallet*, has been replaced by a *wh*-pronoun and then brought to the front of the sentence. In addition, subject–operator inversion has taken place. In this case, the primary auxiliary *do* has been added to fulfil the operator function. A similar process has taken place in the following example, but this time the question word replaces an adverbial element:

declarative				interrogative				
S	V	O	A	$A_{Wh\text{-}}$	V_{op}	S	V	O
We	*'ll finish*	*this job*	*today*	*When*	*will*	*we*	*finish*	*this job?*

You can also see from this example that the verb phrase contained an auxiliary so it was unnecessary to supply an operator. We saw that in *yes-no* questions we do not need to add an operator for the lexical verb *be*. The same is true of *wh*-questions. Also, when the subject of a sentence, whatever the lexical verb, is substituted with a *wh*-word, no inversion takes place:

declarative			interrogative		
S	V	C	S$_{Wh-}$	V	C
Lima	*is*	*the capital of Peru*	*What*	*is*	*the capital of Peru?*
S	V	O	S$_{Wh-}$	V	O
Pippa	*married*	*Mick*	*Who*	*married*	*Mick?*

In the examples we have looked at so far the *wh*-word, which is normally either a *wh*-pronoun or *wh*-adverb, replaces a complete clause element. However, the *wh*-word may replace just part of a phrase.

declarative			interrogative			
S	V	O	O$_{Wh-}$	V$_{op}$	S	V
Lloyd	*is wearing*	*his pink shirt*	*Which shirt*	*is*	*Lloyd*	*wearing?*

In this example the *wh*-determiner *which* replaces only part of the NP *his pink shirt*. However, the *wh*-element of the sentence is still brought to the front as in constructions where the *wh*-word replaces an entire element.

There is one other method of asking questions. This is the use of a **tag question**. A **question tag** is added to a declarative sentence to produce a rather different type of interrogative structure. Here are some examples:

declarative	question tag
He said he'd be here by six,	*didn't he?*
The cat <u>has</u> had its supper,	*hasn't it?*
They <u>couldn't</u> come to the party tonight,	*could they?*
Tracy <u>hasn't</u> been to your flat,	*has she?*

The tag is formed from an auxiliary verb and a pronoun. The auxiliary verb is the operator from the verb element in the main clause of the declarative sentence. Where no operator is present in the declarative, as in the first example, *do* is used in the tag. The pronoun refers back to the subject of the declarative sentence. You will also notice that when the declarative sentence is positive the tag is negative and vice versa. Normally, a negative tag expects the answer *yes* while a positive one anticipates *no* as a response.

☐ *wh*-pronouns ⇨ 2.8, 2.13
☐ *wh*-determiners ⇨ 2.9, 2.13

7.5 IMPERATIVE SENTENCES

An imperative sentence is normally used to direct someone to do something, as you can see from the following examples:

Shut the door at once
Have a good day
Please stop making that noise
Do be quiet

The meaning of the imperative may be quite strong or forceful as in *Shut the door at once* or it may be more gentle and positive as in *Have a good day*. The third example above is introduced by the **politeness marker** *please* which softens the abruptness of *stop making that noise*.

In an imperative sentence the subject element is normally omitted and the lexical verb is in the base form:

A	S	V	O
	Ø	*Shut*	*the door*
	Ø	*Have*	*a good day*
Please	Ø	*stop*	*making that noise*

The verbs in declarative and interrogative sentences will correspond to their subject in terms of first, second or third person. Because the imperative doesn't normally have an overt subject, the question of person is less relevant. However, imperatives are assumed to be in the second person. If the subject were present it would take the form of the second person pronoun *you: You have a good day! You be good!* Very occasionally, the imperative is in the third person in which case it has an overt subject:

S	V	O
Nobody	*drink*	*my gin and tonic*
Latecomers	*see*	*me*

Auxiliaries do not normally occur in imperatives although the auxiliary *do* can be used to soften the imperative as in *Do be quiet*. In addition, *do* is used to make the imperative negative as this auxiliary must precede the negative particle *not*: we could contrast *Stop talking* with *Don't stop talking* therefore.

☐ 1st, 2nd & 3rd person ⇨ 2.8

7.6 EXCLAMATIVE SENTENCES

Exclamative sentences resemble interrogative sentences in so far as a *wh*-word is used in their construction and the *wh*-element is fronted. Here are some examples:

What a lovely day it is
What nonsense you talk
How quickly you did that
How they gossip

Exclamatives only use the *wh*-words *how* and *what* so in this respect they are dissimilar to interrogatives which use a much wider range of *wh*-words. The other major difference is that there is no subject–operator inversion. The *wh*-word is attached to one of the sentence elements and that element is then brought to the front of the sentence. The rest of the sentence structure remains unchanged:

declarative	exclamative	fronted element
It is a lovely day	*What a lovely day it is*	complement
You talk nonsense	*What nonsense you talk*	object
You did that quickly	*How quickly you did that*	adverbial
They gossip (a lot)	*How they gossip*	adverbial

In the last example above *how* is not attached to another element but fills the place of an assumed adverbial such as *a lot* or *a great deal*.

Sometimes you will find that exclamatives consist of simply the *wh*-element and the rest of the sentence is omitted or understood:

full exclamative	reduced exclamative
What a lovely day it is	*What a lovely day*
What nonsense you talk	*What nonsense*
How amazing that is	*How amazing*

Exclamatives are rarely used for anything other than to express exclamations. In this they differ from the other sentence types which have more flexibility of function as we have already seen.

7.7   OTHER STRUCTURAL VARIATIONS

We will look now at some other ways in which sentence structure can vary. In these instances, however, the structural variation does not result in a new sentence type or in a change of voice from active to passive, but in the placing of greater focus on one part of the sentence or in the better balancing of the sentence's structure. The variations we will be looking at may involve the change in position of a clause element or the removal of an item from its normal position within a phrase.

We will begin by looking at **extraposition**. As the name suggests, this involves moving a linguistic item (normally a subordinate clause) out of its normal clause position and placing it later in the clause or sentence, usually after the other obligatory elements. Here is a typical example:

SVC structure

S		V	C
That Jane is very thoughtful		*is*	*common knowledge*

structure after extraposition

dummy S	V	C	extraposed S
It	*is*	*common knowledge*	*that Jane is very thoughtful*

The first example above shows the regular declarative SVC structure of the sentence. The subject of the sentence is a subordinate *that*-clause *That Jane is very thoughtful*. This is quite a problematic structure despite conforming to the SVC pattern. Most typically, subjects are noun phrases rather than clauses. Subordinate clauses are often easier to process when they follow the main verb of the sentence rather than precede it. Further, the complexity of the subject element causes quite a high information load at a point where the main verb, which has a pivotal function in a sentence, has not yet been introduced. These are all reasons why we should extrapose the subject. In the reorganised sentence above the subject has been moved to a position after the complement. However, this leaves the subject position empty and so it is filled with the dummy subject *it*. Because the dummy subject is signalling the removal of the actual subject to a later position in the sentence, it is referred to as **anticipatory *it***.

Extraposed subjects are always clauses but they need not necessarily be finite *that*-clauses. Here is an example with a non-finite *-ing* clause as the subject:

SVC structure

S	V	C
Keeping bees	*can be*	*rather tricky*

structure after extraposition

dummy S	V	C	extraposed S
It	*can be*	*rather tricky*	*keeping bees*

It needn't be the subject of a clause which is extraposed. Here is an example of the object of a ditransitive verb being extraposed:

SVOC structure

S	V	O		C_o
* *The teacher*	*made*	*that coursework was due in*		*clear*

structure after extraposition

S	V	dummy O	C_o	extraposed O
The teacher	*made*	*it*	*clear*	*that coursework was due in*

In this example, it is so natural for speakers to extrapose the object that the SVOC structure is grammatically unacceptable. This is due to the high information load in the object element preceding the far simpler complement element. The other advantage of the extraposed structure is that the most important part of the information in the sentence, namely *that coursework was due in*, is postponed until the end of the sentence where it will receive greater attention.

Another type of extraposition is when a relative clause is removed from the noun phrase in which it occurs:

> *A book which reveals new information about the religious beliefs*
> *of William Shakespeare* (S)   *was published* (V)   *today* (A)

The subject noun phrase here contains a very long relative clause which postmodifies the head noun *book*. This results in the part of the sentence preceding the main verb being uncomfortably longer than the adverbial which closes it. Without the adverbial, the sentence would seem even more awkward. In order to redress this problem, the relative clause can be removed from the noun phrase and positioned at the end of the sentence, even after the non-obligatory adverbial:

S	V	A	extraposed rel.cl.
A book	*was published*	*today*	*which reveals...*

Immediately, the sentence seems more balanced. In addition, attention is now focused on the most important information in the sentence, which is contained in the relative clause and concerns Shakespeare's religious beliefs.

Another structure which, like some of the examples of extraposition, makes use of *it* as a dummy subject is the **cleft sentence**. The purpose of this structure is again to place more focus on a particular piece of information within the sentence. Consider this example:

S	V	O	A
Terry	*plays*	*jazz piano*	*for fun*

Here, we may wish to place emphasis on *Terry* to distinguish him from, say, *Clive*. We can do this by rearranging the sentence as follows:

dummy S	V(*be*)	C (focus + relative clause)
It	*is*	*Terry who plays jazz piano for fun*

The rearranged sentence is introduced by a dummy subject, followed by the verb *be*, then the focus of the sentence, *Terry*, and finally the rest of the information in the sentence placed in a relative clause. If we wanted to place the emphasis on *jazz piano*, this is equally possible:

dummy S	V(*be*)	C (focus + relative clause)
It	*is*	*jazz piano that Terry plays for fun*

We could even if we wish place the focus on *for fun* (as a contrast perhaps to *for a living*) and contain the rest of the information in a *that*-clause:

dummy S	V(*be*)	C (focus + *that*-clause)
It	*is*	*for fun that Terry plays jazz piano*

As you can see, a cleft sentence provides a versatile structure for drawing attention to the information given by a variety of sentence elements.

We saw in section 6.3 that *there* can function as a dummy subject as well as *it*. *There* is used as a dummy subject in conjunction with the verb *be*. Consider this example as a possible response to being asked what was in the wine rack:

*Six bottles of white wine and four of red are

Here the respondent is using the verb *be* to state the existence of something, namely six bottles of white wine and four bottles of red wine. The reason this answer is grammatically unacceptable, however, is that the verb *be* is a copular verb and needs to be followed by a complement. (Only very rarely can this verb be used without a complement: *I think therefore I am* is an example.) A possible way to make the answer grammatically complete might be to add *in the wine rack*:

S	V	C
? Six bottles of white wine and four of red	*are*	*in the wine rack*

An alternative, and more natural response (partly because the inclusion of *in the wine rack* seems rather redundant) is to move the subject noun phrase into complement position and insert the dummy subject *there* into the subject slot:

dummy S	V	C
There	*are*	*six bottles of white wine and four of red*

The sentence is now grammatically complete and sounds completely natural as a response to the question (not, of course, that sentences of this structure are only used as answers to questions). The noun phrase which was formerly the subject has moved into the complement position although interestingly it still possesses two key features of a grammatical subject: first, it provides the information on which the main verb is predicated. Secondly, it still controls whether the verb is singular or plural as these examples demonstrate:

dummy S	V	C
There	*has been*	*an accident*
There	*have been*	*two accidents*

This SVC structure, then, is unusual in this respect. When *there* is used as a dummy subject in this way to state the existence of whatever is referred to by the noun phrase in complement position, it is known as **existential *there***.

The existential *there* construction may be used to change the focus of a sentence as well as to achieve the kind of grammatical completeness which we have just been considering. A sentence containing a lexical verb other than *be* could be rearranged in this way:

S	V	A
A raven	*is flying*	*towards us*

dummy S	V	C
There	*'s*	*a raven flying towards us*

The rearranged structure has the property of giving more emphasis to the subject of the original sentence, *a raven*. You will notice how the rest of the information is placed as a non-finite postmodifying clause to *raven*. A full relative clause might also occur:

S	V	O
Only three students	*have gained*	*A grades*

dummy S	V	C
There	*are*	*only three students who have gained A grades*

In these two examples, the SVO sentence is perfectly natural grammatically. However, the rearranged sentence gives even greater emphasis to *only three students*.

So far, we have seen that many sentences are restructured in order to achieve greater emphasis on one of their elements. The part of the sentence whose content is of most importance is the **focus**. We normally expect this to come at the end of a sentence – what is known as **end-focus** – and we have seen already how extraposed and cleft structures enable large units of important information to be moved to this position or at least away from initial position. However, it is possible to change the focus of a sentence without the addition of the dummy subjects *there* and *it*. One way to do this in speech is to place greater stress on one element. In writing this is sometimes achieved by underlining as you can see if you compare the following two examples:

> Philip had <u>three fillings</u> at the dentist's
> <u>Philip</u> had three fillings at the dentist's

The underlining in the first example implies that the writer hadn't expected Philip to have any treatment at all, while the underlining in the second sentence suggests there was some confusion as to who had the fillings. An alternative method of indicating the focus of a sentence is to move an element out of its normal position:

O	S	V	A
Three fillings	*Philip*	*had*	*at the dentist's*

Here the object element has been moved to the front of the sentence and this unusual position enables the speaker to focus on *three fillings* and thus imply surprise at the subject's need to have dental treatment. The process of moving an element to the beginning of a sentence in this way is known as **fronting**.

In contrast to fronting, **end-shift** may be employed to move a subject to the end of the sentence:

> Keith hates kidney beans and chick peas
> Hates kidney beans and chick peas does Keith

The rearranged sentence above has the advantage of giving prominence both to the verb element *hates*, emphasising the strength of feeling, and to the subject *Keith*, drawing attention to who exactly is doing the hating. You will notice that the auxiliary *does* is added at the end (as if from *Keith does hate...*) although it is sometimes possible simply to remove the subject to the end:

Showed themselves to be an absolute dead loss <u>the Conservative government</u>

Sometimes, a sentence may exhibit both fronting and end-shift:

C	V	S
Of most concern	*has been*	*the cause of the disease*

Here, there are several reasons why we instinctively know that an exchange of subject and complement positions has taken place as opposed to this being an SVC structure. First, we would judge *The cause of the disease has been of most concern* to be the most natural arrangement for the example. Further, the complement here is a prepositional phrase and it is highly unlikely that this form would fulfil the subject function. *The cause of the disease* is typical of a subject element in that it is a noun phrase but it also governs whether the verb is singular or plural as the following example shows:

C	V	S
Of most concern	*<u>have</u> been*	*the <u>causes</u> of the disease*

There are many possible variations on basic clause and sentence structure. While some variations are used so that sentences perform different functions such as asking a question or issuing a command, others are used, as we have seen in this section, to change the emphasis of a sentence or to make it more manageable or balanced.

- ☐ subject element ⇨ 6.3
- ☐ dummy subject ⇨ 6.3
- ☐ object element ⇨ 6.5
- ☐ complement element ⇨ 6.6
- ☐ subordinate clauses ⇨ 6.11

7.8 SIMPLE SENTENCES

At the beginning of this chapter we noted that a sentence may consist of just one clause. Such a sentence is a **simple sentence**. The clause in a simple sentence has to be a main clause. In other words, it has to contain a finite verb and must be grammatically complete as it stands. If for instance the clause were introduced by the subordinating conjunction *because*, then it would not be a simple sentence but the subordinate part of a larger sentence. Neither of the following could be termed simple sentences even though they only contain one clause:

S	V	O
Lloyd	*overcoming*	*his fear of spiders*

scj	S	V	O
Because	*Lloyd*	*overcame*	*his fear of spiders*

Both examples contain only one clause which has an SVO structure. The first example however is not a main clause because the verb is non-finite. The second example is not a main clause as the presence of the subordinating conjunction *because* prevents it from being grammatically complete. The first example could be converted into a main clause by adding a tensed auxiliary to the verb phrase – *Lloyd is overcoming his fear of spiders* – while the second would be an independent clause if *because* were removed to give *Lloyd overcame his fear of spiders*. Both of these examples are now simple sentences.

When we talk about a sentence being a simple sentence we are referring to its grammatical structure not to the information load it contains. The following example is a simple sentence despite its length and relative complexity:

S
The venerable precentor of Gloucester Cathedral whom I met last summer
V   O
has been organising   a musical tour of antipodean churches

This is a long sentence and it is complex in that it contains some quite specialised vocabulary and the subject noun phrase in particular contains a lot of modification. Grammatically, however, this sentence is simple, its structure being SVO.

By contrast, the shortest declarative sentence possible could consist of only two words:

S	V
Someone	*coughed*

Here, the subject takes the form of a noun phrase which consists of just the pronoun *someone*. The verb phrase is in the simple past tense and so it contains no auxiliary verbs. Because the verb *cough* is intransitive, the sentence is complete without the need for any verb complementation. Of course, it is possible to expand any simple sentence by adding adverbials.

Provided these adverbials are not themselves clauses, then the sentence remains a simple one:

A	S	V	A	A
Suddenly	*someone*	*coughed*	*loudly*	*in the next room*

The adverbials which have been added here take the form of two adverbs (*suddenly* and *loudly*) and one prepositional phrase (*in the next room*).

A simple sentence need not be declarative. Imperative, interrogative and exclamative sentences are simple as long as they contain a main clause only:

Fetch my newspaper	imperative
Where's my newspaper	interrogative
What a useless newspaper this is	exclamative

It is important to make a clear distinction between sentence type and sentence structure. Sentence type will be either declarative, imperative, interrogative or exclamative. The structure of a sentence will be simple, compound or complex. We have also looked at function (statement, question, directive or exclamation) as a further aspect of sentences.

So far we have seen that simple sentences contain one verb element and that this occurs within a main clause. Consider the following example which contains two verb elements:

S	V	O
I	<u>*know*</u>	*a man who <u>has</u> an irrational fear of spiders*

This sentence is an SVO main clause which has *know* as its verb. The object element of the clause is a noun phrase which has *man* as its head. You will see though that *man* is postmodified by the relative clause *who has an irrational fear of spiders*. Since the sentence contains this subordinate clause, it might not seem like a simple sentence. However, compare it with this sentence:

S	V	O
The man	*knows*	*that his fear of spiders is irrational*

Here, the object element is not a phrase but a subordinate *that*-clause:

scj	S	V	C
that	*his fear of spiders*	*is*	*irrational*

If we remove this subordinate clause then the sentence will be incomplete:

S	V	O
The man	*knows*	*Ø*

This incompleteness results from the fact that the object element was realised by a clause. If we remove the subordinate relative clause from *I know a man who has an irrational fear of spiders* then a complete grammatical sentence remains:

S	V	O
I	*know*	*a man*

This is because the subordinate clause was only part of the object noun phrase and therefore had a rather different function in the sentence from the subordinate clause which constituted the entire object element. When a sentence which contains only one main clause has a subordinate clause as part of one of its elements and that subordinate clause can therefore be removed without loss of grammatical completeness, then that sentence is still a simple sentence. So we treat *I know a man who has an irrational fear of spiders* as a simple sentence. If, on the other hand, a subordinate clause (finite or non-finite) makes up an entire element in a clause and grammatical incompleteness will result if it is removed, then the sentence is not simple but **complex**. We will deal with complex sentences in section 7.10.

☐ relative clauses ⇨ 6.13

7.9   COMPOUND SENTENCES

There are two ways of incorporating more than one clause into a sentence (apart from embedding one of them in a phrase). One option is to link two or more clauses on an equal basis so neither clause is dependent on the other. The alternative is to place clauses in an unequal relationship so that one is grammatically dependent on the other. The latter method produces a **complex sentence**, the former a **compound sentence**. The process of forming a compound sentence by joining two or more clauses on an equal grammatical footing is known as **coordination.**

We saw in Chapter 5 that the words in a sentence are grouped together first and foremost into phrases and that every word is part of a phrase even if that phrase only contains one word. There is however an exception to the principle that all words are grouped into phrases and this exception concerns conjunctions, particularly when they are used to join clauses. The conjunctions which we use to join clauses on an equal basis and thus form compound sentences are **coordinating conjunctions**. **Coordinator** is an alternative term for a coordinating conjunction.

There are three central coordinators. These are *and, but* and *or*. Here is an example of two main clauses joined with *and* to form a compound sentence:

S	V	O	ccj	S	V	O
I	*read*	*a book*	*and*	*she*	*watched*	*a film*

This compound sentence consists of two main SVO clauses. In this example, it would be possible to reverse the sequence of the clauses:

S	V	O	ccj	S	V	O
She	*watched*	*a film*	*and*	*I*	*read*	*a book*

The coordinating conjunction must remain between the two clauses, however. This is in contrast to a subordinating conjunction such as *while* which can occur at the beginning of the sentence:

> *She watched a film <u>and</u> I read a book*
> * *<u>And</u> I read a book she watched a film*
> *She watched a film <u>while</u> I read a book*
> *<u>While</u> I read a book she watched a film*

The reason it is impossible to place a coordinating conjunction anywhere other than between the two clauses which it joins is that the conjunction is a linking element joining the clauses on an equal grammatical basis. A subordinating conjunction by contrast introduces a clause and makes it subordinate to the main clause in a sentence. Because it is attached to a specific clause in this way rather than linking two clauses, if the clause moves its position, then the subordinating conjunction will move with it.

There is a restriction on the order of the main clauses which *and* joins if the clauses refer to events which occurred in a particular sequence:

> *The attendant opened the front door and I entered the hotel*
> * *I entered the hotel and the attendant opened the front door*

The restriction evident in the second example above is a semantic one and not a grammatical one.

A compound sentence contains at least two main clauses but more are possible. The coordinators *and* and *or* can be used to join three or more main clauses:

> *Jo can come to your house <u>or</u> you can go to hers <u>or</u> you can meet at the pub*
> *The phone rang <u>and</u> the doorbell went <u>and</u> the dog was barking all at once*

By contrast, *but* can only join two main clauses. This is not due to any grammatical property possessed by this conjunction, but to its semantic function of expressing contrast or the opposite of what is expected:

> *William likes Baba the Elephant but Benedict prefers The Teletubbies*
> *The task was difficult but they enjoyed themselves*

There is then a greater restriction on *but* in its capacity to link clauses than there is on the conjunctions *and* and *or*.

The coordinator *or* is sometimes accompanied by *either* at the beginning of the first clause in a compound sentence. This gives emphasis to the alternatives expressed:

> <u>*Either*</u> *Gregory will cook the supper <u>or</u> Clare will fetch a takeaway*

The pair *either/or* are **correlative**. You will see here that *either* occurs at the beginning of the first clause in the compound. In section 5.7 we saw that coordinators can join phrases as well as clauses. There are two more correlative pairs *both/and* and *neither/nor*: these have the capacity to join phrases but not clauses:

> *Both Terry and Julia washed up*
> * *Both Terry washed the dishes and Julia dried them*
> *Julia liked neither her job nor the commuting*
> * *Neither Julia liked her job nor she liked the commuting*

It is important to distinguish between coordination of clauses and coordination of phrases since this enables us to explain why only two of the sentences above are grammatically possible.

There are two further, less central, coordinators which we will mention briefly here. One is *nor*, which is the negative counterpart of *or*. This coordinator replaces *or* when the first clause in a compound sentence is negative:

> *The pizza hadn't been delivered nor had the restaurant phoned*

Like *or, nor* can coordinate more than two clauses. It can also coordinate phrases as well as clauses.

The coordinator which we have not yet considered is *for*. In many respects this behaves like one of the central coordinators. We can compare it to *and* in terms of the position in which it occurs, for example:

> *We were feeling cold and it was snowing*
> *We were feeling cold for it was snowing*
> * *And it was snowing we were feeling cold*
> * *For it was snowing we were feeling cold*

However, *for* differs from the other coordinators in that it is restricted to the linking of main clauses. It is like *but* in that it can only link two main clauses. However, it cannot link phrases nor can it link two subordinate clauses on an equal basis, a property which the other coordinators possess.

In a compound sentence we very often repeat in the second clause some of the information given in the first:

> 1a   *Terry cut the grass and <u>Terry</u> weeded the flower beds*
> 2a   *Terry painted the ceiling and Julia <u>painted</u> the walls*

In example 1a the subject *Terry* occurs in both clauses while in example 2a the verb *painted* occurs in both clauses. Sometimes we reiterate information for the purpose of emphasis, but often there is no need to repeat an item just given. Therefore we simply omit the item which would have been repeated because it will still be understood by our audience. This omission of retrievable information is known as **ellipsis**. Ellipsis can be indicated by using the Ø symbol. Here are examples 1a and 2a reformulated using ellipsis:

> 1b   *Terry cut the grass and Ø weeded the flower beds*
> 2b   *Terry painted the ceiling and Julia Ø the walls*

Ellipsis is a feature very commonly found in compound sentences and is another example of the economy we practise in language. Similar omission, however, is not possible when one clause is subordinate to another:

> 1c   *Since <u>Terry</u> cut the grass, <u>he</u> also weeded the flower bed*
> 1d   * *Since Terry cut the grass, Ø also weeded the flower beds*
> 2c   *Terry <u>painted</u> the ceiling while Julia <u>painted</u> the walls*
> 2d   * *Terry painted the ceiling while Julia Ø the walls*

This is a significant constraint on ellipsis and indicates one of the important differences between clauses joined through coordination and those joined in an unequal relationship through subordination.

> ☐ conjunctions ⇨ 2.12
> ☐ coordination of phrases ⇨ 5.7
> ☐ ellipsis ⇨ 8.5

7.10   COMPLEX SENTENCES

A **complex sentence** contains at least two clauses. However, in contrast to a compound sentence where the clauses are equal grammatically, one of the clauses will be subordinate and will constitute an entire element of the main clause. We saw in section 6.11 that a range of clause types can be subordinate and we will look more fully at this range shortly. For the sake of completeness in this section we will also be reiterating some of the points made in section 6.12 and we will be looking again at how subordinate clauses function as clause elements.

The verb element of a clause has to be a verb phrase so it is impossible for an entire clause to fulfil this function. However, a clause can function as any of the other clause elements. First, we will consider how clauses can act as the subject, object or complement element in a higher level clause. For the time being, we will use examples of *that*-clauses rather than other types of subordinate clauses:

Clause as subject
S   V   C
That Brian has the flu   is   obvious to everyone

Clause as object
S   V   O
Guy   knows   that Brian has the flu

Clause as complement
S   V   C
The problem   is   that Brian has the flu

In all three examples above, one of the clause elements is a subordinate clause. This means that all these examples are complex sentences. When a subordinate clause acts as an obligatory clause element in this way, the subordinate clause is **embedded** in the main clause. Figure 7.1 gives a diagrammatic illustration of the relationship of the embedded subordinate clause to the main or **superordinate** clause.

Sometimes, however, the function of a subordinate clause is less central than this. This is when the subordinate clause functions as a non-obligatory adverbial element of the superordinate main clause.

A	S	V	O	A
When Brian recovers from the flu	*he*	*will ride*	*his bike*	*again*

There are two adverbials in this complex sentence. The adverbial at the end of the sentence is the adverb *again*. The adverbial element at the start of the sentence however is a subordinate clause and it is the presence of this clause in the sentence which makes it a complex one.

We will now look more fully at the range of possibilities for the form which a subordinate clause can take. We will select just one of the clause elements – the object element – for our range of examples. First, the subordinate clause may be non-finite:

		bare infinitive		
		S	V	O
without subject	1	*Fenella*	*dared*	*jump in the deep end*
with subject	2	*Alissa*	*watched*	*Jane wash up*

		to-infinitive		
		S	V	O
without subject	3	*Phil*	*wants*	*to start a record company*
with subject	4	*Jane*	*wants*	*Phil to start a record company*

		-ing participle clause		
		S	V	O
without subject	5	*Emma*	*likes*	*driving her new car*
with subject	6	*Tajal*	*saw*	*Emma driving her new car*

		-ed participle clause		
		S	V	O
with subject	7	*Bill*	*saw*	*Chris beaten to a pulp*

An almost complete range of non-finite clauses, both with and without overt subjects, can fulfil the object function of a superordinate clause (and of course the range of non-finite clauses can function as subject, complement and adverbial elements too).

The subordinate clause which functions as a clause element can also be

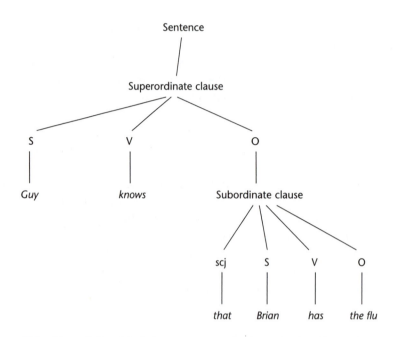

Figure 7.1   The relationship between superordinate and subordinate clauses

a finite clause. Here is an example of a finite *that*-clause functioning as the object element:

	S	V	O
8	*Jo*	*knew*	*that her new job offered excellent prospects*

If we analyse the subordinate clause in this example, you will see that it is declarative in structure:

scj	S	V	O
that	*her new job*	*offered*	*excellent prospects*

We could compare this finite clause to any of the non-finite subordinate clauses given previously, such as this one from example 6:

S	V	O
Emma	*driving*	*her new car*

Even the subordinate clauses from examples 1, 3 and 5 above which lack an overt subject can be analysed as having a declarative structure particularly since the subject can be understood by retrieving it from the main clause. If we take example 3, *Phil wants to start a record company*, it is clear that the understood subject of *to start* is *Phil:*

S	V	O
(Phil)	*to start*	*a record company*

This non-finite clause is declarative in structure since it has an implied subject followed by the verb and the object which complements the verb *start*.

So far, all our examples of subordinate clauses have been declarative, whether they have contained finite or non-finite verb elements. However, subordinate clauses can also be interrogative or exclamative. A finite declarative clause, when functioning as a subject or object or possibly a complement element, will be a *that*-clause. If the subordinate clause is finite but interrogative then the subordinators will be either *if* or *whether* when the interrogative is a *yes-no* question:

S	V	O
Clare	*wondered*	*whether Gregory was back (Is Gregory back?)*
Simon	*asked*	*if he could use the phone (Can I use the phone?)*

If the interrogative, however, is a *wh*-question, then it will begin with a *wh*-word (pronoun, adverb or determiner):

S	V	O	
Clare	*asked*	*who had phoned*	(*wh*-pronoun)
Clare	*wondered*	*where Gregory had gone*	(*wh*-adverb)
Clare	*inquired*	*what time it was*	(*wh*-determiner)

We saw in section 7.4 that in *wh*-interrogatives, the *wh*-word is brought to the front of the clause and there is subject–operator inversion unless the *wh*-word is the subject of the sentence. In subordinate interrogative clauses this subject–operator inversion does not take place:

interrogative main clause

A_{Wh-}	V_{op}	S	V
Where	*has*	*Gregory*	*gone?*

interrogative subordinate clause

	A_{Wh-}	S	V
(Clare wondered)	*where*	*Gregory*	*had gone*

One of the signals of subordination here, in addition to the fact that the subordinate clause is functioning as the object of the main clause, is that the subject–operator inversion normally found in interrogatives does not occur. Non-finite clauses can also be subordinate *wh*-interrogatives but only when the non-finite verb is a *to*-infinitive:

S	V	O
Terry and Julia	*have decided*	*where to go for their holiday*
Terry and Julia	*did not know*	*whether to go to America*

The first subordinate interrogative above – *where to go for their holiday* – is a *wh*-interrogative while the second example – *whether to go to America* – is a *yes-no* interrogative. Neither of these non-finite clauses contains an overt subject and the subject of the infinitive has to be inferred from the main clause.

Subordinate clauses can be exclamative as well as declarative or interrogative. However, the range of clause types is far more limited here as the subordinate exclamatives only begin with *how* or *what* in the same way as a main clause exclamative. There is no word order variation:

main clause
What a nuisance homework can be

exclamative as embedded subordinate clause
Viren knows what a nuisance homework can be

main clause
How disappointing that film was

exclamative as embedded subordinate clause
Jon told Gill how disappointing that film was

Subordinate exclamative clauses are considerably more restricted in their range than interrogative and declarative clauses.

Complex sentences, then, contain a subordinate clause which functions as an element of the superordinate or main clause. When a subordinate clause occurs where a noun phrase would more typically occur (usually as the subject or object of the main clause), then the subordinate clause is a nominal clause and is embedded in the main clause. Sometimes, however, a subordinate clause is linked to the main clause in a more peripheral way. This is when the subordinate clause functions as the optional adverbial element of the main clause. It is these **adverbial clauses** which we will look at in the next section.

In this section and the preceding two sections, we have seen that sentences are essentially simple, compound or complex. Very often, however, a sentence will not fit neatly into one of these categories. Consider this example:

> *Sara wanted a new bike and Heidi wanted one too if she could afford it*

Here, the main clauses *Sara wanted a new bike* and *Heidi wanted one too* are coordinated with the conjunction *and*. However, the second main clause also has a subordinate clause *if she could afford it*. This combination of two coordinated main clauses and one subordinate clause means the sentence is **compound-complex**. Similarly, a complex sentence may contain two subordinate clauses which are coordinated:

> *Heidi wanted a new bike if she could afford it and if she saw one she liked*

The main clause here is *Heidi wanted a new bike*. The sentence contains an adverbial element *if she could afford it and if she saw one she liked* which consists of two subordinate clauses coordinated with *and*. Other combinations of main and subordinate clauses are possible. This wider range of options for sentence construction in no way detracts, however, from the salience of the three-way division between simple, compound and complex sentences.

> ☐ subordinate clauses ⇨ 6.11
> ☐ clauses as clause elements ⇨ 6.12

7.11   ADVERBIAL CLAUSES

We saw in section 6.7 that the adverbial element in a clause may be an adverb phrase or a prepositional phrase. These repeated examples illustrate this:

Julia speaks French <u>very fluently</u>	AdvP
Terry was digging up the weeds <u>in his garden</u>	PP

In addition, the adverbial element of a clause may be another clause, although this clause will be subordinate. In the following example, the subordinate clause which functions as the adverbial element is introduced by the subordinating conjunction *since*:

A	S	V	O
Since it was very cold	*Terry*	*lit*	*a fire*

We noted in section 2.7 that adverbs as a word class can be subdivided into adjuncts, disjuncts and subjuncts according to their function. Similarly, adverbial elements – which of course function like adverbs whatever form they take – can also function as adjuncts, disjuncts or subjuncts. The same is true for adverbial clauses, although these largely function as adjuncts or disjuncts.

Adjuncts usually express manner, time, place or degree. Here are some examples of adverbials expressing the first three of these:

adverbial of manner	
He walked <u>awkwardly</u>	AdvP
He walked <u>with a limp</u>	PP
He walked <u>as if he had hurt his foot</u>	subordinate clause
adverbial of place	
He sat <u>here</u>	AdvP
He sat <u>in the garden</u>	PP
He sat <u>where he could</u>	subordinate clause
adverbial of time	
He arrived <u>yesterday</u>	AdvP
He arrived <u>in the morning</u>	PP
He arrived <u>after I left</u>	subordinate clause

Adverbs function as disjuncts when they comment on what is said or the way that something is said. Adverbials can also function in this way:

1	*<u>Frankly</u>, I don't think this is a good idea*	AdvP
2	*<u>In all honesty</u>, I don't think this is a good idea*	PP
3	*<u>If I'm honest</u>, I don't think this is a good idea*	subordinate clause
4	*<u>Surprisingly</u>, the party was a success*	AdvP
5	*<u>In spite of the band</u>, the party was a success*	PP
6	*<u>Although the band was dire</u>, the party was a success*	subordinate clause

In examples 1 to 3 the adverbial element provides a comment on the way something is said, while in examples 4 to 6 it comments on the content of the main clause.

Adverbials which function disjunctively often express condition, concession, reason, purpose or result. **Conditional clauses** often begin with the subordinating conjunction *if*, although other subordinating conjunctions such as *provided, supposing, unless* and *as long as* can also introduce them, as can some *wh*-words:

If you want, we can go and see the new James Bond movie
Provided you're free, we can go and see the new James Bond movie
Whenever you're free, we can go and see the new James Bond movie

Concessive clauses, which express an unexpected qualification to the content of the main clause, normally begin with *although, though* or *while*:

Although you're angry, I'm going to do this anyway
While I appreciate you're angry, I'm going to do this anyway

Reason clauses are typically introduced by *as, because, for* and *since*:

I'm going to bed because I don't feel well
I'm going to bed for that is the only way I can get rid of this flu

Adverbial clauses can also be **purpose clauses** or **result clauses**:

So that he could see better, the boy stood on the box	purpose
The boy stood on the box so then he could see better	result

The subordinating conjunctions which normally introduce purpose clauses are *in order that, in order to, so, so as to* and *so that*, while *so* and *so that* can also introduce result clauses.

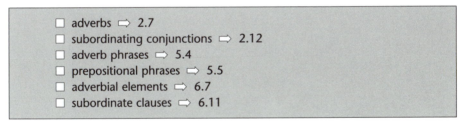

☐ adverbs ⇨ 2.7
☐ subordinating conjunctions ⇨ 2.12
☐ adverb phrases ⇨ 5.4
☐ prepositional phrases ⇨ 5.5
☐ adverbial elements ⇨ 6.7
☐ subordinate clauses ⇨ 6.11

Part IV
DISCOURSE FRAMEWORKS

8 Beyond Sentences

8.1 DISCOURSE

In Part III we looked in considerable detail at syntactic structures: we saw how to construct increasingly larger units, moving from phrases to clauses and then from clauses to sentences. The structure of a sentence is the point at which grammar traditionally stops. This is because it is possible to delimit what a sentence might be, but virtually impossible to delimit anything larger than a sentence. After all, sentences are used to build all kinds of larger units ranging from short notes to letters to newspaper articles to short stories to epic novels. There would, however, be an incompleteness about our study of the frameworks of English if we did not pay some attention to the way in which we join sentences together and this is what this short section is about. Here, then, we will be studying **discourse**. Discourse is any sequence of sentences which make up a complete unit or **text** (although in principle a text could consist of just one sentence, for example in a proverb such as *Too many cooks spoil the broth*). Sometimes the term discourse is used specifically to refer to conversation, but here we are mainly using it in the more general sense of a linguistic unit larger than a sentence.

We have already explored a considerable number of aspects which make a linguistic unit complete and grammatical. This sense of completeness goes beyond the level of a sentence and is something we can identify in groups of sentences. Consider the following extract:

> *Anything said in a normal way bounced off me. One of the most impressive ruins in England, this former royal castle was besieged by parliamentary forces in 1646. Twoflower was a tourist, the first ever seen on the discworld. It was darkening slowly outside. In another minute Tod and Terry found themselves in the street just in time to catch a tram for Nelson's Pillar. His comments prompted speculation that the Clinton administration was not concerned about the dollar's weakness. I'm going to be sharing a flat with three others. Joe Hogan makes sciobs, traditional baskets for straining and serving potatoes. In Victorian times, it was the home of the local blacksmith and today it*

forms a comfortable base for exploring this delightful corner of Devon.
Put the lower-section battens in place under the top-section battens and
measure down from the top to the bottom edge of the lower batten.

You won't have read more than a couple of lines before you realised that there was something rather strange about this 'text'. It consists of ten sentences but it is quite clear that these sentences do not follow in a sequence nor do they together add up to a coherent and complete passage. The perfectly straightforward explanation for this is that each sentence was selected at random from a range of different texts and the new 'text' created is therefore entirely artificial. The randomness of the selection of the sentences is evident to a reader and, in addition, most speakers of English would have little difficulty in suggesting the source of each individual sentence in the extract. The final sentence, for example, was taken from a DIY manual, while the penultimate sentence comes from a catalogue of properties for self-catering holidays. The very fact that a reader would be able to identify this extract as a 'non-text' shows that we all possess a very clear sense of what a coherent text or group of sentences is like. The phenomenon of sentences belonging together is known as **textuality**. In this chapter we will be exploring exactly what it is that gives a text textuality. In general terms this is brought about by **cohesion**. Cohesion is a blanket term for a range of linguistic signals and strategies which enable us to know that sentences belong together and in a particular sequence. In sections 8.2 to 8.7 we will be studying a variety of cohesive devices.

8.2 LEXICAL COHESION

Cohesion can operate on both a lexical level and a grammatical level and we begin by considering how words and the meanings of words can give a text cohesion. The lack of lexical cohesion was one of the indicators that the extract given in the previous section was not an integrated whole. Consider the key lexical words from the first three sentences:

1 *said normal way bounced*
2 *impressive ruins England former royal castle besieged parliamentary*
 forces
3 *Twoflower tourist first ever seen discworld*

Not only is there no repetition of any word but, more significantly, there are no lexical words in sentence one which have a connection with any of those in the other two sentences, and the same can be said for sentences two and three. In a cohesive text, we would expect there to be lexical links between sentences. Compare this extract of text which is taken from the opening of a front page article in the *Sunday Times* in October 1999:

Revealed: Britain's secret nuclear plant

A secret nuclear fuel plant processing radioactive material a mile from the centre of a British city has been revealed to have serious safety flaws.

Nuclear fuel more volatile than the uranium which caused the recent radioactive leak at a Japanese facility is being secretly manufactured in the Rolls-Royce plant in Derby.

Highly enriched uranium fuel is processed at the factory for the Ministry of Defence (MoD) – although this has never before been disclosed and the local population has not been told because the work is classified. They are only aware that the factory makes engines for Trident nuclear submarines.

A reader would be in no doubt here that this text is a cohesive one. The lexis is one of the main indicators that these four sentences belong together. For one thing, several lexical words are repeated: the central adjective *nuclear,* which signals the theme of the article and is used in the headline, appears twice in the compound *nuclear fuel* and also in *nuclear submarine.* The adjective *radioactive* occurs twice as does the noun *uranium.* Furthermore, *nuclear, radioactive* and *uranium* are all linked by their meanings. In other words they belong to the same **semantic field**. The article is about a supposedly secret nuclear plant and there is frequent reference to the location of the work which is taking place. The *plant* is mentioned twice and the noun *factory,* which belongs to the same lexical set as *plant,* is also used twice. In addition, the noun *facility* is used to refer to the Japanese processing plant. The work itself is referred to through the verbs forms *processing, processed* and *manufactured.* There are concerns about the nuclear processing and this theme is carried in *serious safety flaws, more volatile than the uranium* and *recent radioactive leak.* Finally, there is a semantic field of secrecy established not only through *secret* and *secretly* but also through *classified* and through its antonyms *revealed* and *disclosed.*

You can see then that in a cohesive text there are many lexical signals which establish the unity of the text and, as it were, reassure the reader (or listener) that what they are receiving is a deliberate sequence of sentences. The particular extract we have just considered is quite dense in the number of lexical and semantic connections that exist but any text will contain comparable connections. Lexical cohesion, then, can be established either through the repetition of lexical items or through the meaning relationships of lexical items within particular semantic fields or lexical sets.

☐ lexical words ⇨ 2.3
☐ antonyms & other meaning relations ⇨ 3.9

8.3   REPETITION

Repetition is another method of achieving cohesion in a text. The repeated items may recur within a given sentence or in more than one sentence. The repeated item may be a single lexical word, a word group, a clause, a particular structure or even a sound.

In the previous section we saw how the repetition of certain lexical words such as the adjectives *nuclear* and *radioactive* and the nouns *uranium*, *plant* and *factory* not only played a part in developing the subject matter of the news report, but also gave a sense that we were reading a cohesive text. It is important to make a distinction between repetition of lexical and of grammatical words. This is because we need to repeat grammatical words all the time due to their particular syntactic function. The choice of a lexical item, by contrast, is more topic-specific and has a deliberateness about it which the selection of grammatical words does not typically have. Most of the time we barely notice the repetition of grammatical words. In this paragraph alone, the definite article (*the*) has been used 13 times and the coordinating conjunction *and* has been used 6 times.

Phrases of more than one word or parts of phrases may also be repeated. In the *Sunday Times* article the *secret nuclear fuel plant* referred to in the headline is inevitably referred to several times throughout the article. Here are the references to it in the first ten paragraphs:

A secret nuclear fuel plant	paragraph 1
... the Rolls-Royce plant in Derby.	paragraph 2
... the plant ...	paragraph 4
... the plant.	paragraph 5
The plant ...	paragraph 8
The plant ...	paragraph 9

You will notice that the first two mentions of *the plant* provide more specific detail about it, but thereafter a simple noun phrase is sufficient to refer to the topic of the article. You will also see that in paragraph one it is <u>*A*</u> *secret nuclear fuel plant*. Once its identity has been established, however, it is referred to as *the plant* throughout the rest of the text.

Repetition of single words or word groups is a common strategy for giving a text cohesion. Less common, because more obviously deliberate, is the repetition of larger units of construction. Very often, when this occurs, it will be within a persuasive, rhetorical or literary context. Consider this extract from one of Sir Winston Churchill's famous wartime speeches:

> *We shall go on to the end. We shall fight in France. We shall fight on the seas and oceans. We shall fight with growing confidence and growing strength in the air. We shall defend our island, whatever the cost may be. We shall fight on the beaches. We shall fight on the landing grounds. We shall fight in the fields and in the streets. We shall fight in the hills. We shall never surrender.*

This example is full of repetition. If we rearrange the layout of this extract, it becomes easier to see the patterns of repeated elements and how they operate:

we shall go on		*to the end*
we shall fight		*in France*
we shall fight		*on the seas and oceans*
we shall fight		*with growing confidence and*
		growing strength in the air
we shall defend	*our island*	*whatever the cost may be*
we shall fight		*on the beaches*
we shall fight		*on the landing grounds*
we shall fight		*in the fields and in the streets*
we shall fight		*in the hills*
we shall never surrender		

In this extract, there is extensive repetition of the subject and verb combination *we shall fight*. The extract opens with a comparable structure *we shall go on*. *We shall fight* then occurs three times, *we shall defend* provides a brief variation, and finally there are four more occurrences of *we shall fight* building to the climax of *we shall never surrender* (which is made more forceful by the inclusion of the adverb *never)*. All these clauses have the first person plural pronoun *we* as their subject (emphasising of course the unity of the British people in time of war) and they all employ the modal auxiliary *shall* which gives a greater sense of determination than the alternative *will*.

Not only is there repetition of subject and verb elements in this extract, there is also repetition in the adverbial elements:

to	*the end*
in	*France*
on	*the sea and oceans*
with	*growing confidence and growing strength*
in	*the air*
on	*the beaches*
on	*the landing grounds*
in	*the fields*
in	*the streets*
in	*the hills*

If you analyse these structures you will see that they are all prepositional phrases (including two compound prepositional phrases *on the seas and oceans* and *with growing confidence and growing strength*). The first example, *to the end,* expresses time, while *with growing confidence and growing strength* indicates manner, but the rest indicate location. There is a sense in which we are given a list of all the places where the war will be fought, and this accumulation also contributes to the build-up which concludes with *we shall never surrender.* The repetition shown here is different in kind from the verbatim repetition of *we shall fight.* Here it is the structure of the prepositional phrase (a preposition with a noun phrase as its complement) which is repeated. Structural repetition of this kind is called **parallelism.**

Finally, we will look briefly at phonological repetition. Just as clausal repetition and parallelism give a text a sense of being more consciously crafted, phonological effects achieved through repetition probably do this to an even greater extent. Consider this chapter opening from the novel *Waterland* by Graham Swift:

> *The Great Ouse. Ouse. Say it. <u>Ouse</u>. Slowly. How else can you say it? A sound which exudes slowness. A sound which suggests the slow, slug-gish, forever oozing thing it is. A sound which invokes quiet flux, minimum tempo; cool, impassive, unmoved motion. A sound which will calm even the hot blood racing in your veins. Ouse, Ouse, Ooooooouse ...*

In this extract, Swift is describing a river in East Anglia. He uses the repeated /uː/ sound, which occurs not only in the name of the river but also in *exudes, oozing* and *unmoved,* in order to suggest the heavy motion of the river. This is possibly the most noticeable example of repetition in this extract but you can see that Swift also uses lexical repetition as well as extensive parallelism through the structure of the noun phrase *a sound* ... where the head word *sound* is postmodified by a relative clause introduced by *which*. This level of crafting and repetition would be highly unexpected in everyday speech or even in informative language such as a newspaper report, but it is a common feature of more polished and literary discourse.

8.4   ENDOPHORIC REFERENCE

Endophoric reference is the process by which one item in a text refers to another item within the same text, and both items share the same **referent**. In other words, they are **co-referential**. We saw in the previous section that repetition is often used when there is a need to make frequent reference to a particular item or in order to achieve a particular effect. Sometimes when frequent reference is required, however, repetition can seem unnecessary and clumsy. This is particularly the case when an item is repeated not long after it has first been mentioned. Consider this example:

> *The orchestra is touring Europe. The orchestra will perform first in Berlin.*

The repetition of *the orchestra* in the second sentence is unnecessary and seems unnatural because we would normally replace the second instance of this noun phrase with a pronoun:

> *The orchestra is touring Europe. It will perform first in Berlin.*

In this example, the pronoun *it* signals a co-reference to some other piece of information which needs to be retrieved in order to complete the meaning of *It will perform first in Berlin*. In this instance, the referent of *it* is retrieved from the preceding sentence and we are able to deduce that *it* refers to *the orchestra*. When an element (most typically a pronoun but possibly a determiner or adverb) refers to a previous element in this way it is an **anaphor**, and its reference is **anaphoric**. The item to which the anaphor refers us back is its **antecedent**.

Anaphors enable us to avoid needless repetition and are used frequently in discourse. Less common but nevertheless of importance in cohesion is **cataphor** or **cataphoric** reference. Cataphors refer forward:

> *This is what I want you to do: go to the shop, buy a turkey, come home and cook it.*

Here, the cataphor is the demonstrative pronoun *this*. Since no information has already been given which might provide a referent for *this*, it would be assumed by a listener or reader that the referent has not yet been given. In other words, *this* is a cataphor and it refers forward here to quite an extensive unit: *go to the shop, buy a turkey, come home and cook it.* In fact anaphors and cataphors can refer to anything from a single word to any number of sentences. The advantage of using a cataphor is that it sets up an expectation of information to come and alerts the audience to pay attention to what follows.

Anaphors and cataphors can occur both within sentences and as a device to connect sentences. As we noted above, anaphors and cataphors are most typically pronouns (as in the examples we have considered so far in this section) but they can also be determiners or adverbs. Here are some further examples:

anaphoric determiner
There were ten different cheeses on the cheeseboard. <u>This</u> huge selection made it very difficult for Louise to choose what she wanted.

anaphoric adverb
Annette and Ashley finally settled in Chester. They were happy <u>there</u> for many years.

cataphoric determiner
<u>These</u> presents are what Harriet asked for: a mobile phone, a trip to London and a new pair of trainers.

cataphoric adverb
<u>Here</u> is the point in the story when the truth emerges. It's just after the letter is discovered...

Although the process of retrieving the reference of an anaphor or cataphor is normally straightforward, there are restrictions on the scope of the reference. If the reference is anaphoric, the referent is the most recently mentioned item which could fulfil the reference. (If the reference is cataphoric, it is the next feasible item to be mentioned.) That is why the following example is confusing:

<u>Laurence</u> has just returned from Moscow. There were some tricky moments at the embassy there involving a <u>protestor</u>. <u>He</u> found it quite difficult to deal with the situation.

What is clearly meant here is that Laurence and not the protestor found the situation difficult to deal with. Grammatically, though, the text is confusing because the *he* of the third sentence would at first be taken to refer to the more recently mentioned person, the protestor (whom we therefore assume to be male). To make this text clear, we would need to re-establish the subject of the third sentence by replacing *he* with *Laurence*.

The examples of anaphors and cataphors which we have discussed so far have all had referents within the text in which they occur. In other words, they are all endophoric references. By contrast, a reference may be **exophoric** and refer to something related to the situation or context in which the discourse occurs rather than something within the discourse itself. Imagine the following example uttered by an exasperated parent walking into their child's bedroom:

> *Look at the mess you've made in this room.*

Here, the determiner *this* refers not to any room recently mentioned or about to be mentioned in the parent's utterance but to the actual room in which the speaker stands at the moment of utterance. The determiner *this* is therefore used contextually rather than textually here. This is an example of exophoric reference.

Exophoric references, because they are context-bound, are normally **deictic**. **Deixis** refers to the way certain words indicate time, place or person within the context of utterance. In the example *Look at the mess you've made in this room*, the use of *this* implies that the room in question is the one in which the speaker is standing. If, by contrast, the speaker had said *Look at the mess you've made in that room* then the inference is that the speaker is not actually in the room referred to. Written texts may also contain exophoric reference which are deictic. A notice in a self-service restaurant which reads *Please leave your trays here when you have finished* would be inviting customers to leave their trays close to the notice, presumably on a rack of some kind.

Deictic words often operate in contrasting pairs. Here are some more examples:

indicating time	indicating location	indicating person
now/then	*here/there*	*I/you*
today/yesterday	*this/that*	*I/we*
today/tomorrow	*these/those*	*he/they*

☐ adverbs ⇨ 2.7
☐ pronouns ⇨ 2.8
☐ determiners ⇨ 2.9

8.5 ELLIPSIS

Ellipsis was introduced in section 7.9 with the examples:

> *Terry cut the grass and Ø weeded the flower beds*
> *Terry painted the ceiling and Julia Ø the walls*

Ellipsis is essentially the omission from a clause or sentence of an element which can nevertheless be inferred, usually because it is recovered from elsewhere in the text. We are able to identify that something is understood because we are aware of a syntactic gap in a structure. In the first of the above examples, we are aware that the subject of the second clause *weeded the flower beds* is missing and we are able to find this missing information by referring to the subject of the first clause, namely *Terry*. In the second example, it is the verb element *painted* which is missing, and we again refer to the preceding clause to find the missing element. We saw in Chapter 6 that English syntax is based on a typical clause structure of subject and verb plus any verb complementation. Often it is our implicit knowledge of what a complete clause should be which enables us to identify that an element (or elements) has been ellipted. The reason why ellipsis occurs in syntactic structures has already been touched on: essentially, we use language in an efficient and economic way and do not favour repetition unless it is for emphasis or for clarification. Some repetition can be avoided by using anaphors: ellipsis is basically another method of avoiding repetition.

The examples given at the start of the previous paragraph showed ellipsis operating within compound sentences. It is also possible for ellipsis to operate across sentence boundaries and it is therefore another important cohesive device in discourse. Consider this example:

> *You may think that DVD is the best thing since sliced bread. Well it isn't.*

The second sentence here, if considered in isolation, is clearly grammatically incomplete. The reason for this is that the verb in the sentence is *be*, which is normally followed by a complement. Here, however, the complement has clearly been ellipted and needs to be retrieved from the preceding clause:

S	V	C
it	*is (n't)*	*Ø*
DVD	*is*	*the best thing since sliced bread*

The full meaning of *It isn't* is *It isn't the best thing since sliced bread*. However there is no need to repeat the complement a second time, hence the ellipsis. (You may also have noticed that this sentence contains an anaphor since *it* refers to the antecedent *DVD*.)

Ellipsis is particularly common in conversation, where speakers are often involved in question and answer or in comment and response exchanges:

A   *Are you intending to come to the cinema tonight?*
B   *Yes I am*

The explicit meaning of *Yes I am* is *Yes I am intending to come to the cinema tonight*. The ellipsis here is more extensive than in the previous examples we have considered. Speaker B could simply have replied *yes* to A's question in which case the ellipsis would then have been of the complete clause *I am intending to come to the cinema tonight*. Here is another example of a possible conversational exchange:

A   *That was terrible news about the stock market crash*
B   *Absolutely dreadful*

Here, B has substituted A's adjective *terrible* with the adjective *dreadful* and has emphasised *dreadful* by using the intensifier *absolutely*. In isolation *absolutely dreadful* would be fairly meaningless since we would not know what it referred to but in the context of the exchange it is clear that B means *That was absolutely dreadful news about the stock market crash*. There is no likelihood, however, that A would misunderstand B despite B's extensive use of ellipsis in their response. Conversation would seem very laboured and long-winded if we did not use ellipsis wherever possible.

In Part III of this book we saw other examples of omitted elements in certain structures which we might now interpret as examples of ellipsis. One such instance is a verbless clause. We discussed this structure in 6.16. For example, we considered:

Although unhappy with the decision, Debra agreed to help

The adverbial element *Although unhappy with the decision* is a verbless clause. We justified our interpretation of this as a clause on the grounds that it was introduced by a subordinating conjunction and that the subject and verb elements – *Debra* and *was* respectively, could be understood from the rest of the sentence. The ellipted elements are found not in a preceding part of the text, but in the following main clause.

In the previous section, we identified the difference between endophoric and exophoric reference. Endophoric reference occurs within the text and therefore, whether it is achieved through anaphor or cataphor, is a textual cohesive device. By contrast, an exophoric reference refers to the context or situation in which discourse occurs. Ellipsis is normally endophoric but can be exophoric. For example, a sign by an escalator saying *Keep to the right* would clearly mean *Keep to the right of the escalator*, while someone buying tickets at a cinema box office might simply say to the cashier *three adults please* meaning *I'd like tickets for three adults please*.

> ☐ clause structures ⇨ 6.8

8.6   CONJUNCTS

We have already examined conjuncts as a way of linking sentences in section 2.7 but we will revisit them here. Conjuncts are typically adverbs which perform the function of linking one sentence to another, usually to the preceding one. We considered the following example:

> *It looked as if it might rain. They decided to go for a picnic <u>nevertheless</u>.*

Here, the conjunct *nevertheless* links the second sentence to the first. Like other types of adverb, conjuncts can occur in a variety of positions:

> <u>*Nevertheless*</u>*, they decided to go for a picnic*
> *They decided <u>nevertheless</u> to go for a picnic*

Like other cohesive devices, it is possible for conjuncts to link more than two sentences:

> *Jonelle's essay was going very well. <u>So</u> she decided to stop*
> *for a cup of coffee. <u>In any case</u>, she needed a cigarette.*

In the above example, the adverb *so* links the second sentence to the first while the prepositional phrase *In any case* links the third sentence to the second and also to the first since it implies that Jonelle would have stopped working on her essay in order to have a cigarette.

Although conjuncts most typically link one sentence with a preceding sentence, some can set up the expectation of a list:

> *First* *I'd like to welcome you to this college. *Next* I'd like to*
> *introduce Jackie ...*

Conjuncts are typically adverbs or prepositional phrases. If they are prepositional phrases, such as *in any case*, *as a result* and *on the other hand*, they are
usually frozen collocations: for example, *as a result* is an expected combination. We would not expect to find a similar phrase like *as an outcome* fulfilling
the conjunctive role although we could of course find this prepositional
phrase in a different context. Very occasionally, conjuncts are clauses:

> *I'd like to live in the country.*
> *What is more*, I want to live in a cottage with an open fire.*

In this example, *what is more*, like the prepositional phrases we discussed above
such as *as a result*, is a frozen collocation used only for this particular conjunctive function.

> ☐ adverbs as conjuncts ⇨ 2.7

8.7   REGISTER

So far, we have been looking at cohesive devices such as anaphors and
conjuncts which make connections across sentence boundaries (although
some devices may also make connections within sentences). Linguistic features
like these are cohesive strategies used in all kinds of discourse. In other words,
you are just as likely to find them in a short story as you are in a business letter
or a telephone answering machine message. They are all internal cohesive
devices which link sentences and signal to the reader that the text has unity.

However, there is a further aspect of cohesion which relates not to the
internal cohesive devices of a text but to the context in which it is used. This
aspect of discourse is known as **register**. Register is the collective term for
various situational and functional aspects of a text. In other words, register is
the sum of a text's subject matter, its purpose, its **mode** (essentially, spoken or
written), its **genre** (the type of text it is) and the relationship that exists
between its participants (namely, the writer or speaker and the audience).
These factors all work together to influence the choices language users make
when constructing discourse. Compare these two short examples:

1 **8.30 Delia's How to Cook – Part Two**
   Delia looks at the world of cheese, with recipes and tips on

buying, storing and cooking. Tonight's recipes include Welsh rabbit with sage and onions, cheese-and-herb fritters, and curd cheesecake.

Director Philip Bonham Carter; Executive producer David Willcock (S) 3070

2 **Parmesan Toast**
a thin loaf of bread – ciabatta, baguette etc.
butter
grated Parmesan cheese

Split the bread horizontally to give two flattish pieces. Like thick slices of toast. Splitting the loaf by hand will give a rough surface which is more interesting to eat than a flat, knife-cut surface. Spread lavishly with butter, sprinkle thickly with grated Parmesan. Grill till the cheese melts and the toast drips with butter. The bread should be golden in patches. Wolf immediately.

Example 1 is a television listing from the *Radio Times* and example 2 is a recipe from Nigel Slater's *Real Cooking*. Although these examples are both very short texts, it is possible to identify some cohesive devices within them such as lexical cohesion and ellipsis. In terms of register, there are also some distinctive features to identify.

The subject matter of both examples is cooking with cheese. However, example 1 gives you information about a programme on this subject while example 2 actually gives you some instructions for a simple recipe involving cheese. These different purposes are reflected in the way the pieces are written. Example 1 uses declarative sentences and the present tense (*Delia Smith looks ...*, *Tonight's recipes include ...*) while example 2 uses imperatives (*Split ...*, *Spread ...*, *Sprinkle ...*). These grammatical differences are part of the **field** of each text, namely its purpose and context of use as well as the subject matter.

Both texts are in the written mode. Example 1 follows a prescribed format with programme time and title as a heading, then the information about the programme, and finally details of the director and producer of the series. Coded abbreviations are used, namely (S) for subtitles and the number *3070* for video programming. Different font sizes and types are used and these conform to the pattern for all *Radio Times* listings. Example 2 also has a heading, this time the name of the recipe. A list of ingredients and the actual instructions follow. Again, the text has a prescribed design in terms of font size and type. These two examples show that mode is not simply a matter of the choice between speech and writing. Written texts also involve choices with regard to layout and whether the text is typed or handwritten, while spoken discourse requires the speaker to adopt an appropriate intonation pattern as well as a suitable voice quality, speed and volume.

Another important aspect of register is **tenor**. This concerns the relationship between the writer or speaker and their audience: in other words, the relationship between the participants in the discourse. This relationship determines how formal or informal a text is. If you look again at the *Radio Times* entry in example 1, the tenor is fairly formal. The writer is unknown and the audience for which the listing is written is a wide and not especially specific one. Therefore, the lexis chosen is not too colloquial (although neither is it very specialised or elevated), there is no direct address to the reader, and the sentences are grammatically complete. By contrast, example 2 has a more informal feel. This is because the writer, Nigel Slater, is trying to establish a friendly relationship with the cook who is using his book. He clearly wants them to enjoy the cooking and not become too serious about it. The informality is signalled by the use of ellipsis and the informal vocabulary such as *flattish* and *Wolf*.

Finally, the concept of genre can be helpful when looking at different types of discourse. A genre is a particular type of speaking or writing identifiable by a distinct style and form. Language users are aware of the conventions for a huge variety of different genres, although some are more clearly defined than others. Written examples include television listings, recipes, letters (both business and personal), postcards, birthday cards and school reports, to name just a few. Spoken examples include conversation (although this could easily be subdivided), business transactions, telephone messages, news bulletins, weather reports, court hearings and so on. Experience teaches us what to expect from different types of discourse and the patterns to use for them. When we go up to the counter in a clothes shop, for example, we expect the sales assistant to begin with a question such as *Can I help you?* Equally, we are aware of any failure to follow conventions of genre. Comedians often make use of this awareness for comic effect. There might be humour in describing a surgical operation in the style of a football commentary, for instance.

When we create a text, then, we not only use lexical and grammatical devices to link the sentences of that text together, but we also adopt the appropriate pattern and style for that particular text. Unity in discourse is ultimately achieved therefore through the working together of cohesive devices on both a textual and a contextual level.

Part V
PHONOLOGICAL FRAMEWORKS

9 Phonetics and Phonemes

9.1 PHONETICS AND PHONOLOGY

Phonetics is the study of the sounds of speech – how we produce speech, how we perceive speech, and what characterises each particular sound. There are several branches of phonetics but we will only be concerned here with **articulatory phonetics**. This is the area of phonetics which deals with the actual production of speech sounds. When we talk about speech sounds we are referring to the individual sounds which make up words. A simple word like *bat*, for example, is made up of three distinct sounds. We will be concerned here with discovering what precisely we do in physiological terms in order to produce individual sounds such as these and many others.

Closely related to phonetics is **phonology**. Whereas phonetics deals with the physical production and perception of speech, phonology is more concerned with sounds systems and patterns. The main aspects of phonology which we will be exploring are the set of speech sounds which occur in English, the way these sounds combine to form syllables and words, and the aspects of speech such as stress and intonation which affect syllables, words and strings of words.

Although phonetics is distinct from phonology, for the sake of simplicity phonetics is included here as part of the **phonological frameworks** which are dealt with in this final section of the book. Clearly, both phonetics and phonology, which relate to sound and sound systems, are in contrast to the other frameworks we have covered which are concerned with lexical, grammatical and discourse structure. In this chapter, we will begin by looking at speech production (a branch of phonetics), but in conjunction with this we will also move beyond the realm of phonetics proper in order to identify the system of speech sounds – or **phonemes** – which characterise English. In the following chapter we will look at the way in which these speech sounds combine to form syllables and words. Then in Chapter 11 we will conclude our exploration of the phonological frameworks of English by looking at features such as stress and intonation which affect syllables, words and strings of words.

One important point to make before we begin to consider speech sounds and their production concerns the primacy of speech. Because most of us have never struggled with speech in the way we may have struggled with reading and writing, it is easy to take spoken language for granted and to rate it as less valuable than the written language. Speech is important not only because it provides us with a versatile and instant means of communication but also because human language materialises first and foremost as speech. This is why no study of the frameworks of English would be complete without a specific study of phonology.

9.2   A REPRESENTATIVE ACCENT

In Chapter 1 we discussed the desirability of having one particular variety of English to refer to when looking at lexical and grammatical frameworks. The variety selected was **Standard British English**. This was chosen because it has common currency: even if people do not speak Standard English, they will almost certainly write it sometimes and they will be very familiar with it as a national dialect used, for example, in newspapers, in business and legal documents, and in much public broadcasting.

Standard English is a **dialect**: in other words, it is a variety characterised by certain lexical and grammatical features. All speakers of English have a dialect, be it Standard English or some other variety. Similarly, all speakers have an **accent**. Accent is the term we use to refer to characteristics of pronunciation. Often, we can identify where someone comes from by their accent. Through television and film, and through our everyday experiences, most of us are familiar with the accents of Belfast, Glasgow, Edinburgh, Cardiff, Liverpool and Newcastle to name just a few of the regional accents of the United Kingdom. (And most of us are also adept at recognising accents from Australia, America, Asia and so on.) An accent which has become particularly widespread in recent years is the accent associated with London and the Home Counties (although it is rapidly spreading further afield). This accent is known as **Estuary English** and is spoken by, for example, the comedian Paul Merton or the MP Ken Livingstone.

Selecting a representative accent for our study of the phonology of English is not an entirely straightforward matter. We cannot simply select the accent used by speakers of Standard English since they do not all speak the same accent. There are valid arguments for selecting Estuary English as our yardstick accent, since it is so widely spoken. However, Estuary English is a fairly recent phenomenon and linguists have traditionally selected an accent known as **Received Pronunciation** (often abbreviated as **RP**) to represent British English and this, therefore, is the accent we will use here. The Queen speaks RP but hers is a variety associated with the aristocracy and with older speakers which is known as **conservative RP**. In this book, what is meant by RP will be the **mainstream** variety of the accent. You can hear this spoken by many national newsreaders and by well known media or public figures such as Joanna Lumley, Stephen Fry and Jeremy Paxman.

There is an irony about selecting RP to study in that relatively few people (3–5 per cent is the usual estimate) have an RP accent. However, it is perceived as representative of English in that it is the accent taught to many foreigners and it is the pronunciation given in dictionaries. Although it has the disadvantage of sometimes being associated with social privilege, it also has the advantage of not being associated with any specific geographical region.

9.3 PHONEMES

In this chapter, then, we are looking at the way sounds are produced and at the range of sounds which occur in English as represented by Received Pronunciation. We have already seen that words are the chief building blocks of language, although it is possible to analyse words in terms of the smaller units of meaning (or morphemes) which comprise them. On a phonetic level, we can analyse words in terms of distinct, individual sounds. To repeat our earlier example, in the word *bat* you can distinguish three separate sounds. We can test the theory that there are three distinct sounds in *bat* by seeing if each sound can be substituted with another and whether a different word is the result of this substitution. The first sound of *bat* could be replaced to form *rat*, the second to form *bet*, the third to form *bad*. (Of course, the first element of *rat* could be substituted with /br/ to give *brat*, but the fact that /br/ can be divided into /b/ and /r/ means it is not a minimal or smallest possible unit of sound.) Each of these words – *bat*, *rat*, *bet* and *bad* – must, then, be made up of three distinct sounds. If a single sound substitution enables us to make a distinction between two different words (as in *bat* and *rat*), this is proof that the two sounds involved are each meaningful sounds in the language.

Sometimes, a particular sound can be pronounced in different ways depending on the position or context in which it occurs. For instance, compare the way you pronounce /l/ at the start of *loop* with /l/ at the end of *pool*. Word-initial /l/ is different from word-final /l/ in that the latter involves far more spreading of the back of the tongue against the roof of the mouth. The word-initial /l/ is known as **clear *l*** while the word-final /l/ is **dark *l***. Despite this difference of pronunciation, however, we are unlikely to claim that these two sounds are distinct sounds in the way that /b/ and /p/ are. On the contrary, they represent different surface realisations of the same underlying sound. Similarly, some Scots speakers might pronounce *rat* with a slightly rolled /r/ at the beginning, whereas an RP speaker is unlikely to roll the /r/. This does not mean that the Scots speaker is uttering a different word from the RP speaker, merely pronouncing the same word in a slightly different way. We can conclude therefore that there is a difference between the underlying 'model' sounds which make up words and the surface realisation of these sounds by various speakers. These underlying sounds are **phonemes**. Phoneme is an abstract concept in the way that lexeme is also abstract, as we saw in Chapter 2. The surface forms of the phonemes, which vary depending on the position of a sound or on the speaker's accent, are **allophones**. Clear *l* and dark *l* are allophones of the phoneme /l/ just as the various pronunciations of the sound at the beginning of *rat* are allophones of the phoneme /r/. The study and identification of allophones is beyond the scope of this chapter since we are primarily concerned with discovering how we produce sounds and with identifying the set of phonemes which underpin the sound system of the language. We will continue to use the term phoneme on occasions but in many instances the terms **sound** or **speech sound** will be sufficient for our purposes.

Using the method of contrasting pairs of words (such as *bat/rat*, *bat/bet*, *bat/bad*) we can work out how many distinct sounds or phonemes a language possesses. The complete set of phonemes in a language or in a particular accent of a language is known as a **phoneme inventory**. If you collected together all the phonemes which occur in every language of the world you would discover that the phonemes of English make up only a proportion of all the possible sounds which occur in human speech. Some languages have fewer phonemes than English, others more. The number of sounds in a language may or may not be significant. What is certainly of interest though is the actual selection of sounds. Language is not a haphazard phenomenon and this awareness should prompt us, when we have collected together the phonemes of English, to see what patterns we can find in the selection and to see how the sounds are related.

☐ morphemes ⇨ 3.2

9.4   THE INTERNATIONAL PHONETIC ALPHABET

One of the problems of writing down speech sounds, or making a **transcription**, is indicating them clearly to the reader. It is fairly easy to show that *bat* contains three speech sounds because it is easy to grasp the relationship between each of the three letters of the written word and the sounds they represent. However, the letters <b,a,t> (remember that angled brackets < > are used in linguistics to identify letters) do not always stand for the sounds they represent when *bat* is pronounced. For example, <a> represents different sounds in *harp, pace* and *asleep* and <t> represents different sounds in *nation, hatch* and *theme,* while <b> doesn't represent any sound at all in *dumb.*

This problem of there not always being the same correspondence between letters and sounds led a group of linguists concerned with the teaching of foreign languages (and who formed themselves into the **International Phonetic Association**) to devise a special alphabet in which one symbol always represented the same sound and in which there was a symbol for every possible sound a language learner might need. This special alphabet is known as the **International Phonetic Alphabet (IPA** for short) and it is an indispensable tool for the study of phonetics and phonology as it makes the task of identifying and referring to sounds much easier. However, when working on phonetics, you will need to remember that it is the sound of a word which is of importance and not its written form. You need to take care to transcribe words into the phonetic alphabet according to their sounds not their spellings: *dumb,* for example, only has three phonemes (/d, ʌ, m/) even though it has four letters. We write phonetic symbols in slant brackets / / in order to distinguish sounds from letters. Essentially, the symbols in slant brackets represent the underlying phonemes but do not give any detailed information about how these phonemes are realised, such as whether or not a /r/ sound is rolled. This type of transcription is known as a **broad** transcription. It is possible to use additional symbols and special markings called **diacritics** in a transcription in order to indicate allophones. An allophonic or **narrow** transcription of speech is placed within square [ ] brackets.

One word of warning: despite the principle outlined above of one symbol to one speech sound in the IPA, it is not impossible that you will come across some variations in the course of your studies. This is largely because American linguists use a slightly different set of symbols from British linguists. The symbols used in this book are in common use, however, so you need have no worries about them being recognised should you use them yourself.

☐ list of IPA symbols ⇨ pp. 253–4
☐ diacritics ⇨ p. 254

9.5 THE VOCAL TRACT

Before looking at the English phoneme system and the consonants and vowels it contains, we need to take a brief look at the **vocal tract** where the sounds are produced. The vocal tract begins at the **voice box** or **larynx** and ends at the **lips**. The larynx is essentially a casing of cartilage rings at the top of the **trachea**. The front of the larynx protrudes slightly below the chin and jaw (especially in men) and so you can probably feel it. In the larynx are two small but extremely important muscles, stretching from front to back, which can open and close. These are the **vocal cords** (although you may occasionally find them referred to as the **vocal folds**). The space between them is known as the **glottis**.

The section of the vocal tract between the larynx and the **uvula** (the piece of flesh which hangs down at the back of the mouth) is known as the

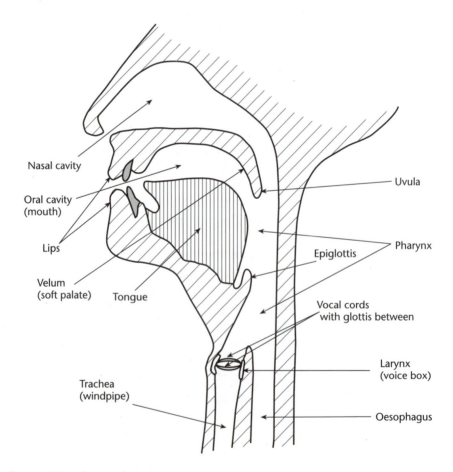

Figure 9.1   The vocal tract

pharynx. Above the pharynx, the vocal tract branches into the **nasal cavity** and the **oral cavity**. For the majority of sounds in English, the **soft palate** (or **velum**) is raised, blocking off the nasal cavity. However, there are three nasal consonants in English for which the soft palate is lowered (as in Figure 9.1), allowing air to pass through the nasal cavity.

Our interest in the production of the sounds of English is centred on the larynx and everything above it. However, the **lungs** are crucial to the production of sound. English phonemes are made by the air passing from the lungs, up the trachea, then through the larynx and the rest of the vocal tract. This flow of air is known as an **airstream**. If the airstream flows out from the lungs it is an **egressive pulmonic airstream**. All sounds in English are made by using an egressive pulmonic airstream. (Some languages make use of an **ingressive pulmonic airstream**, which involves air being drawn into the lungs as the sound is made.) It is the action of the vocal folds at the top of the larynx and the shape of the mouth that determine which sound is produced.

9.6 THE CONSONANTS OF ENGLISH

Many people traditionally distinguish between **consonants** and **vowels** in terms of the letters of the alphabet: <a, e, i, o, u> and sometimes <y> are the vowels and the rest are consonants. Again, you need to forget about letters and spellings and think about sounds or phonemes. In phonetics, a consonant involves some kind of narrow, partial or complete **closure** (or **stricture**) in the vocal tract – usually in the mouth. This closure is brought about by different parts of the mouth making some kind of contact with each other. By contrast, a vowel sound involves no closure or contact of this kind and the airstream flows unobstructed out of the mouth. Try saying aloud once more the separate sounds of *bat* and you will discover that only the middle sound is a vowel. (The first sound involves the lips closing together, and the third sound requires the tongue to come into contact with the ridge which runs behind the upper teeth, while the middle sound has the tongue lying fairly flat in the mouth, with no obstruction being caused to the airstream.)

The English of Received Pronunciation is based on a system of 24 consonants. (There is very little variation for other accents.) The IPA symbols for the consonants are given in Table 9.1 in something resembling alphabetical order to make it easier for you to learn them. Many of the IPA symbols are the same as the letters from our Roman alphabet which you would probably associate with that sound anyway. Some of the other symbols are drawn from the Greek alphabet (/θ/) or from Anglo-Saxon orthography (/ʒ, ð/). Two symbols (/ŋ, ʃ/) are modifications of Roman letters.

Table 9.1   RP consonants

/b/	bead
/d/	deed
/dʒ/	jet
/f/	feed
/g/	get
/h/	heed
/j/	yet
/k/	keep
/l/	let
/m/	met
/n/	net
/ŋ/	ring
/p/	pet
/r/	reed
/s/	seed
/ʃ/	shape
/t/	tape
/tʃ/	cheat
/θ/	thin
/ð/	then
/v/	vet
/w/	win
/ʒ/	measure
/z/	zone

Although it is helpful to see the IPA symbols for the first time in some-thing approximating to alphabetical order, this strategy does little to illumi-nate the patterns which underlie the consonant system of English. There are ways of looking at the above consonants which tell us much more about their relationship to each other. So far, we have no way of describing what differ-entiates one consonant from another, although we have seen how exchanging phonemes results in different words being produced. By looking at specific characteristics of the individual consonant sounds, we will be able to perceive their relationship to each other and also understand how they are produced in the vocal tract. We classify consonants according to three aspects:

place of articulation
manner of articulation
presence or absence of voice

If you take a closer look at the mouth as depicted in Figure 9.2, it is possible to identify various **places of articulation**. A place of articulation is the part of the

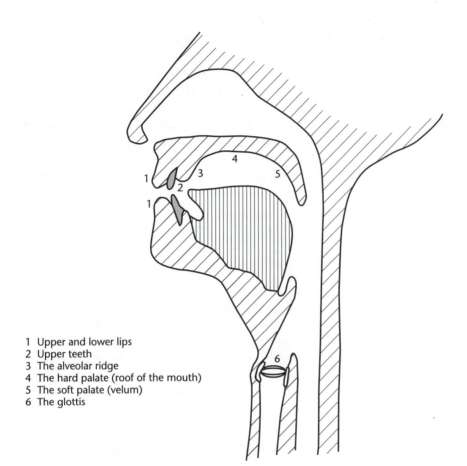

Figure 9.2   Places of articulation

1 Upper and lower lips
2 Upper teeth
3 The alveolar ridge
4 The hard palate (roof of the mouth)
5 The soft palate (velum)
6 The glottis

vocal tract where the closure necessary for a consonant sound is made. The places of articulation used in the consonant phoneme system of RP are the **lips**, the **upper teeth**, the hard ridge behind the upper row of teeth known as the **alveolar ridge**, the roof of the mouth or **hard palate**, the **soft palate** at the back of the mouth (also known as the **velum**), and the **glottis**.

The parts of the mouth involved in making speech sounds are called **articulators**. Three parts of the mouth cannot move: the upper teeth, the alveolar ridge and the hard palate. These are therefore known as **passive articulators**. The other parts can move and are the **active articulators**. The **tongue** is a very important active articulator as it is often brought into contact with another part of the mouth in order to make a closure. It is useful to distinguish the different parts of the tongue, namely the **tip**, the **blade**, the **front** and the

back, and also the **sides**. The blade is the tapered front part of the tongue with the tip at its extremity. When the tongue is at rest, the front lies opposite the hard palate and the back opposite the soft palate.

Although the tongue is such an important articulator, the special terms which refer to the various places of articulation refer to the other articulators involved and not the tongue. For example, although the tongue is involved in the articulation of /t/ when it makes contact with the alveolar ridge, /t/ is described simply as an alveolar sound. If you go through the list of consonants in Table 9.1 and make the various sounds, you will be able to work out which articulators are involved and thus identify the places of articulation. They will all fall into one of the following categories:

Type of sound	Articulators involved
bilabial	the lips
labio-dental	the upper front teeth placed against the lower lip
(inter-) dental	the tongue (tip and sides) between the front teeth and touching the upper teeth
alveolar	the tongue (tip or blade, and sometimes sides) against the alveolar ridge
palato-alveolar	the tip or blade of the tongue making contact with the alveolar ridge, while the front of the tongue is raised towards the hard palate
palatal	the tongue (front and/or sides) against the hard palate
velar	the back of the tongue against the velum (or soft palate)
glottal	the vocal cords

You will find that some sounds are very easy to classify, while others may be a little trickier. Table 9.2 shows where the sounds are made.

Another means of classification needs to be introduced if further relationships between the consonants are to be seen. This involves looking at the **manner of articulation**. Consider the four bilabial phonemes identified in Table 9.2. They are all made at the same place of articulation (namely the lips) but it is impossible that they are all made in the same manner or we would not be able to distinguish between them. Identifying the manner of articulation allows us to classify sounds according to what happens to the airstream as it passes through the vocal tract. We can distinguish five types of sound in terms of manner of articulation. A sound may be a **plosive**, a **nasal**, a **fricative**, an **affricate** or an **approximant**.

Table 9.2 Places of articulation for RP consonants

Bilabial	Labio-dental	Dental	Alveolar	Palato-alveolar	Palatal	Velar	Glottal
/b/	/f/	/θ/	/d/	/ʤ/	/j/	/g/	/h/
/m/	/v/	/ð/	/l/	/ʃ/		/k/	
/p/			/n/	/ʧ/		/ŋ/	
/w/			/r/*	/ʒ/			
			/s/				
			/t/				
			/z/				

An example of a plosive sound is /b/ at the start of *bead*. As /b/ is a bilabial sound, the lips are the articulators involved in its production and the lips are also therefore the place of articulation. The lips are closed as air passes from the lungs and up the trachea into the mouth (where the soft palate is raised, shutting off the nasal cavity). When the air reaches the mouth, because the lips are closed there is a build-up of air pressure behind them. When the lips open, the pressure is suddenly released and this causes a small explosion or plosive sound to result.

In the production of /m/ (as in <u>m</u>et), which is a nasal sound in terms of the manner of articulation but also a bilabial sound as far as place of articulation is concerned, the lips are closed as for /b/. However, in contrast to plosive sounds, the soft palate is lowered so that released air can also pass through the nasal cavity. As with a plosive sound, pressure builds up in the mouth but the pressure is lower as some of the air can escape through the nasal cavity. When the air is released by opening the lips there is a small burst or explosion of air as with a plosive sound but it is less prominent due to the lower air pressure in the mouth before the air is released. The sound also has a different quality because there is resonance in the nasal cavity as the air escapes. If you hold your hand close to your face and then utter /b/ and /m/ alternately, you will feel the difference in the strength of the explosion. For /m/ you will also feel some air escaping through your nostrils. Because both plosives and nasals involve a complete closure or stopping off of the vocal tract at one of the places of articulation before the release of air, these two types of sounds are collectively known as **stops**.

An example of a fricative sound is /s/ (as in <u>s</u>eed). As with plosives, the nasal cavity is blocked off through the lowering of the velum. This consonant is an alveolar sound, so the blade of the tongue is touching the alveolar ridge. However, in contrast to plosive and nasal sounds, the closure isn't so tight that no air at all can escape. The air passes through but there is friction because of the proximity of the tongue to the alveolar ridge. This gives the sound its turbulent or fricative quality. Fricatives also contrast with plosives and nasals in that they can be extended as long as you have breath to articulate them. Stop consonants, on the other hand, are momentary.

An affricate sound is a combination of a plosive and a fricative. An example is /ʧ/ (as in <u>ch</u>eat). This sound begins as a plosive /t/ with the airstream blocked by the tongue being positioned against the alveolar ridge. The air which has built up in the mouth is released more gently than in a plosive consonant: as a result the closure is partially maintained, and this causes a brief fricative sound – in this case /ʃ/ – to follow. Affricates are fairly rare consonants in all languages. There are only two in English: /ʧ/, which we have just discussed, and /ʤ/ (as in <u>j</u>et) which is a combination of /d/ followed by /ʒ/.

The four approximant sounds in RP – /w, l, r, j/ – are slightly problematic consonants. Some phoneticians call them **semi-consonants**, and others call them **semi-vowels**, which gives an indication as to why they are problematic. When approximant sounds are produced, the restrictions to the air passage are less than those for the preceding four types since closure in the vocal tract is never total, nor is friction ever produced at the place of articulation. This makes approximants more like vowels. However, a good argument for treating them as consonants relates to their positions in words, since they appear where consonants rather than vowels normally occur: compare *back* and *tack* to *whack, lack, rack* and *yak*. Also, there is some contact between articulators in the production of the approximants – although the obstruction to the airstream is only partial.

The consonant /l/ is sometimes referred to as a **lateral** (meaning 'at the side') or **lateral approximant** to distinguish it from /r/, which is a **central approximant**. It is lateral because the blade of the tongue touches the alveolar ridge above the front teeth and the air escapes at the sides of the mouth; /r/ is central because the sides of the tongue are very close to or touching the alveolar ridge above the back teeth and the air escapes down the middle of the mouth. You can contrast the tongue positions for /l/ and /r/ by sucking in instead of uttering these sounds. For /l/ you will feel the the sides of your tongue tingle as the air is sucked over them while for /r/ you will feel this sensation on the blade of your tongue. The term **liquid** (or **liquid approximant**) refers to the two approximants /l/ and /r/.

The consonant /w/ is produced by a partial closure of the lips (and is therefore a bilabial approximant), but the back of the tongue is raised towards the soft palate so we describe /w/ as having a secondary velar articulation. Finally, /j/ is a palatal approximant since the sides (and to some extent the front) of the tongue are raised towards the hard palate (try contrasting /j/ and /r/) and the air, as with /w/ and /r/, escapes down the centre of the mouth.

If you now work through the rest of the consonants (/p, f, v, θ, ð, d, n, t, z, ʃ, ʒ, g, k, ŋ, h/) you should be able to identify their manner of articulation. It is then possible to combine the features of place and manner of articulation in a table to show how the consonants of English are classified. This is shown in Table 9.3 which reveals that in many instances there are still two phonemes which fulfil a particular description. For example /s/ and /z/ are both alveolar fricatives. A further feature must be identified which will enable us to distinguish between these two phonemes, and this feature is **voicing**. The presence or absence of voice when a phoneme is produced is caused by the state of the vocal cords in the larynx. If the folds are open when the air passes through the larynx then the airstream flows freely and the phoneme is voiceless. On the other hand, if the vocal cords are almost closed then the air causes them to vibrate as it passes through and the sound is voiced. You can test this by putting your finger on your larynx and saying the sounds /s/ and /z/ alternately. You will be able to feel your larynx vibrate when you make the /z/ sound.

In English, a distinction between a voiceless phoneme and its voiced counterpart is only found in plosives, fricatives and affricates. For all the pairs of consonants in Table 9.3 (excluding /l/ and /r/ which are both voiced), one is voiced and the other voiceless. The fricative /h/ (sometimes also referred to as an **aspirate**) is unlike the other consonants in being produced at the glottis, not in the mouth. It is voiceless because to produce it the vocal cords need to be more open than for voiced consonants but not fully open as when breath-

Table 9.3 Consonants of RP showing place and manner of articulation

	Bilabial	Labio-dental	Dental	Alveolar	Palato-alveolar	Palatal	Velar	Glottal
Plosive	/p/ /b/			/t/ /d/			/k/ /g/	
Fricative		/f/ /v/	/θ/ /ð/	/s/ /z/	/ʃ/ /ʒ/			/h/
Affricate					/tʃ/ /dʒ/			
Nasal	/m/			/n/			/ŋ/	
Approximant	/w/			lateral /l/ central /r/		/j/	(/w/)	

ing out normally and silently. (The friction for /h/ is partly produced at the glottis, but there is likely to be some friction in the rest of the vocal tract too.) In English, all three nasal phonemes and all the approximants are voiced. In Table 9.3, the voiced plosive, fricative and affricate phonemes appear on the upper line, the voiceless ones on the lower.

Now that the 24 consonants have been arranged on a grid, you have all the information you need to refer to each one individually. Of course, you can refer to them by phonetic symbol, but you may find that for some reason you will need to give a more specific definition. When describing a consonant in full, begin by stating whether or not it is voiced (if there is a contrast), then state the place of articulation and finally the manner. So /g/ is a voiced velar plosive and /m/ is a bilabial nasal.

The advantage of having arranged the consonants in a grid as shown in Table 9.3 is that we can observe the entire consonant system of RP in terms of the distribution of these speech sounds. One interesting feature is that more phonemes are articulated at the alveolar ridge than at any other point, but the lips are also frequently used. This fact leads us to infer that these places of articulation are particularly important in human language generally. A considerable amount of work has been done examining the phonemes of other languages. In many ways, English turns out to be fairly typical, both in the number of phonemes it possesses and in the way they are distributed. Most of the consonants which occur in English are frequently found in other languages. Some of the less common consonants which occur in English are the affricates /tʃ/ and /dʒ/ and the fricatives /ʒ, θ, ð/ (and it is worth noting that children are often slower to master these consonants than most of the others). English is quite unusual in having nine fricatives, and in having more fricatives than plosives. The study of phoneme universals has also revealed that languages do not normally have nasals unless they have plosives at the same place of articulation, and this is of course true of English.

9.7   THE VOWELS OF ENGLISH

All consonants are produced by a specific kind of closure in the mouth. This closure is either total (for plosives, nasals and affricates), almost total so that the airstream causes friction at the place of articulation (affricates again and fricatives) or partial and not close enough to cause friction (approximants). By contrast, no such closures are used for vowels, which rely instead on the shape of the lips and the position of the tongue in the mouth, without the tongue coming into contact with the other articulators as it does for consonants. With this knowledge, it is possible to draw up a descending scale of closure and

Table 9.4 Degrees of consonant and vowel closure

Is the sound dependent on contact between articulators?	Type of contact between articulators	Consonant or vowel?
yes	total closure	consonant (plosive, nasal, affricate)
yes	almost total closure (+ resulting friction)	consonant (affricate, fricative)
yes	partial closure of the mouth (no friction)	consonant (approximant)
no	none necessary	vowel

articulator contact as shown in Table 9.4. Vowels might be viewed as being at one end of a **continuum** of closure (or **narrowing**) and as being distinct from consonants in that they are not dependent for their production on contact between the articulators. To get a clearer idea of how this narrowing continuum works, consider the following set of sounds:

/t/   total closure, with the tip/blade (and sides) of the tongue against the alveolar ridge

/s/   almost total closure, with the tip/blade (and sides) of the tongue against the alveolar ridge but not so tightly as for /t/ since friction is produced

/l/   partial closure, with the tip/blade of the tongue against the front of the alveolar ridge (and the front of the tongue raised towards the hard palate) but no contact between the tongue and the ridge at the sides of the mouth

/i/   (the vowel sound in *keen*) – no contact between the tongue and other articulators but the blade/front of the tongue is moved towards the alveolar ridge (and the hard palate)

These four sounds all involve the same part of the mouth, utilising the tip, blade or front of the tongue and the alveolar ridge. If you say them in a sequence you should be able to distinguish between the four types of closure and the way in which the vowel narrowing differs from the other three types. For /i/, the front section of the tongue is very close to touching the alveolar ridge or the hard palate. However, no contact is made between the front of the tongue and the alveolar ridge nor are the articulators close enough for any friction to be caused. The airstream has a free passage through the mouth. (You may feel the sides of the back of the tongue touching the back upper teeth. The tongue is a large muscle and will often inadvertently touch other parts of the mouth without this being essential to the production of a particular sound.) Not all vowels rely on the same amount of narrowing in the mouth as the vowel /i/, so the vowels themselves may also be said to be on a narrowing continuum. Table 9.5 lists the vowels of RP in 'alphabetical' order in terms of the phonetic symbols which represent them. This is again for the purposes of introducing these sounds. However, the vowels have already been divided into two types – **monophthongs** and **diphthongs**. (The <ph> in these terms is pronounced /f/.) A monophthong is a pure vowel. In other words, when the vowel is spoken in isolation, the position of the mouth remains unchanged. By contrast, a diphthong is a **glide** from one vowel position towards another. As you pronounce a diphthong you will feel the shape of your mouth alter slightly.

There are 20 vowels in RP. As with the IPA symbols for consonants, some vowel symbols resemble or are letters of the Roman alphabet, while others look a little less familiar. Diphthongs are represented by two symbols, the first being the vowel with which the glide begins and the second being the vowel towards which the glide moves. Be careful not to confuse /ɑ/ and /a/. In writing, these symbols are simply different shapes for the same letter, but in the IPA they represent two distinct sounds. In addition you need to take care not to confuse /ɜ/ and /ɛ/ (the same shape but facing different directions), and /i/ and /ɪ/ (the latter is written as a capital <I> but should be the same size as the other symbols). The symbol /ə/ is an upside down <e>, /ɒ/ an upside down <ɑ> and /ʌ/ an upside down <v>. In RP, /a/ and /ɛ/ only occur in diphthongs.

The fact that diphthongs are each represented by two symbols may be misleading as it suggests that a diphthong is not one phoneme but two. The

Table 9.5   The vowels of RP

monophthongs	/æ/	bat	diphthongs	/aɪ /	buy
	/ɑ/	bard		/aʊ/	bough
	/e/	bet		/eɪ/	bay
	/ɜ/	bird		/ɛə/	bear
	/ə/	about		/əʊ/	beau
	/i/	bead		/ɪə/	beer
	/ɪ/	bit		/ɔɪ/	boy
	/ɒ/	bomb		/ʊə/	tour
	/ɔ/	board			
	/u/	food			
	/ʊ/	book			
	/ʌ/	but			

diphthongs are, however, treated as distinct phonemes because they are not simply sequences of one vowel followed by another, but single elements of a slightly more complex nature than monophthongs in that the tongue glides from one position to another. For example, the diphthong represented by /eɪ/ is not the phoneme /e/ followed by the phoneme /ɪ/. To pronounce /e/ and /ɪ/ as a sequence of two monophthongs vowels would yield two separate syllables, while the diphthong /eɪ/ is a single syllable. Further, the initial part of a diphthong is always more prominent than the latter part, suggesting some relationship between these two positions. Finally, all the diphthongs share a characteristic of some of the monophthong vowels, that feature being **length**.

We need now to move away from simply listing the vowels of RP and find a systematic way of classifying them just as we did for the consonants. You will recall that consonants were classified according to place of articulation, manner of articulation and the presence or absence of voice. These three aspects enabled us to formulate Table 9.3 which showed a full classification of the 24 consonant phonemes of RP. They also enabled us to give each consonant its own specific description. We saw just now how vowels are distinct from other sounds in that they do not rely on contact between articulators or on the same degree of closure in the mouth. Also, a contrast between voiced and voiceless vowels is impossible because all vowels are voiced. However, the classification by place and manner of articulation which we used for consonants has some bearing on how we can classify vowels systematically. A slightly different method must be found for classifying the vowels, although for the sake of economy and unity it is undesirable to make our classification too different. Something else which needs to be borne in mind when classifying vowels is that, because of the nature of their production, there must inevitably be a degree of approximation in mapping them.

Manner of articulation cannot be applied in the same way to vowels as to consonants since there are no contrasts between plosive, nasal, fricative, affricate and approximant sounds. However, we can make a contrast of **length**. Although this is quite difficult to measure and it is possible also to prolong vowels at will, it is true to say that in RP some vowels are regularly or typically given greater duration than others. Therefore we can use length to make an initial division of the monophthong vowels (diphthongs need not concern us here since they possess the feature of length by being glides).

A concrete way of demonstrating that some vowels are longer than others can be provided by looking at some simple **monosyllabic** words (words of one syllable). A contrast can be made between monosyllabic words which end in a consonant and those which end in a vowel. Table 9.6 contrasts examples of words with the **closed** structure CVC (consonant–vowel–consonant) with those of an **open** CV (consonant–vowel) structure, where the vowel is not

Table 9.6 The occurrence of monophthongs in CVC and CV words

Monophthong	CVC word	Phonetic transcription	CV word	Phonetic transcription
/æ/	bat	/bæt/	–	–
/ɑ/	bard	/bɑːd/	bar	/bɑː/
/e/	bet	/bet/	–	–
/ɜ/	bird	/bɜːd/	burr	/bɜː/
/ə/*	–	–	–	–
/i/	bead	/biːd/	bee	/biː/
/ɪ/	bit	/bɪt/	–	–
/ɒ/	bomb	/bɒm/	–	–
/ɔ/	board	/bɔːd/	bore	/bɔː/
/u/	food	/fuːd/	boo	/buː/
/ʊ/	book	/bʊk/	–	–
/ʌ/	but	/bʌt/	–	–

*/ə/ can appear without a following consonant, but normally not in a monosyllabic word. The occurrence of /ə/ is discussed in sections 10.3, 11.2 and 11.3.

followed by a final, closing consonant. The table shows that only five of the twelve monophthongs appear in RP in an open CV structure. This is linked to the fact that they have the feature of length. Length is indicated by a modified colon ː after the vowel in question (although a regular colon : is sometimes used). From now on the five long monophthong vowels of RP will normally be written with a length mark to distinguish them from the short vowels. It was mentioned above that diphthongs, because they involve a glide from one vowel to another, have the feature of length. It is not surprising therefore that, like the long monophthong vowels, they appear in open CV structures (for example, *bear* /bɛə/ and *boy* /bɔɪ/, and all the other examples in Table 9.5).

So far, then, we have seen that all vowels are voiced. They cannot be distinguished in terms of manner of articulation in the same way as consonants, but we can make a contrast between short and long vowels. Short vowels are always monophthongs while long vowels may be monophthongs or diphthongs. We can now consider whether the concept of place of articulation has any bearing on how we might classify vowels, although we clearly cannot refer to the role of articulators in the same way we did for consonants. (It is worth mentioning here that in English the soft palate is normally raised for vowels, so that air escapes through the oral cavity only. This feature is usually taken for granted when describing RP vowels.)

For consonants, we have seen how the contrast between, say, a bilabial sound and an alveolar one involves a difference in the shape of the mouth at the moment of articulation because of the different articulators involved.

Similarly with vowels, the mouth does not retain the same shape. You can tell this if you contrast /ɪː/ with /ɑː/ or /e/ with /uː/, for example. As you contrast these phonemes, you should be able to feel your tongue moving into different positions and your lips changing shape. It is these changes which give the vowels their distinctive qualities. These two aspects of vowel articulation – tongue position and lip shape – can be used to complete the classification of vowels.

The tongue position for monophthong vowels is usually plotted by a dot on a grid that relates to the shape of the mouth. The idea of a grid was introduced by the phonetician Daniel Jones (1881–1967). The shape in which it is usually drawn now is very similar to his original design. To understand the grid, you need first to imagine its lines being plotted in the mouth as shown in Figure 9.3, which shows a cross-section of the head. The grid has been superimposed on the mouth in such a way that each corner of the grid indicates the points, front and back, where the tongue will be at its highest or lowest, particularly when the mouth is opened quite wide. In Figure 9.3,

Figure 9.3   The vowel grid superimposed on the mouth

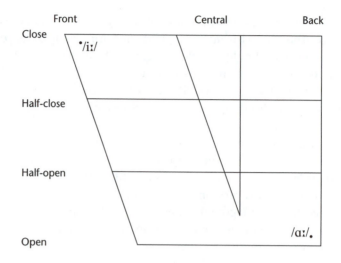

Figure 9.4 The vowel grid with /iː/ and /ɑː/ positions

however, the mouth is only slightly open and the tongue is in a neutral position. If you now look at Figure 9.4 which shows the grid in greater detail, you will see that various labels have been added. The labels at the top – **front**, **central** and **back** – refer to the front, central (the back of the front and the front of the back) and back areas of the tongue. You will remember that the front of the tongue lies opposite the hard palate, while the back of the tongue lies opposite the soft palate. For a front vowel, the front of the tongue will be raised towards the alveolar ridge and the hard palate; for a back vowel, the back of the tongue will be raised towards the soft palate. For central vowels, the tongue tends to be flatter than for front or back vowels. The labels at the side of the grid denote the height of the tongue and therefore the amount of space between the tongue and the hard and soft palates when the vowel is produced. A **close vowel** will have a relatively small cavity between the tongue and the palate, while an **open vowel** will have a relatively large one, especially since the jaw is slightly lowered for open vowels. There are two intermediate measures of tongue height – **half-close** and **half-open**. So to produce the vowel /iː/, the tongue is pushed slightly forward and up towards the alveolar ridge and the hard palate (similar to the position it takes to articulate /t/, as we saw earlier). By contrast, the /ɑː/ sound requires the tongue to be low. This is why doctors ask you to 'say ah' when they examine your throat: it forces you to lower your tongue. The two vowels /iː/ and /ɑː/ have been marked on Figure 9.4 using a dot. The dot is placed on the grid to show the highest point the tongue reaches in the production of any particular vowel. The dot also indicates which part of the tongue is raised highest. The vowel /iː/, then, is a close

/iː/

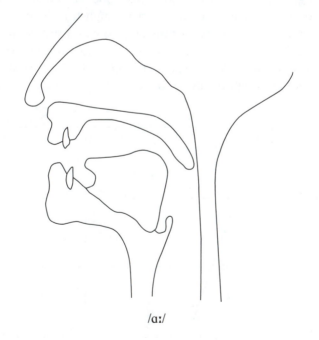

/ɑː/

Figure 9.5   Tongue positions for the vowels /iː/ and /ɑː/

front vowel while /ɑː/ is an open back vowel. Figure 9.5 shows the contrasting tongue positions of these two vowels.

The shape of the lips was also mentioned above as a feature which contributed to the distinctive quality of each vowel. Try once more contrasting the sounds /iː/ and /ɑː/: you will notice your lips are far more spread for /iː/ than for /ɑː/. Now try positioning your tongue for /iː/ but rounding your lips: you will find that the vowel you produce is distinct from /iː/ (and of course has its own IPA symbol – /y/). When classifying vowels, the shape of the lips is usually given less attention than the height of the tongue and the part of the tongue that is raised, but we will return to this in a moment.

You will probably have noticed that the vowels /iː/ and /ɑː/ appear very near two extremes of the vowel grid. This means they are very useful as points of reference. Daniel Jones identified eight reference points around the grid, working out which vowels would be produced if the tongue fell from high to low at the front or back of the mouth in equal measures. These reference vowels are known as **cardinal vowels** and are shown in Figure 9.6. When cardinal vowels are written they are often preceded by *C* as an indication that the phonetic symbol represents a cardinal vowel, which is a positional reference point, rather than a phoneme, which is part of the set of speech sounds of a given language. Another point to notice about the eight cardinal vowels is that they do not all have a counterpart in English or in RP. The cardinal vowel /ɛ/ is not considered as part of the English vowel system. In pronunciation it is quite close to /ə/ but the tongue is raised further forward in the mouth. It is close to the vowel at the end of *resident*. Similarly /a/ does not have an RP equivalent although it can be found in the first vowel sound in *cham-*

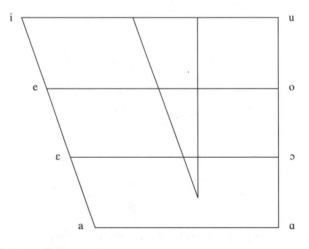

Figure 9.6   The eight cardinal vowels

pion when pronounced in a Geordie accent. The cardinal vowel /o/ is found in French in the pronunciation of, for example, *beau* meaning 'beautiful'. The /iː/ and /ɑː/ of RP are not normally plotted at the extremes which the cardinal vowels represent.

You may now like to try pronouncing the cardinal vowels yourself. If you utter the vowel sounds from the following words in the sequence below, then you are essentially moving your tongue through the range of positions on the cardinal vowel grid, starting with C/i/, then working down the left side of the grid and back up to C/u/. When you listen to the eight cardinal vowels you may find it difficult to hear some of the differences between them, especially between the half-open and half-close sounds C/ɛ/ and C/e/, and C/ɔ/ and C/o/. If you practise producing these vowels, you should find the distinctions will become clearer:

C /i/	as in RP *bead*
C /e/	as in RP *bed*
C /ɛ/	as in RP *resident*, approximately
C /a/	as in Geordie *champion*
C /ɑ/	as in RP *bard*
C /ɔ/	as in RP *board*
C /o/	as in French *beau*
C /u/	as in RP *food*

When you work through this sequence, you will also notice the way the shape of your lips changes as you go. For /i/ (point 1), the lips are spread; they are still spread for /a/ but less so than for /i/; when you reach /u/ (point 8) you will find your lips have become very rounded. So these cardinal vowels move from spread to rounded lips. This aspect of the cardinal vowels is often assumed rather than mentioned explicitly, but it is important to remember that lip shape is a factor in producing these vowels. The eight cardinal vowels examined here are the eight **primary cardinal vowels**. If you start again at 1 with lips rounded – reversing the process – you will produce the eight **secondary cardinal vowels**. However, the secondary set is not of relevance here since the English vowels relate most closely to the lip shapes of the primary set.

Now we have a fuller frame of reference for plotting vowels, we can position the RP monophthongs on the grid. Figure 9.7 shows the eight (primary) cardinal vowels labelled on the outside of the grid, with the 12 monophthong phonemes of RP labelled within the grid. As mentioned above, not all the primary cardinal vowels have a counterpart in RP. This is not especially significant, bearing in mind that the cardinal vowels are only points of reference. What is interesting is that the vowels are fairly evenly distributed between the

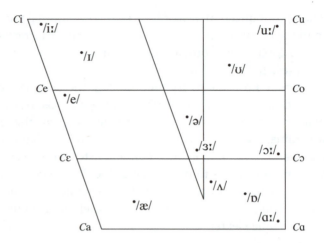

Figure 9.7   Cardinal vowels and RP monophthongs

front and the back of the mouth. It would be rather surprising if they were nearly all at the front or nearly all at the back. Also, many phonologists consider it significant that most of the monophthongs can be grouped into pairs which are phonetically similar, with one short and one long vowel in each pairing. Five such pairings can be identified in RP: /ɪ/ and /iː/, /æ/ and /ɑː/, /ɒ/ and /ɔː/, /ʊ/ and /uː/, /ə/ and /ɜː/.

The 'neutral' sound /ə/ which occurs more or less in the middle of the grid is of particular interest. It is so common in English that it has a special name – **schwa**. To pronounce schwa you have your mouth in what is likely to be its most natural position. Keep your tongue in what might be called its resting position, open your lips slightly (neither spreading them nor rounding them), and add voice: /ə/ is the sound you will probably produce, or something quite close to it. One of the reasons why schwa is so common in English is because vowels in unstressed syllables normally revert to it. More will be said about this in Chapter 11.

The grid (Figure 9.7) used for plotting pure (monophthong) vowels can also be used to plot the eight diphthongs of RP, using an arrow to indicate the direction of the glide in terms of tongue height and which part of the tongue is highest. This is shown in Figure 9.8. You will notice from Figure 9.8 that three diphthongs move towards /ɪ/, and another two towards /ʊ/. In all five instances, the finishing vowel position is more close (that is, there is less distance between the highest part of the tongue and the hard or soft palate) than the starting position. These five diphthongs are often therefore referred to as **closing diphthongs**. The other three diphthongs move towards /ə/ as the finishing position and, since /ə/ is a central vowel, these diphthongs are often

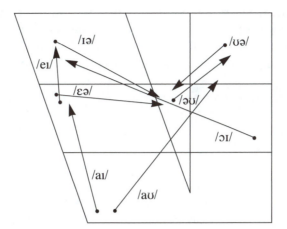

Figure 9.8   Tongue height and direction in RP diphthongs

referred to as **centring diphthongs**. Table 9.7 summarises these findings.

We have now completed our survey of the twenty vowels of RP. As with consonants, it is acceptable to refer to the vowels simply by their phonetic symbols. However, you may want to distinguish between length and type so you might, for instance, refer to the short monophthong /æ/, the long monophthong /ɑː/ or the diphthong /aː/. If you want to give more detail about how the vowels are articulated you should do so in terms of the vowel grid. Begin by indicating the tongue height and then refer to the part of the tongue raised: so /e/ is a half-open front vowel, /ɜː/ is a half-open central vowel and /uː/ is a close back vowel. (Schwa is termed a mid central vowel.) You may also wish to add information about whether the lips are rounded or unrounded. So /uː/ is a rounded vowel or, more fully, a close back rounded vowel.

Diphthongs can be described as closing or centring. The closing diphthongs can be divided between those for which the tongue movement is

Table 9.7   RP diphthongs

closing dipthongs	gliding to /ɪ/	/eɪ/
		/aɪ/
		/ɔɪ/
	gliding to /ʊ/	/əʊ/
		/aʊ/
centring diphthongs	gliding to /ə/	/ɪə/
		/ɛə/
		/ʊə/

towards the front of the mouth (towards /ɪ/) and those for which the movement is towards the back of the mouth (towards /ʊ/). If you need to be more specific than this, you will need to make reference to the vowel which occurs at the starting point of the glide and the vowel which the glide moves towards.

☐ schwa in unstressed syllables ⇨ 11.2

9.8 PHONETIC TRANSCRIPTIONS

It is very likely in the course of your language studies that you will need to transcribe speech. In order to study someone's vocabulary, there is no point in transcribing what they say phonetically (that is, using phonetic symbols). On the other hand, to make a study of their accent, or to study the speech of a young child to see how many of the phonemes of English they have mastered, you will need to use the phonetic alphabet to make some or all of your transcription.

A few tips about transcribing speech might therefore be valuable here. Since it is almost impossible to transcribe speech in real time, the normal practice is to make the transcription from a recording. Until you become very quick and confident, it is probably best to begin by transcribing in ordinary English spelling, and then go back over a few words at a time, converting the words to the IPA. It's not a good idea to do this from memory: you will need to listen to that section of the recording again. One reason for this is that the speaker's accent may be different from yours and you may imagine them saying a word as you would say it. Another reason is that speakers aren't always consistent in their pronunciation and you may well need to identify any variations in their speech. It is also important to remember that, although when we write we leave spaces between words and sometimes between letters, when we speak we run sounds and words together. The result of this **connected speech** is that many speech sounds change their character slightly or are even lost altogether because they are influenced by the sound which precedes or succeeds them. For example, the words *next* and *day* spoken in isolation are pronounced [nekst] and [deɪ], but when spoken together the /t/ at the end of *next* is often lost because the following sound (the /d/ of *day*) is similar in every feature except voicing. The utterance that results will probably be [neks deɪ]. The same is true of *prime minister*, which is often pronounced not as [praɪm mɪnɪstə] but as [praɪmɪnɪstə] because the first word ends with the same phoneme that begins the second word.

When transcribing in phonetic symbols, it is usual to leave gaps between words as you would in speech. However, if you feel a speaker is almost treating two words as one (as some people seem to treat *prime minister*) you could do so too. IPA transcription does not employ punctuation nor is there a distinction between capital and lower case letters. Brackets are only needed at the beginning and end of your transcription.

You may find when transcribing English that you can hear a new sound for which you do not know the symbol. Some of the additional symbols you may need are given with the list of phonetic symbols at the back of this book, along with a list of diacritics (the marks which enable us to give additional information about the pronunciation of phonemes). If you still need a new symbol you can look it up in the *Phonetic Symbol Guide* (by Pullum and Ladusaw, 1986) or you may have another suitable reference book available. Alternatively, there is no reason why, for the purposes of your transcription, you couldn't invent a symbol – but remember to identify it in a key.

☐ connected speech ⇨ 10.6
☐ additional symbols and diacritics ⇨ pp. 253–5

10 Segmental Phonology

10.1 WHAT IS SEGMENTAL PHONOLOGY?

In Chapter 9, we were concerned with phonetics – with the way in which the consonants and vowels of English (as represented by RP) are produced and how they can be classified. We touched briefly on some of the interesting features which emerged from the classification. In this chapter, we move on to look more closely at the **phonology** of English. Whereas phonetics is chiefly concerned with the production of individual speech sounds, phonology is concerned with the phoneme systems of languages and with the individual sounds – or **segments** – when they are no longer in isolation but grouped together in syllables and words. Phonology is often divided into two broad areas – **segmental phonology** and **suprasegmental phonology**. Suprasegmental phonology deals with aspects of speech such as pitch and intonation which colour speech at the syllable level and beyond. We will cover suprasegmental phonology in Chapter 11. Segmental phonology deals with the distribution of the phonemes, how they vary in different environments, and how phonemes group together to form syllables and words.

We have already seen how we can classify the sounds of a language as a set of distinct segments which we have termed phonemes. We have also touched on the fact that the realisation of a phoneme may vary from accent to accent or from speaker to speaker (an example was given of the /r/ at the beginning of *rat* sometimes being rolled). Phonologists consider that the phoneme is an abstract concept. In other words, a phoneme is an idealised or stylised version of the sound in question and isn't 'real'. Phonologists therefore make a contrast between phonemes, which make up the sound system of a language on an abstract level, and allophones, which are the sounds speakers actually produce.

To summarise, we have already touched on two aspects of segmental phonology in Chapter 9: namely, the phoneme system which underpins the RP accent of English and the fact that phonemes have varying surface realisations which are termed allophones. In this chapter, we will move away from considering speech sounds in isolation and look instead at how speech sounds operate in combinations with each other.

☐ phonemes and allophones ⇨ 9.3

10.2 THE DISTRIBUTION OF CONSONANTS

In Chapter 9 we formulated a table which showed the 24 consonants of RP in terms of place and manner of articulation, and also voicing. For easy reference, this table is repeated here as Table 10.1. We discovered that RP has 6 plosives, 2 affricates, 9 fricatives, 3 nasals and 4 approximants. This distribution shares several features with other languages of the world, which enables us to conclude that the consonant phoneme inventory of English is not especially remarkable, except perhaps in its abundance of fricatives.

So far, then, we have mainly examined these phonemes in isolation. We now need to move on to see how they combine to form syllables and words. The distribution of its phonemes, along with any allophonic variants, are two phonological features which give English its own particular flavour. What is said here about English phonemes is not necessarily true of other languages, although there are bound to be some features in common. If you speak or are studying any other languages, you will probably find it interesting to make some comparisons.

We will begin our study of the distribution of consonants in syllables and words by looking at the positions in which they occur. First, we will examine **monosyllabic** and **disyllabic** words (disyllabic words have two syllables) to see which consonants occur singly in the positions we identify. To

Table 10.1 Consonants of RP showing place and manner of articulation

	Bilabial	Labio-dental	Dental	Alveolar	Palato-alveolar	Palatal	Velar	Glottal
Plosive	/p/ /b/			/t/ /d/			/k/ /g/	
Fricative		/f/ /v/	/θ/ /ð/	/s/ /z/	/ʃ/ /ʒ/			/h/
Affricate					/tʃ/ /dʒ/			
Nasal	/m/			/n/			/ŋ/	
Approximant	/w/			lateral /l/ central /r/		/j/	(/w/)	

keep things simple, then, the monosyllabic words will have the structure CVC (where C stands for consonant and V stands for vowel), and the disyllabic words will be CVCV(C). (We will consider groups of consonants or **consonant clusters** later in this chapter.) The words used as examples will be transcribed into the phonetic alphabet in order to focus on their pronunciation. There are three positions in which the consonants can occur: **word-initial** (at the beginning of a word), **word-final** (at the end of a word) and **word-medial** (between vowels in a word of two syllables or more, and therefore at the boundary of two syllables). Table 10.2 lists the possible positions of the 24 consonants.

As you can see from Table 10.2, most of the consonants occur in all three positions specified. The six plosives, the two affricates and most of the fricatives have full distribution in English. Of the other fricatives, /ʒ/ is something of an oddity, appearing at a later stage in the development of the language than the other fricatives. Word-initially, /ʒ/ only occurs in a handful of French loan words such as *genre* and *gigolo* (although it is hard to say how many speakers consider them to be 'foreign') and we also use it in French phrases such as *je ne sais quoi*, *joie de vivre* and *le mot juste*. The words in which /ʒ/ appears word-finally are also of fairly recent French origin and many speakers pronounce these words with /dʒ/ rather than /ʒ/ to give /beɪdʒ/ *beige* and /gærɪdʒ/ *garage*, for example. (Some speakers also replace the /ʒ/ at the start of *gigolo* with /dʒ/.) The word-medial /ʒ/ developed historically in sequences where /z/ was followed by /j/ or /ɪ/. Generally, /ʒ/ is fairly rare. However, it is probably sufficiently established in Modern English for speakers to feel comfortable with it, despite its rarity and the frequently occurring word-final variant /dʒ/ .

The consonant /h/ presents a slightly different picture. /h/ is common at the beginning of words, although rarer word-medially. However, it never occurs in English at the end of a word. Although in Old English /h/ occurred in word-final position (as in *neah*, meaning *near*), its place and manner of articulation have perhaps influenced the way it is used in Modern English. Because /h/ is articulated at the glottis, the mouth is able simultaneously to be shaped ready for the following vowel. The fricative /h/ has therefore come to be a period of aspiration or audible breath preceding the start of a vowel. Since no vowel follows the final /h/ in an isolated word, /h/ has become redundant in this position.

Phonologists often claim that the two affricate phonemes of English – /tʃ/ and /dʒ/ – are redundant members of the phoneme inventory. The manner of articulation for affricates – a plosive followed by a short fricative sound – suggests we might make our inventory more streamlined if we dropped the affricates altogether and treated /tʃ/ and /dʒ/ instead as a plosive + fricative sequence. (The phonetic symbols themselves suggest they are sequences rather

Table 10.2 The distribution of consonants in RP

Consonant	Word-initial		Word-final		Word-medial	
Plosives						
/p/	pet	/pet/	cup	/cʌp/	taper	/teɪpə/
/b/	bead	/biːd/	dab	/dæb/	baby	/beɪbiː/
/t/	tape	/teɪp/	bat	/bæt/	matter	/mætə/
/d/	deed	/diːd/	bad	/bæd/	raider	/reɪdə/
/k/	keep	/kiːp/	back	/bæk/	backer	/bækə/
/g/	get	/get/	bag	/bæg/	nugget	/nʌgɪt/
Affricates						
/tʃ/	cheat	/tʃiːt/	teach	/tiːtʃ/	teacher	/tiːtʃə/
/dʒ/	jet	/dʒet/	hedge	/hedʒ/	lodger	/lɒdʒə/
Fricatives						
/f/	feed	/fiːd/	doff	/dɒf/	tuffet	/tʌfɪt/
/v/	vet	/vet/	save	/seɪv/	cover	/kʌvə/
/θ/	thin	/θɪn/	bath	/bɑθ/	python	/paɪθən/
/ð/	then	/ðen/	lithe	/laɪð/	mother	/mʌðə/
/s/	seed	/siːd/	mass	/mæs/	NASA	/næsə/
/z/	zone	/zəʊn/	maze	/meɪz/	razor	/reɪzə/
/ʃ/	shape	/ʃeɪp/	rush	/rʌʃ/	rasher	/ræʃə/
/ʒ/	(genre)	(/ʒɒnrə/	(beige)	(/beɪʒ/)	measure	/meʒə/
/h/	heed	/hiːd/	-	-	ahead	/əhed/
Nasals						
/m/	met	/met/	bomb	/bɒm/	timer	/taɪmə/
/n/	net	/net/	learn	/lɜn/	tiny	/taɪniː/
/ŋ/	–	–	wrong	/rɒŋ/	singer	/sɪŋə/
Approximants						
/w/	win	/wɪn/	–	–	toward	/təwɔd/
/r/	reed	/riːd/	–	–	carer	/kɛərə/
/l/	let	/let/	hill	/hɪl/	pillar	/pɪlə/
/j/	yet	/jet/	–	–	–	–

than distinct phonemes, although they are sometimes represented by /č/ and
/ǰ/ rather than /tʃ/ and /dʒ/.) There are good arguments both for the single
phoneme analysis and for the two-phoneme sequence analysis, but since the
argument cannot easily be resolved (if at all) and since many of the other textbooks you are likely to use will treat these sequences as separate phonemes, we
will retain the two affricates here as separate phonemes of the inventory.

Of the nasals, /m/ and /n/ appear in all three positions but /ŋ/ does not
appear at the beginning of words. The reason for this is also historical. Old
English had no /ŋ/ phoneme, but when /n/ preceded the velar plosives /k/ or

/g/ speakers gave it a velar as opposed to an alveolar articulation, creating the allophone [ŋ] for /n/. Later, southern English lost /g/ from the word-final cluster [ŋg] and /ŋ/ became a separate phoneme. This resulted in a distinction between, for example, *thin* /θɪn/ and *thing* /θɪŋ/. The fact that /ŋ/ is derived originally from a cluster of two consonants which itself never occurred word-initially explains why /ŋ/ is never found in that position.

The approximants are the phonemes with the most limited distribution in single consonant occurrences, although they are very productive in clusters. This is perhaps not surprising given their ambivalent position somewhere between the other consonants and the vowels. All four approximants occur word-initially. In RP, only /l/ occurs word-finally, although in many other accents so does /r/. (Most Americans will say *bar* /bɑr/ and *her* /hɜr/, for example. Accents where /r/ appears in positions where it would not be realised in RP are known as **rhotic** accents.) Both /l/ and /r/ appear frequently word-medially. The bilabial approximant /w/ appears word-medially but is fairly rare, while /j/ does not appear word-medially in English. In fact /j/ appears to be a rather marginal consonant of English, being the only palatal consonant. Of the four approximants, the alveolars /l/ and /r/ seem the most productive as single consonants.

Clearly, the distribution of the consonants is not quite as cut and dried as we might like it to be. The grey areas may prompt us to ask questions about the phoneme inventory but they do not invalidate the process of classifying the phonemes. Too many patterns are visible for the distribution to be a matter of coincidence. The grey areas not only make us question our classification constructively but also help us to focus on aspects such as regional variations, and (although this is not within the scope of this book) the way the language has changed over the centuries and is still changing. In addition, although all languages operate within identifiable frameworks, it would be naïve to expect any language to evolve into some preconceived idea of 'perfection'.

Phonemes are realised in speech by allophones. Phonemes are subconsciously given certain allophonic variants by speakers either because of the influence of adjacent phonemes in neighbouring words or because of the position of the phoneme in a word. We will consider the influence adjacent phonemes have on each other later in this chapter. For the purpose of illustration, we will refer here to two key instances in English where an allophone is linked to consonant position.

The first instance is one which we have already discussed in Chapter 9 and concerns the approximant /l/. We saw how word-initial /l/ differs from word-final /l/, a distinction between what are known as **clear *l*** and **dark *l***. (Dark *l* is represented by the symbol [ɫ].) Dark *l* also occurs before another consonant in words such as *shelf* [ʃeɫf], *field* [fɪɫd], *pulse* [pʌɫs], and *film* [fɪɫm]. Another example of allophonic variation which is a key feature of RP is the **aspiration** of word-initial /p, t, k/. This means that the articulation of these voiceless plosives when they occur at the beginning of a word (but not in a cluster) is followed by a short period of glottal friction (as for /h/) before the following vowel begins. This is in contrast to a word-final voiceless plosive which is not followed by aspiration. Aspirated sounds can be indicated by a superscript ʰ : [pʰ, tʰ, kʰ]. In a narrow transcription, then, words like *cup* and *tart* will be written as [kʰʌp] and [tʰɑːt] respectively.

☐ **RP consonants** ⇨ 9.6
☐ **Connected speech** ⇨ 10.6

10.3   THE DISTRIBUTION OF VOWELS

RP has seven short vowels, five long monophthong vowels and eight diphthongs, which are also long vowels. The two vowel grids – one showing the monophthongs, the other showing the diphthongs – are repeated here as Figure 10.1. In section 10.2 we looked at the distribution of RP consonants to see which ones have full distribution (that is, word-initially, word-medially and word-finally) and which ones have some limitation on their occurrence. It is valuable to do the same with vowels. You can see this in Table 10.3. Here, the vowels are shown both in **closed syllables**, which means they are preceded and followed by a consonant (CVC) or simply followed by a consonant (VC), and in **open syllables** (CV) where no consonant follows. Only monosyllabic words are shown.

We have already seen that in RP the short vowels do not occur in open CV syllables: this enabled us to distinguish them from the other vowels. There are two further gaps in the table for short monophthongs. The first is /ʊ/ not occurring in VC monosyllables. In fact, no words begin with /ʊ/ in RP. This vowel does, however, occur in this position in other accents to give, for example, /ʊp/ *up*, /ʊðə/ *other*, and /ʊndə/ *under*. In RP, all these words have /ʌ/ initially. This phoneme is a later addition to English (from about the seventeenth century) which has not been introduced into all accents. In RP, however, /ʌ/ has replaced /ʊ/ word-initially as well as in other positions.

The other gap here relates to **schwa**. It is difficult to discuss schwa without discussing stress (which we do in Chapter 11) since schwa only occurs in unstressed syllables. This accounts for the absence of schwa in monosyllabic words which, in isolation, are cited with the full, stressed value given to their vowels. (This also raises the question of whether schwa is a true phoneme of

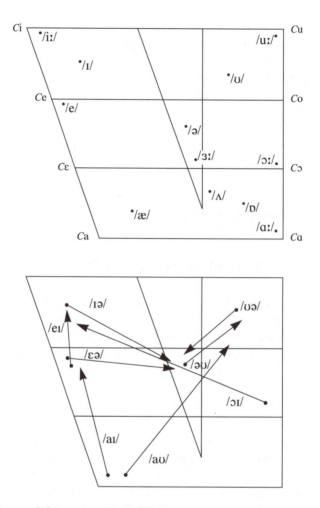

Figure 10.1   RP monophthongs and RP diphthongs

English or simply an allophonic variant of other vowel phonemes. This is not an issue we will pursue here, however.)

Of the long vowels and diphthongs, the only gaps relate to the centring diphthongs in VC structures. /ɪə/ and /ɛə/ occur alone in RP in *ear* and *air*, while in **rhotic** accents (those in which /r/ occurs in positions where it has been lost in RP) they occur in a VC structure as /ɪər/ and /ɛər/. We also have *aired* /ɛəd/ in RP derived from *air* plus an *-ed* verb inflection. This evidence suggests that all the long vowels and diphthongs are used very productively in English, with the possible exception of /ʊə/. It is difficult to find examples of /ʊə/ in monosyllables (although it is easier when /ʊə/ is preceded by /j/ as in

Table 10.3 The distribution of vowels in RP

vowel	CVC		VC		CV	
Short monophthongs						
ɪ	bit	/bɪt/	it	/ɪt/	–	–
e	bet	/bet/	egg	/eg/	–	–
æ	bat	/bæt/	at	/æt/	–	–
ɒ	bomb	/bɒm/	of	/ɒv/	–	–
ʊ	book	/bʊk/	–	–	–	–
ʌ	but	/bʌt/	up	/ʌp/	–	–
ə	–	–	–	–	–	–
Long monophthongs						
ɪː	bead	/biːd/	eave	/iːv/	bee	/biː/
ɑː	bard	/bɑːd/	art	/ɑːt/	bar	/bɑː/
ɔː	board	/bɔːd/	ought	/ɔːt/	bore	/bɔː/
uː	food	/fuːd/	ooze	/uːz/	boo	/buː/
ɜː	bird	/bɜːd/	irk	/ɜːk/	burr	/bɜː/
Closing diphthongs						
eɪ	bait	/beɪt/	age	/eɪdʒ/	bay	/beɪ/
aɪ	bite	/baɪt/	ice	/aɪs/	buy	/baɪ/
ɔɪ	void	/vɔɪd/	oil	/ɔɪl/	boy	/bɔɪ/
əʊ	bode	/bəʊd/	ode	/əʊd/	beau	/bəʊ/
aʊ	fowl	/faʊl/	out	/aʊt/	bough	/baʊ/
Centring diphthongs						
ɪə	beard	/bɪəd/	(ear)	(/ɪə/)	beer	/bɪə/
ɛə	laird	/lɛəd/	(air)	(/ɛə/)	bear	/bɛə/
ʊə	gourd	/gʊəd/	–	–	tour	/tʊə/

/pjʊə/ *pure* and /kjʊə/ *cure*). Interestingly, words with /ʊə/ often have variable pronunciation such as [pɔː] or [pɔə] rather than [pʊə] for *poor*. In 1947, the phonetician D. B. Fry made a study of how frequently each of the various phonemes of RP occurred. The diphthong /ʊə/ was found to account for only 0.06 per cent of all phoneme occurrences, and was at the bottom of the frequency scale. There is some support for the view that this particular phoneme might be lost from RP in the future.

One allophonic feature of vowels which you may find it useful to know about is **nasalisation**. This occurs when the velum has been lowered during the articulation of the vowel and air passing through the nasal cavity gives the vowel a slightly different quality from usual. The diacritic ˜ indicates that a vowel has been nasalised. Nasalised vowels usually precede nasal consonants. They don't occur frequently in English but speakers occasionally use them in words of French origin like *restaurant* [restərõn(t)].

> ☐ RP vowels ⇨ 10.6
> ☐ schwa in unstressed syllables ⇨ 11.2

10.4   SYLLABLE STRUCTURE

So far, we have examined the phonemes of English either in isolation or in terms of the positions in which consonants and vowels occur. We now move on to study **phonotactics**, which is the way phonemes group together in English to form syllables. Syllables vary in the way they are constructed but they nevertheless conform to a set pattern and we shall be concerned in this section with discovering what that pattern or **syllable template** is.

Central to the structure of a syllable is a vowel. A long monophthong may be a monosyllabic word on its own (*are* /ɑː/, for example) as may a diphthong (for example, in *ear* /ɪə/). By contrast, a single consonant cannot constitute a word. In a monosyllabic word, the vowel may be preceded and succeeded by a consonant or consonants. If, on the other hand, a consonant is preceded and succeeded by a vowel, as in *other* /ʌðə/, a disyllabic word results. This suggests that there is a direct relationship between the number of vowels and the number of syllables in a word. If we work on the premise of one vowel to one syllable, having already established that a vowel can occur on its own or with consonants either side, we can start with a preliminary syllable template of consonant – vowel – consonant. In the following diagram, +/- indicates that there may or may not be a consonant in this position. Also, there may be more than one consonant.

+/– consonant(s)	vowel	+/– consonant(s)

Table 10.3 showed that most of the vowels can begin syllables in English as can most consonants. What we now need to discover is which consonant groups can occur at the beginning of a syllable. For the time being, we will continue to concentrate as far as possible on monosyllabic words so that word and syllable structure coincide, and we will move on to words of more than one syllable when we have established the full syllable template.

If you work your way through a random selection of words, you will quickly discover that the maximum number of consonants which can begin a syllable in English is three. Examples of this include *spread* /spred/, *squirm* /skwɜːm/ and *scrape* /skreɪp/. However, there are restrictions on which consonants can form a cluster of this kind. You won't be able to find any words beginning with, say, /gdn/ or /θph/.

We saw in section 10.2 that all the consonants except /ŋ/ can begin a word in English. They represent a central group known as **initial consonants**. Any consonants which can precede them are **pre-initial consonants** and those which can follow are **post-initial consonants**. This means we are looking at a word-initial structure of

monosyllabic word / syllable				
+/- consonant(s)			vowel	+/– consonant(s)
pre-initial consonant	initial consonant	post-initial consonant	V	C

We can deduce which two-consonant sequences can begin an English word by trying out the various combinations. Table 10.4 shows the consonants which occur in pre-initial and in post-initial position. What emerges is that the options are systematically limited. The pre-initial consonant can only be /s/

Table 10.4   Word-initial two-consonant clusters

Pre-initial consonant /s/	**Initial consonant**	Post-initial consonant /w/	Post-initial consonant /l/	Post-initial consonant /r/	Post-initial consonant /j/
spin	/p/		play	pray	puny
	/b/		bleed	breed	beauty
stick	/t/	twin		train	tune
	/d/	dwell		drain	dune
skin	/k/	queen	clean	creep	cute
	/g/	(Gwent)	glean	grin	
	/tʃ/				
	/dʒ/				
sphinx	/f/		flip	frail	few
	/v/				view
	/θ/	thwart		threat	(enthuse)
	/ç/				
	/s/	swim	slip		(suit)
	/z/				(Zeus)
	/ʃ/	(schwa)		shred	
	/ʒ/				
	/h/				hue
small	/m/				muse
snail	/n/				news
	(/ŋ/)				
swim	/w/				
slip	/l/				(lewd)
	/r/				
(suit)	/j/				

and it can only be followed by nine other consonants: the voiceless plosives /p, t, k/, the voiceless labio-dental fricative /f/, a nasal (but not /ŋ/, which doesn't occur word-initially) or an approximant (but not /r/). Of these, /sj/ is not a particularly common combination. Although it is used by speakers of conservative RP, it is far more common to hear, for example, /suːt/ rather than /sjuːt/. It is significant that the plosives and the fricative which can follow /s/ are all, like /s/, voiceless.

The post-initial consonants are all approximants. A number of combinations appear, but the gaps are worth noting. The six plosives combine very productively with the approximants although not all combinations are possible. The affricates do not occur in consonant clusters at all, while the combinations of fricative + approximant and nasal + approximant are fairly limited. In some instances, variant pronunciations are found – such as suːt for *suit* (already discussed) and /luːd/ for *lewd*. /θj/ may be possible given *enthuse* but there are no /θj-/ words in current usage. Sometimes, combinations seem possible because proper names exist which have them word-initially, such as /gw/ in *Gwent* and /zj/ in *Zeus*. It is difficult to decide whether they should be included as representative or not. *Schwa* is an example of /ʃw-/ but the only other examples of this combination are proper names, so /ʃw-/ is probably not representative of a typical English consonant cluster.

Moving on to three-consonant clusters, we find that they are related to the combinations possible for two-consonant clusters. For example, /spr-/ (as in *spring)* is only possible as an English cluster because the initial consonant /p/ can be preceded by /s/ and followed by /r/ in two-consonant clusters. In Table 10.5, the shaded areas indicate that the combination in question will not occur. The unshaded areas show which combinations can, in theory, occur, and contain examples of those which actually do. It is difficult to say precisely

Table 10.5 Word-initial three-consonant clusters

Pre-initial + initial consonant /s/ + C	Post-initial consonant /w/	Post-initial consonant /l/	Post-initial consonant /r/	Post-initial consonant /j/
/sp/		splash	spray	spew
/st/	–		string	stew
/sk/	squeak	sclerosis	scream	skewer
/sf/		–	–	–
/sm/				–
/sn/				–
/sw/				
/sl/				–
/sj/				

why possible combinations such as /stw-/ and /slj-/ fail to occur. It could be that they are **accidental gaps**, meaning that it would seem perfectly natural to a native speaker to have a word beginning with this combination but there happens not to be one, or there may be some other reason relating, perhaps, to the rarity of part of the combination such as /sf-/ or /lj-/.

Although it is not a matter which we will pursue here, phonologists have given a considerable amount of attention to which vowels can follow word-initial consonants and consonant clusters, and which ones can precede word-final consonants and consonant clusters. Some consonants and consonant clusters combine with many of the vowels while others have far fewer partners: /j/, for instance, in clusters such as /fj-/, /stj-/ and so on, almost always occurs before /uː/.

Word-finally, the consonant picture is rather different and certainly less simple than for word-initial clusters. Whereas word-initial clusters have up to three consonants, word-final clusters have a maximum of four consonants. We have already seen that all the consonants occur alone word-finally with the exception of /h, w, j/. The approximant /r/ does not occur word-finally in RP although it does in rhotic accents. The large group of singly-occurring consonants can be said to fill the **final consonant** position. Consonants which precede them are **pre-final**, and those which follow are **post-final**. This means we have a similar template for final consonants to the one established for initial consonants, with the addition of a second post-final slot for those words which end in a four-consonant cluster or in certain three-consonant clusters:

monosyllabic word / syllable							
+/− consonant(s)			vowel	+/- **consonant(s)**			
pre-initial consonant	initial consonant	post-initial consonant	V	**pre-final consonant**	**final consonant**	**post-final consonant**	**(post-final consonant)**

Table 10.6 shows which pre-final consonants can combine with the final consonants.

In pre-final position, the consonant will be a nasal, the voiceless alveolar fricative /s/, or the lateral approximant /l/. (The approximant /r/ also occurs in rhotic accents.) If we compare these final combinations with the pre-initial + initial consonant combinations, we discover an interesting contrast: only /s/ occurs in the pre-initial consonant position whereas the pre-final consonant position has not only /s/ but also four other consonants – /m, n, ŋ, l/ – as options. The final + post-final combination also has several possibilities, as Table 10.7 shows.

You will notice that a number of the examples in Tables 10.6 and 10.7

Table 10.6 Word-final two-consonant clusters (pre-final C + final C combinations)

Pre-final consonant /m/	Pre-final consonant /n/	Pre-final consonant /ŋ/	Pre-final consonant /l/	Pre-final consonant /s/	**Final consonant**
bump	–	–	help	wasp	/p/
–	–	–	bulb	–	/b/
–	tent	–	kilt	haste	/t/
slammed*	hand	hanged*	bold	–	/d/
–	–	chunk	hulk	whisk	/k/
–	–	–	–	–	/g/
–	hunch	–	filch	–	/tʃ/
–	sponge	–	bulge	–	/dʒ/
bumf	–	–	elf	–	/f/
–	–	–	shelve	–	/v/
warmth	tenth	–	health	–	/θ/
–	–	–	–	–	/ð/
–	tense	–	else	–	/s/
Thames	cleanse	wings*	falls*	–	/z/
–	–	–	Welsh	–	/ʃ/
–	–	–	–	–	/ʒ/
–	–	–	–	–	(/h/)
–	–	–	film	–	/m/
–	–	–	kiln	–	/n/
–	–	–	–	–	/ŋ/
–	–	–	–	–	(/w/)
–	–	–	–	–	/l/
–	–	–	–	–	(/r/)
–	–	–	–	–	(/j/)

are marked with an asterisk. This is to show that they are the result of adding an **inflection** to an existing word. This may be the plural ending for nouns which is articulated as /-s/ or /-z/ depending on whether the final consonant of the noun is voiceless or voiced. So *toff* /tɒf/ adds /-s/ while *bag* /bæg/ adds /-z/. Alternatively, the inflection may be a verb ending as in *hushed* or *raised*. Again, whether the final consonant is voiceless or voiced is relevant to the final consonant of the verb in its **base** form: *hush* /hʌʃ/ will add /-t/, while *raise* /reɪz/ will add /-d/. (/s/ and /z/ can also be verb inflections as in *speaks* or *listens*.) Some consonant clusters only exist word-finally because they occur as the result of an inflection being added to a noun or verb.

You can see the correlation between voiced and voiceless consonants in clusters throughout Table 10.7, not just in the asterisked words, but in examples such as *lapse* and *tuft*. If you examine Tables 10.6 and 10.7 together, however, you will find that some consonants – particularly the nasals /m/ and

Table 10.7   Word-final two-consonant clusters (final C + post-final C combinations)

Final consonant	Post-final consonant /s/	Post-final consonant /z/	Post-final consonant /t/	Post-final consonant /d/	Post-final consonant /θ/
/p/	lapse	–	opt	–	depth
/b/	–	sobs*	–	sobbed*	–
/t/	blitz	–	–	–	eighth
/d/	–	adze	–	–	–
/k/	axe	–	act	–	–
/g/	–	bags*	–	bagged*	–
/tʃ/	–	–	thatched*	–	–
/dʒ/	–	–	–	hedged*	–
/f/	toffs*	–	tuft	–	fifth
/v/	–	loves*	–	loved*	–
/θ/	meths	–	bathed*	–	–
/ð/	–	lathes*	–	writhed*	–
/s/	–	–	haste	–	–
/z/	–	–	–	raised*	–
/ʃ/	–	–	hushed*	–	–
/ʒ/	–	–	–	garaged*	–
/h/	–	–	–	–	–
/m/	–	Thames	–	slammed*	–
/n/	tense	cleanse	tent	hand	tenth
/ŋ/	–	wings*	–	hanged*	–
/w/	–	–	–	–	–
/l/	else	falls*	kilt	bold	health
/r/	–	–	–	–	–
/j/	–	–	–	–	–

/n/ and the approximant /l/ – are able to combine with both voiced and voiceless consonants.

We now move on to consider word-final three-consonant clusters. Table 10.8 lists the pre-final + final combinations and gives examples showing which of the five post-final consonants can follow them. (You will remember from examining the word-initial clusters that a three-consonant cluster only occurs if its first two elements and its last two elements occur separately as two-consonant clusters. The same principle applies to word-final combinations.) Again, the shaded areas indicate impossible combinations. Interestingly, the majority of the examples here are the result of adding the kind of noun or verb inflections discussed above. Only a handful of the examples end in three-consonant clusters in their own right, as it were. These are words such as *glimpse* /glɪmps/ and *twelfth* /twelfθ/ (although the latter is often reduced to [twelθ]).

Table 10.9 gives examples of final + post-final clusters which can be followed by a further post-final consonant. Almost all of these are, again, the result of adding inflections. The only exceptions are *next* /nekst/, *thousandth* /θaʊzəntθ/ and *sixth* /sɪksθ/. *Sixth* is unusual in that although there are instances of /-ks/ word-finally (as in *axe* /æks/) there are no instances of /-sθ/. If /-ksθ/ is not to be seen as an impossible combination (which it clearly isn't)

Table 10.8 Word-final three-consonant clusters (pre-final C + final C + post-final C combinations)

Pre-final + final consonant	Post-final consonant /s/	Post-final consonant /z/	Post-final consonant /t/	Post-final consonant /d/	Post-final consonant /θ/
/mp/	glimpse		prompt		–
/mb/		–		–	–
/md/		–			
/mf/	nymphs*		galumphed*		–
/mθ/	–		–		
/mz/				–	–
/nt/	tents*				thousandth
/nd/		hands*			
/ntʃ/			pinched*		
/ndʒ/				sponged	
/nθ/	tenths*		–		
/ns/			tensed*		
/nz/				cleansed	–
/ŋd/		–			
/ŋk/	minx		defunct		
/ŋz/				–	
/lp/	helps*		sculpt		–
/lb/		bulbs*		–	
/lt/	kilts*				–
/ld/		holds*			
/lk/	hulks*		milked*		
/ltʃ/			filched*		
/ldʒ/				bulged*	
/lf/	gulfs*		engulfed*		twelfth
/lv/		shelves*		shelved*	
/lθ/	healths*		–		
/ls/			pulsed*		
/lz/				–	
/lʃ/			welshed*		
/lm/		films*		filmed*	
/ln/		kilns*	–	–	–
/sp/	wasps*		gasped*		–
/st/	masts*				–
/sk/	whisks*		whisked*		–

Table 10.9   Word-final three-consonant clusters (final C + post-final C + post-final C combinations)

Final + post-final consonant	Post-final consonant /s/	Post-final consonant /z/	Post-final consonant /t/	Post-final consonant /d/	Post-final consonant /θ/
/ps/			lapsed*		
/pt/	opts*				–
/pθ/	depths*		–		
/bz/				–	
/bd/		–		–	
/ts/			blitzed*		
/tθ/	eighths*		–		
/dz/				–	
/ks/			next		sixth
/kt/	acts*				–
/gz/				–	
/gd/		–			
/tʃt/	–				
/dʒd/		–			
/fs/			–		
/ft/	tufts*				–
/fθ/	fifths*		–		
/vz/				–	
/vd/		–			
/θs/			–		
/θt/	–				–
/ðz/				–	
/ðd/		–			
/st/	masts*				–
/zd/		–			
/ʃt/	–				–
/ʒd/		–			
/mz/				–	
/md/		–			
/ns/			tensed*		
/nz/				cleansed*	
/nt/	tents*				thousandth
/nd/		hands*			
/nθ/	tenths*		–		
/ŋz/				–	
/ŋd/		–			
/ls/			pulsed*		
/lz/				–	
/lt/	kilts*				–
/ld/		holds*			
/lθ/	healths*		–		

the only solution is to treat /-sθ/ as an accidental gap. You may like to consider which of the gaps in Tables 10.6 and 10.7 are accidental, and which are truly impossible combinations given the restrictions on some voiced and voiceless consonants combining.

You may also have noticed that several of the examples in Tables 10.8 and 10.9 occur in highlighted boxes. This is because they occur in both tables. This highlights the fact that, for some combinations, two analyses are possible. The /-nts/ ending of *tents*, for example, could be treated as:

pre-final consonant	final consonant	post-final consonant
n	t	s

or as

final consonant	post-final consonant	post-final consonant
n	t	s

Given that *tents* is the plural of *tent*, it is probably preferable to accept the former analysis as this gives /t/ as the final consonant of the word in its uninflected form.

There are words in English which end in four-syllable clusters, but such clusters are rare. The words in which they occur are all either nouns which end in a three-consonant cluster and which have been given the plural inflection /-s/, or verbs which have a /-s/ inflection in the third person singular of the present tense (for example, *(s/he) sculpts*). In other words, there are no four-consonant final clusters in uninflected words in English.

10.5   THE SYLLABLE TEMPLATE

Now we have discovered which consonant clusters occur at the beginnings and ends of monosyllabic words in English, we have almost completed our syllable template. It is important to remember that consonants are an optional element of syllables while vowels are obligatory. We can therefore offer the following as a syllable template:

syllable							
+/− consonant(s)			vowel	+/− consonant(s)			
pre-initial consonant	initial consonant	post-initial consonant	V	pre-final consonant	final consonant	post-final consonant	(post-final consonant)

At the moment, we are presupposing that the three main slots of the template are, so to speak, equal and are a linear ordering of the phonemes which make up any particular syllable or monosyllabic word. However, this is something we need to reconsider as a special link can be found between the vowel and the consonants which succeed it. There is, after all, the phenomenon of rhyme. In rhyming pairs such as *sad* and *glad*, *straight* and *hate*, it is the vowel plus any following consonants which provide the rhyme – the constant element – while the word-initial consonant or consonants change. In addition, many phonologists have noted a link between the length of the vowel and the consonants which follow it. We have already seen how short monophthongs have to be followed in RP by one or more consonants, whereas almost all vowels (excepting only /ʊ/ and /ʊə/) can occur without a preceding consonant. These two aspects are sufficient here to indicate the special relationship between a vowel and any succeeding consonants, and lead to the following as a more appropriate syllable template:

syllable							
onset *(optional)*			rhyme				
			peak	coda *(optional)*			
consonant(s)			vowel	consonant(s)			
pre-initial consonant	initial consonant	post-initial consonant	V	pre-final consonant	final consonant	post-final consonant	post-final consonan)

Here, the syllable template has been slightly restructured and some new labels have been introduced. The syllable has been divided into an **onset** – the opening consonant, if present – and a **rhyme**, which is the obligatory vowel followed by any final consonant. The vowel is termed the **peak** of the syllable because it is the 'centre' of the syllable where the **sonority** or volume of the voice is at its greatest. Any consonants which conclude a syllable are known as the **coda**. This analysis of the syllable is preferable to our original version in showing the special link between the peak and the coda, and we will use it from now on.

So far, our study has concentrated as far as possible on monosyllabic words since they automatically provide examples of possible syllables in English. We can now go on to consider how we might interpret the strings of consonants we find between syllable peaks in words of two syllables or more. Some of the clusters which occur word-finally will not occur word-medially because they are the result of adding inflectional endings. However, many combinations do occur word-medially and we must decide how to allocate the consonants in question to either the preceding or succeeding syllable.

In an example such as *toaster*, we find that the consonant cluster which occurs between its two syllables – /st/ – is acceptable both as a syllable onset (as in s<u>t</u>ir), and as a syllable coda (as in toa<u>st</u>). So the onset/coda test alone cannot provide us with an answer to our question of which syllable /st/ belongs to. In matters of **syllabification** – the way in which a word is divided into syllables – we have to be guided by pronunciation. If you asked someone to pronounce the word toaster with a pause between the two syllables, the likelihood is that they would say /təʊ-/ and /-stə/ rather than /təʊst-/ and /-ə/. In fact, provided the cluster in question is an acceptable syllable onset group, the natural tendency in languages generally, not just English, is to treat a cluster which occurs between syllables as the onset of the next syllable rather than the coda of the preceding one. What is interesting is that the process of syllabification (which is phonological) may be at odds with the morphological make-up of a word. So although the noun toaster is formed, as far as its meaning is concerned, from the base toast and the -er suffix to denote 'something that toasts', we don't syllabify it as toast + er.

Of course, sometimes the morphemes in a word will correlate with its syllable structure. In an example such as blackbird, a compound noun, we can easily identify the free morphemes – black and bird – as also being the two syllables of the word. There is no problem therefore in analysing the /kb/ sequence which occurs between the vowels of blackbird: the /k/ is the coda of the first syllable while the /b/ is the onset of the second:

syllable 1				syllable 2		
onset		rhyme		onset	rhyme	
		peak	coda		peak	coda
initial consonant	post-initial consonant	vowel	final consonant	initial consonant	vowel	final consonant
b	l	æ	k	b	ɜː	d

In other examples, impossible strings occur word-medially and the syllabification of a word is not linked to its construction as it is in blackbird. An example of this is magnet. The consonant cluster /gn/ is an impossible onset and also an impossible coda. Instinct and 'broken' pronunciation in fact tell us that the syllabification of magnet is /mæg/ + /net/, the problem of the impossible cluster being solved by the assigning of /g/ to the first syllable, and /n/ to the second, resulting in two well-formed syllables.

In Chapter 9, we examined closely the vowel inventory of RP, dividing the vowels into monophthongs and diphthongs. Sometimes, a closing diphthong is followed by a glide towards schwa. This combination is known as a **triphthong**. Speakers will differ as to whether a triphthong results in one syllable or two. In a word such as *sour* /saʊə/, for example, or *fire* /faɪə/ the number of syllables a listener perceives will probably be influenced by the amount of prominence given to the middle element of the triphthong. In other examples, particularly those made up of a basic stem with an inflectional or derivational ending (such as <-er>), there will probably be general agreement that there are two syllables. This is true of words such as *slower* /sləʊə/ and *buyer* /baɪə/. These words have neither a coda for the first syllable nor an onset to the second (indicated in the chart by the symbol Ø):

syllable 1				syllable 2		
onset		rhyme		onset	rhyme	
		peak	coda		peak	coda
initial consonant	post-initial consonant	vowel	final consonant	initial consonant	vowel	final consonant
s	l	əʊ	Ø	Ø	ə	
	b	aɪ	Ø	Ø	ə	

Finally, we need to consider **syllabic consonants**. We have worked on the assumption that a vowel is an obligatory element in a syllable. However, there is one exception to this principle which is found in words of two syllables or more. This is when a nasal (/m/ or /n/) or an approximant (/l/ and sometimes /r/) functions as the peak of the syllable. This occurs when the vowel in the syllable, because it isn't stressed, becomes so reduced that it effectively disappears, leaving the coda to function alone as the peak. So a word like *button* may be pronounced [bʌ] + [tɒn] in broken pronunciation while in natural speech it will be pronounced [bʌtən] (with the /ɒ/ of the second syllable being reduced to a schwa as it isn't stressed) or even [bʌtn̩]. (The diacritic ˌ is placed below the consonant in order to indicate that it is syllabic.) Syllabic consonants are fairly common in all accents of English but there are restrictions on when they can occur.

10.6 CONNECTED SPEECH

Throughout most of this chapter, we have been working towards an understanding of how consonants and vowels group together phonologically to form syllables and words. We have seen how phonemes are given allophonic variants either as the result of their position in a word (/l/ may be clear or dark, for example) or because they are affected by adjoining phonemes (vowels, for instance, may become nasalised when adjoining nasal consonants). Also, we have to bear in mind that the articulation of phonemes varies depending on the accent of the speaker.

At the end of Chapter 9, we touched on how phonemes vary when in contact with adjacent phonemes from other words. These variations are the result of **connected speech**. When we write, we leave gaps between words so it is easy for the reader to process the text. When we speak, it is unnecessary to leave pauses between words much of the time and it would sound unnatural if we did. Given that segments affect each other within individual words, it is hardly surprising that this influence also operates across word boundaries.

When connected speech was first discussed in section 9.8, we looked at the examples of *next day* and *prime minister*, and noticed how the /t/ at the end of *next* was lost before *day* and how the /m/ at the end of *prime* was lost before the /m/ at the start of *minister*. The term for this loss of a speech segment is **elision**. Elision is particularly likely to occur when clusters of consonants form or when identical segments occur in a sequence and this happens frequently in connected speech. Syllabic consonants are also the result of elision. We saw above how a vowel sometimes becomes so reduced (as in *button*) as to disappear altogether, the syllable peak being filled by the succeeding consonant to give [bʌtn̩] rather than [bʌtən].

In some circumstances, segments may be lost, but it is also common for segments to appear or be added at word boundaries. This phenomenon is known as **liaison**. In English, the segment which usually appears is /r/. RP, you will remember, is a non-rhotic accent, so words which end in /r/ in some accents will not do so in RP. For example, a speaker of a rhotic accent will pronounce *four* as [fɔr] whereas an RP speaker will pronounce it [fɔː]. However, when *four* is followed by a word which begins with a vowel, the /r/ is likely to be pronounced in RP. So, like a speaker of a rhotic accent, an RP speaker may well pronounce *four apes* as [fɔr eɪps], with the /r/ emerging at the end of *four*. This occurrence of /r/ is known as **linking r**.

Because the presence of a linking r is so common in English, speakers frequently add /r/ in constructions where /r/ does not appear in rhotic accents but where the phonological environment is similar to that for linking r. In other words, the /r/ appears at the end of a word which in isolation ends with a vowel but which in connected speech precedes a vowel. For instance, *America* has no /r/ at the end, even in rhotic accents, but if *America* is placed before a word beginning with a vowel, such as *and* in *America and Canada*, the /r/ emerges to give [əmerɪkər ænd kænədə]. (However, because of the way syllabification works, listeners probably perceive the /r/ as the onset of *and* rather than the coda of the last syllable of *America*.) This type of /r/ is known as **intrusive r**.

We have seen how, in connected speech, segments can both disappear and appear. In other circumstances, they will become more like the segments which precede or follow them. This phenomenon is known as **assimilation**. There are three types of assimilation. The first type is **anticipatory assimilation** and it is quite common. In a phrase such as *ten-pin bowling*, the /n/ at the end of *ten* is often pronounced [m] in anticipation of the fact that the following word, *pin*, begins with the bilabial phoneme /p/. In other words, the alveolar nasal becomes bilabial like /p/. This could also happen to the /n/ at the end of *pin* as this too precedes a bilabial phoneme (/b/). In connected speech, then, *ten-pin bowling* will probably be pronounced [tem pɪm bəʊlɪŋ]. Much rarer is the type of assimilation known as **perseverative assimilation**. This is when a feature of one segment 'perseveres' and is found in the following segment. The two elements of the compound *ashtray* in isolation will probably be pronounced [æʃ] and [treɪ]. But in connected speech or simply in the utterance of *ashtray* by itself, it is likely a speaker will say [æʃtʃreɪ]. Here, the fricative quality of the /ʃ/ at the end of *ash* has been carried over to the /t/ at the beginning of *tray*, causing it to surface as [tʃ]. Finally, there is **coalescent assimilation** or simply **coalescence**. This is when two segments merge into one. For example, in connected speech, *haven't you* is likely to be pronounced [hævəntʃuː] with the /t/ at the end of *haven't* and the /j/ at the start of *you* being merged to give [tʃ].

☐ Phonetic transcriptions ⇨ 9.8

11 Suprasegmental Phonology

11.1 WHAT IS SUPRASEGMENTAL PHONOLOGY?

In Chapter 9 we explored the phoneme inventory of English (as far as RP is concerned) and looked at how the consonants and vowels of RP are articulated. In Chapter 10 we considered the way these phonemes combine to form syllables and words and what happens to adjacent phonemes in connected speech. In other words, Chapter 10 covered **segmental phonology**. In this chapter, we will be going beyond the individual speech sounds of English and the patterns in which they occur in order to look at other aspects of speech which affect the way that syllables, words and strings of words are uttered. These aspects are known as **prosodic features** and include, most importantly, **stress**, **pitch** and **intonation**. Less central prosodic features are **voice quality**, **volume** and **tempo**. The study of these aspects is **suprasegmental phonology** although you will often encounter this area of phonology being referred to simply as **prosodics**.

11.2 WORD STRESS

We have already explored in some detail how syllables are constructed and we have seen that words may be **monosyllabic** (consisting of just one syllable), **disyllabic** (two syllables) or **polysyllabic** (three or more syllables). In this chapter, we will also be using the term **trisyllabic** to refer specifically to words of three syllables. We will begin this section by considering some disyllabic words. In the following examples a dot (·) has been used to indicate the syllable boundary:

a·muse	*pa·per*
be·tween	*ba·by*
ex·change	*ear·nest*
to·wards	*peo·ple*

If you utter these words you will notice that one syllable is given more prominence than the other. In fact, the words in the left-hand column give greater prominence to the second syllable while those in the right-hand column give greater prominence to the first syllable. The prominent syllables in these words are referred to as **stressed syllables**. By contrast, the other syllables are **unstressed**. Stressed syllables can be indicated by placing a vertical superscript line in front of them:

a'*muse*	'*paper*
be'*tween*	'*baby*
ex'*change*	'*earnest*
to'*wards*	'*people*

Speech in English, as in many other languages, is made up of both stressed and unstressed syllables. A non-native speaker who is learning English will sound distinctly unnatural, however accurate their grammar and however proficient their choice of lexis, if they do not get **word stress** correct.

Stress, then, is the means by which we give one syllable greater prominence than another. There are various ways in which this prominence is achieved. First, a stressed syllable may be uttered more loudly than an unstressed one. The difference in volume is rarely very marked but the increase in muscular energy which is involved when you make a syllable louder is significant. You will become aware of this if you try a simple experiment. Speak aloud the words in the two columns above and at the same time tap your hand on the desk whenever you utter a stressed syllable. This should prove very easy, the reason being that the muscular effort involved in hand-tapping corresponds with the muscular effort involved in increasing volume. If you now try the reverse – tapping your hand whenever you utter an unstressed syllable – you will find this activity much trickier and may even find yourself giving the unstressed syllables an unnatural amount of prominence. For an example of how volume can indicate the stressed syllable of a word, consider the difference between the noun '*diplomat* and the adjective *diplo*'*matic*. In both these words, the first three syllables are identical in terms of their CV structure. However, *diplomat* is stressed on the first syllable while *diplomatic* is stressed on the third syllable. There is no change to the way the phonemes are realised here so the change of stress must be the result of the volume given to the relevant syllable.

We saw in the previous chapter that a syllable has a vowel as its peak. A syllable may have prominence if it contains a long vowel. This is often in contrast to the vowels in unstressed syllables which are not always given their full value (a point we will return to shortly). Sometimes, though, we may lengthen a vowel in order to achieve contrastive stress. For example, look at the following exchange:

A: Did you say that someone who carries the incense in church is a thurible?
B: No, a thuri<u>fer</u>

When B replies to A here, they change the normal stress pattern of the word *thurifer* in order to highlight the difference between the two rather similar words *thurible* and *thurifer*. The latter is normally uttered with the stress on the first syllable but in B's reply to A the final syllable of *thurifer* is given prominence by lengthening the vowel. The final syllable is [-fɜː] rather than [-fə] and this lengthening gives it prominence for the purpose of clarification.

The third feature which may give prominence to a syllable is that there will be a marked change of pitch on that syllable. Pitch can be better understood by comparing speech to music, where one note differs from another by being higher or lower in pitch. Variations in pitch are caused by a change in the frequency of the vibration of the vocal cords and this occurs in speech as well as in singing. In fact, speakers constantly vary their pitch, albeit not very markedly most of the time. However, a syllable may be stressed by raising or lowering the pitch at which it is spoken by a greater degree than is normally the case. We will look more closely at pitch changes in section 11.4.

Finally, a syllable will achieve prominence if it is in contrast to a syllable where the vowel has been reduced in value. This can be illustrated by returning to our earlier examples, which have been reordered below:

1 a'muse	2 to'wards	3 'paper	4 'people
5 be'tween	6 ex'change	7 'earnest	8 'baby

The unstressed syllables in the first four examples *(a'muse, to'wards, 'paper* and *'people)* contain the neutral vowel which we call schwa: /ə/. This vowel, however, represents a reduction in vowel value. We know this because when we say a word slowly or extra clearly we replace the schwa with a different vowel: for example, the syllable at the start of *a'muse* would be realised by the diphthong [eɪ] rather than by [ə]. *'People* is an interesting example: in an exaggerated pronunciation the second syllable would be realised as [ʊ] to give [piːpʊl] but normally the vowel in the second syllable is reduced to schwa or the vowel disappears altogether and the /l/ becomes a consonantal syllable. The natural pronunciation then is [piːpəl] or [piːpl̩]. In examples 5, 6 and 7 *(be'tween, ex'change* and *'earnest)*, the vowel [ɪ] in the unstressed syllables may again be regarded as a reduction of an underlying vowel. In *ex'change*, the initial syllable would be pronounced [eks-] rather then [ɪks-] if the vowel were given its full value, while the second syllable in *'earnest* would be [-nest] rather than [-nɪst]. In *be'tween,* the underlying vowel in the unstressed syllable is /iː/. This is also the full value for the vowel at the end of *'baby* but in this example, the vowel in the unstressed syllable simply becomes reduced in length. So an exaggerated pronunciation of *baby* would be [beɪbiː] while the natural pronunciation is [beɪbi].

So far we have considered word stress in disyllabic words. When we utter monosyllabic words in isolation, we give a full value to the vowel which they contain. This is true for both lexical words and grammatical words. However, when monosyllabic grammatical words occur in connected speech, the value of their vowels is often reduced so that in context these monosyllabic words become unstressed. The preposition *from,* for example, in isolation would be pronounced [frɒm]. By contrast, in a string such as *the holiday from hell*, the vowel in *from* would be reduced to a schwa to give [frəm].

Many lexical words are polysyllabic and we need to consider their stress patterns. In many words of three syllables, one syllable is stressed and the other two are unstressed. Here are some examples:

ˈdifficult	toˈmato
ˈeditor	ecˈcentric
ˈpineapple	naˈrrator

The stress falls either on the first syllable (as shown in the first column) or on the second syllable (as shown in the second column). In some words of three syllables, the stress will fall on the final syllable but when this occurs it is normal to give a little more prominence to the first syllable. Consider the way you would pronounce the following:

disbelief
counteract
contradict
auctioneer

Each of the above words is stressed on the third syllable. However, when you utter these words you will also give some prominence to the first syllable. This first syllable is not, then, unstressed like the second syllable but nor does it have the same degree of prominence as the final syllable. This degree of prominence somewhere between a stressed syllable and an unstressed one is referred to as **secondary stress**. The degree of stress given to the final syllable in the above examples may, by contrast, be termed **primary stress**. Secondary stress is also indicated by a vertical line in front of the relevant syllable but the line is a subscript rather than a superscript one:

ˌdisbeˈlief

ˌcounterˈact
ˌcontraˈdict
ˌauctioˈneer

The tendency is for words of three syllables to have simply a primary stress on the first or second syllable. If there is primary stress on the third syllable then it is likely that the first syllable will be given a secondary degree of stress. It is not impossible, however, for primary stress to occur on a first or second syllable and for secondary stress to occur on an adjoining syllable. This is particularly likely in compound words since the stress patterns from the two words which form the compound are retained to some extent. Here are some examples of both bisyllabic and trisyllabic compound words:

| ˈblackˌsmith | ˌfreeˈwheel | ˈhamˌburger | ˌmarshˈmallow |
| ˈdiveˌbomb | ˌmidˈair | ˈdareˌdevil | ˌstrong-ˈminded |

In these examples, *blacksmith* and *divebomb* are contrasted with *freewheel* and *midair* in that the first two have a primary stress on the first syllable and a secondary stress on the second syllable while the second two show the opposite pattern. You may wonder how you can be certain that these compound words contain a primary stress and a secondary stress as opposed to a primary stress and an unstressed syllable. If you put the compound words in a slightly fuller context you will be able to determine the different degrees of stress. For instance, if you contrast *I met a* ˈblackˌsmith with *I met a* ˈtiger, there is a clear difference between the value of *a* (which is unstressed in this context) and the value of *smith* whereas *a* and the *-ger* of *tiger* are comparable in both being unstressed.

The trisyllabic compounds *hamburger* and *daredevil* contrast with *marshmallow* and *strong-minded*. In the first pair the primary stress falls on the first syllable and the secondary stress falls on the second syllable, while the pattern is reversed for the second pair. Further examples show other possible patterns for compound words of three syllables. In the noun ˈmake-beˌlieve, for example, the primary stress is on the first syllable while the secondary stress is on the third syllable. In the adjective ˌsecond-ˈhand the primary stress is on the third syllable while the secondary stress is on the first syllable. In general then it is more typical for compound words to contain both primary and secondary stress but it is not impossible that simple or derived words will contain both.

We will now look briefly at words of four syllables. It is possible for four-syllable words to contain only one stressed syllable:

reˈsponsible

re'suscitate
e'cology
de'livery

Most typically, the stress will fall on the second syllable of a four-syllable word. However, the following – less common – examples have stress on the first syllable:

'*delicacy*
'*culinary*
'*automobile*

More typically, a word of four syllables will contain both a primary and a secondary stress. Here are just three examples:

'*funda₁mental*
₁*sui'cidal*
₁*visi'tation*

The typical pattern is for syllables of primary or secondary stress to alternate with unstressed syllables. It is worth remembering here that we are only dealing with words uttered in isolation and that stress patterns change slightly in the context of connected speech.

So far, we have looked at word stress in terms of the position in which stressed and unstressed syllables may occur. We have not really considered what it is that governs where the stress occurs. This is a complex matter and exceptions will always be found to any rules which are established. In very general terms, syllables are likely to attract stress if they either contain a long vowel or they end in a cluster of at least two consonants. Syllables will tend to be unstressed if they contain a short vowel (which is often realised as [ə] or [ɪ]) or if the syllable coda is just one consonant or there is no consonant at all in this position (although this will not apply to word-final syllables). If a word contains only short vowels and there are no other factors to influence where the primary stress might fall, then the likelihood is that it will fall on the first syllable of the word.

Interestingly, there are several words in English where speakers disagree about the position of the primary stress. A salient example of this is the noun *controversy*. Some speakers give this noun a primary stress only, with this falling on the second syllable (*con'troversy*), while other speakers give the word a primary and a secondary stress ('*contro₁versy*). Other examples of words with more than one stress pattern include *kilometre, inventory* and *metamorphosis.*

Of more significance is the variation in stress which we use to indicate a difference of word class. Consider, for example, the noun 'record and the verb re'cord. These two examples of *record* are **homographs**: this means that they are represented in the same way in writing but differ in terms of meaning and pronunciation. The noun is given primary stress on the first syllable while the verb is given primary stress on the second syllable. This results in the vowels in the first syllables of these words having very different values:

noun	'record	[rekɔːd] or [rekʊd]
verb	re'cord	[rɪkɔːd]

Examples of this kind where word class is distinguished by the position of primary stress are nearly always noun/verb pairs. Further, the examples are all derived words consisting of a prefix plus a base. Other examples include *escort*, *access* and *contract*. There are probably about fifty such homographs in total.

- ☐ derived words (affixation) ⇨ 3.4
- ☐ compound words ⇨ 3.5
- ☐ vowels, including schwa ⇨ 9.6
- ☐ syllable structure ⇨ 10.4
- ☐ syllabic consonants ⇨ 10.5
- ☐ pitch variations ⇨ 11.4

11.3   RHYTHM

Rhythm refers to the pattern of stressed and unstressed syllables in speech. We often associate rhythm with a degree of regularity in this pattern in contrast to **arhythmic** speech where the pattern is irregular. The latter is likely to occur when we are nervous or hesitant in our speech. In general, though, our speech tends to be fairly rhythmic. What is of particular significance is the way we adjust the rhythm of our speech in order to make it more regular. Consider the following two noun phrases:

a cup of tea
a piece of cake

In these examples, the stressed syllables would be the monosyllabic nouns *cup*, *tea*, *piece* and *cake* while the grammatical words, *a* and *of*, would be unstressed and would be pronounced /ə/ and /əv/ respectively. The alternation between stressed and unstressed syllables in these examples results in a regular rhythm.

If, however, we join these two phrases with the conjunction *and*, the regularity of the rhythm is slightly disrupted:

>   a ˈcup of ˈtea and a ˈpiece of ˈcake

Here the regularity is broken by the fact that two unstressed syllables now occur between *tea* and *piece*. Of course, in normal spontaneous speech it is highly unlikely that there will be a consistent alternation between stressed and unstressed syllables. What speakers of English normally do to compensate for the irregularity in occurrence of stressed and unstressed syllables is to space the stressed syllables at approximately equal intervals. This adds something like a regular beat to the utterance. Here the example is shown again with dots over the stressed syllables. These dots also represent beats occurring at regular intervals:

>   •   •   •   •
>   a cup of tea and a piece of cake

Often, two or three unstressed syllables occur between stressed ones:

>   •   (1) • (2) •   (1) •   (3)   • •   (2) •   (1)
>   *Nick and Hilary went to Leningrad to see Laurence and Catherine*

In the above example, the numbers in brackets indicate the number of unstressed syllables occurring between the stressed ones. As already mentioned, the likelihood is that speakers will space the stressed syllables at fairly regular intervals irrespective of the number of unstressed syllables which occur between them. Languages which use this strategy as a means of constructing rhythm are known as **stress-timed** languages. English is fundamentally a stress-timed language although there are some varieties of global English (such as Indian English) which have a rather different rhythmic pattern.

We saw in section 11.2 that all words spoken in isolation contain at least one stressed syllable. We have just seen that in connected speech grammatical words such as *a* and *of* in *a cup of tea* will be unstressed. There are quite a number of monosyllabic grammatical words, *a* and *of* amongst them, which will be unstressed in some circumstances but stressed in others. These words are said to have both **strong** (namely stressed) and **weak** (unstressed) forms. They include the following:

>   pronouns   *she/her, he/him, we/us, you, them*

determiners	*the, a/an, some, her, his, your*
modal auxiliaries	*can, could, shall, should, must*
primary auxiliaries	*am/are/was/were, do/does, have/has/had*
prepositions	*as, at, for, from, of, than, to*
conjunctions	*and, but, that, than*

In addition to the above, the primary auxiliaries *am*, *are*, *was* and *were* can also occur in both weak or strong forms when functioning as lexical verbs. There are various reasons why a weak or strong form may be selected. The position of a word in a sentence may affect the form it takes:

The letter came <u>from</u> Milton Keynes	[frəm]
She didn't know where the letter had come <u>from</u>	[frɒm]

In the first of these two examples, *from* is unstressed and the vowel it contains is a schwa. In the second example, where *from* occurs at the end of the sentence, this preposition is realised in its strong form and the vowel is given its full value. Another reason to adopt the strong form of a word might be for the sake of **contrastive stress**:

You know Susan and Bill? Did you see <u>them</u> in the pub last night?	[ðəm]
No, I didn't see <u>them</u> but I did see Mick and Pippa	[ðem]

In the first example, no particular stress is needed on *them*. In the second example, however, stress is placed on this pronoun which refers to *Susan and Bill* in order to set up a contrast with *Mick and Pippa*. Another reason for adopting the strong rather than the weak form of a grammatical word would be simply to give it emphasis, not necessarily in contrast to another word or phrase as we have just seen:

You <u>shall</u> go to the ball, Cinderella	[ʃəl]

expresses a degree of confidence that Cinderella will go to the ball but

You <u>shall</u> go to the ball, Cinderella	[ʃæl]

is far more confident and assertive, an attitude which is conveyed by using the strong form of the modal auxiliary *shall*.

The choice between the strong and weak forms of the words we have just considered can of course have an effect on the rhythm of the sentence in question. Conversely, the rhythm of a sentence may have an effect on the stress patterns within individual words. We saw in the previous section, for example, that some polysyllabic words contain both a primary and a secondary stress. However, in connected speech, the distinction between primary and secondary stress may disappear. Earlier we had the example of ˌsuiˈcidal where in isolation the first syllable carries secondary stress and the third syllable carries primary stress. In the following context, however, this pattern has undergone a change:

The student made a ˈsuiˌcidal aˈttempt *to climb to the roof of the college*

It is likely here that the third syllable of *suicidal* will have no more stress than the first syllable, and possibly even less. This reflects a trend for a primary stress in one word to shift or be less prominent when the next stress which follows it, albeit in a different word, is also a primary stress. This can also be observed with compound words. In our earlier example of ˌsecond-ˈhand, we saw that the primary stress occurs on *hand*. In this sentence, however, the primary stress moves to the start of *second*:

Phil gave Jane some ˈsecond-ˌhand ˈinforˌmation

The occurrence of the primary stress at the start of *information* causes the primary stress in *second-hand* to shift to the initial syllable. We have already seen that stressed and unstressed syllables tend to alternate in speech or that stressed syllables will occur at roughly equal intervals. The above examples show a tendency among speakers to alternate primary and secondary stresses too. The inclination to alternate strong and weak syllables is sufficiently strong at times to move the primary stress not to a syllable of secondary stress but to a previously unstressed syllable. This can be seen in a compound such as *compact disk*. In isolation, the adjective *comˈpact* is stressed on the second sylla-ble but in *compact disk*, the stress in *compact* moves to the first syllable: ˈcompact ˈdisk.

☐ lexical and grammatical words ⇨ 2.3

11.4   INTONATION AND TONE GROUPS

We noted in section 11.2 that syllables are sometimes given prominence by a marked change of pitch and that pitch varies according to the frequency of the vibrations of our vocal cords. **Intonation** is the way in which pitch rises and falls in speech. Pitch may change markedly (for example from a high pitch to a low pitch) on one syllable or it may change across several syllables. For the time being, we will concentrate on changes in pitch on single syllables. The term which we normally give to such pitch contours is a **tone**. Noticeable changes in pitch typically occur on stressed syllables although they might occur on unstressed syllables for the purpose of contrast or emphasis.

Consider the following sentence:

Heather has won a gold medal for swimming

We will focus on the adjective *gold* in this sentence and consider some of the different tones with which it could be said. Whatever tone is adopted, we can be certain that *gold* would be one of the stressed syllables in the example given its status as a monosyllabic lexical word. First of all, if the speaker did not wish to draw any particular attention to this word, then the likelihood is that it would be said without any noticeable change in pitch. In other words, *gold* would be uttered on a **level tone**. We can indicate that a syllable has a level tone by preceding it with a horizontal line: _gold.

However, if the speaker wished to draw more attention to *gold* then they could utter it with a **falling tone**. This means that the pitch of *gold* would move from high to low. At the start of the tone, the pitch will probably be the same or perhaps a little higher than the pitch used previously (ˏgold) but if the speaker wanted to be even more emphatic then they might well start the tone on a noticeably higher pitch (ˋgold). A falling tone is usually used to express certainty or finality. A slightly more exaggerated falling tone with a greater change in pitch will still express certainty and finality but with rather more emphasis.

In contrast to a falling tone, *gold* could be uttered with a **rising tone**. Again, the rise could be relatively gentle (ˏgold) or more marked (ˊgold) depending on the degree of attention the speaker wanted to draw to the word in question. A rising tone, in contrast to a falling tone, tends to suggest surprise or incompleteness. So if *gold* were uttered on a rising tone in the above example, it would probably have the effect of either turning it into a question or making the statement sound incomplete.

1 *Heather has won a ˊgold medal for swimming?*   (*Could you confirm this?*)
2 *Heather has won a ˏgold medal for swimming and a ˏsilver for diving*

In example 1 the **rising tone** on gold begins on a higher pitch and this turns the statement into a question. In the second example, the less marked rise on *gold* suggests the statement is incomplete. This is confirmed when the second part of the utterance – *and a ˏsilver for diving* – is added. You may notice that there is a falling tone on *silver* which suggests that the information is now almost complete.

Level, rising and falling tones are **simple tones**. They may be contrasted with **complex tones**. There are two main possibilities for complex tones: these are the **fall-rise tone**, which is used fairly commonly, and the **rise-fall** tone, which is more unusual. A fall-rise tone is often used to suggest qualified assertion or an element of doubt:

> A ˅*gold medal?*   *(Are you sure it was gold?)*

A rise-fall tone can be used to express a pleasant surprise or it can express an ironic attitude towards what is said:

> A ˄*gold medal*   *(Well that's a turn up for the books!)*

Although speakers often find it quite difficult to identify the specific type of tone on a syllable when studying language, all speakers are able to respond to the tones they hear and make accurate judgements about the implied meaning behind them.

So far, then, we have seen that in any utterance some syllables will be stressed while others will be unstressed. A stressed syllable may be gently prominent simply due to the natural rhythm of speech or it may be especially prominent because particular attention is being drawn to it. We use falling and rising tones, as well as fall-rise and rise-fall tones, to draw greater attention to a particular word as well as to indicate our stance or attitude towards what is said. For example, we can use a particular tone to indicate that we are asking a question or that we have nearly finished what we are saying or that we are doubtful about what we are saying. In any utterance, only some stressed syllables are marked with a noticeable change of pitch, namely with a tone. Such a syllable is referred to as a **tonic syllable** or **nucleus**.

A tonic syllable will normally, unless the utterance is simply a mono-syllabic word (such as *yes* in reply to a question), occur within a **tone group** (or **tone unit**). This is best understood by looking at an example such as the following extract from a BBC documentary where an astronaut is talking about a mission to repair the Hubble space telescope:

> | *the Hubble symbolises man's quest for the bridge between cosmology and phi˅losophy* | *and so when you go '*off *to catch that thing* | *and it appears on the ho˅rizon* | *it's a powerful* ˎ*moment* | *it is not any other* ˎ*spaceship* | *Hubble* ˎ*touches people* | *it touches* ˅*me* |

In this extract, the tone groups have been separated by vertical lines. The tonic syllables have been underlined and the symbol which precedes them indicates the type of tone on each tonic syllable. Tonic syllables, as we have already noted, are those stressed syllables which are particularly prominent because they carry a tone or noticeable pitch change. Most typically, a tonic syllable will occur towards the end of a tone group and often there is a relationship between the tone group and the grammatical structure of the utterance. In other words, there is some correlation between the tone group and grammatical completeness. Usually, the tonic syllable occurs close to a point of grammatical completeness (although this need not necessarily be a full clause) and it occurs on the last primary stress of the group. Sometimes, however, if a speaker wishes to draw attention to an element which occurs earlier in the group, then the tonic syllable will not necessarily be the last stressed syllable of the group. This can be seen in:

| *Hubble ˌtouches people* |

The last stressed syllable in this group is the first syllable of *people* but here the speaker wants to give particular emphasis to the verb *touches* and so the falling tone occurs on the initial syllable of this verb. In the following group

| *and so when you go 'off to catch that thing* |

the position of the tonic syllable is even more noticeable because it falls on a syllable which would not normally be stressed at all since *off* is a grammatical word.

Since tonic syllables vary in position, this raises the question of how exactly you can identify where a tone group begins and ends. Sometimes, speakers will pause briefly or take a breath between tone groups. In addition, what often happens is that the pitch movement for the tonic syllable does not occur simply on that syllable but continues through the next syllable or syllables. When a new tone unit is then started there may be a sense of the speaker returning to what might be regarded as the 'normal' pitch for the utterance.

In most tone groups, then, the tonic syllable – or nucleus – is preceded by what we call the **pre-nucleus** and may be followed by the **post-nucleus**. Here is an example:

pre-nucleus	nucleus	post-nucleus
it is not any other	*ˌspace*	*ship*

Typically, the pre-nucleus will be longer than the post-nucleus. In the above example, the pre-nucleus contains some stressed syllables but none of them have the prominence of *space*. The post-nucleus here consists simply of *ship* and it is probable that this would be uttered with a slight return towards the normal pitch although the following tone group will begin on a noticeably more normal pitch. In the first tone group of the original example (| *the Hubble symbolises man's quest for the bridge between cosmology and phi\losophy* |), however, it is likely that the downward movement in pitch which begins on the second syllable of *philosophy* will continue through the unstressed syllables which make up the rest of this word. Although we can identify tonic syllables because they carry a noticeable change in pitch, this does not mean that the pitch of the rest of the tone group is constant. When making a statement, for example, speakers are likely to lower the pitch slightly as they move towards the tonic syllable. It is on the tonic syllable, however, that the listener would most notice the change in pitch.

11.5   SEMANTIC FUNCTIONS OF INTONATION

Intonation is part of the fabric of spoken language. Intonation can serve two purposes. It can either express the speaker's attitude towards what they are saying, or it can be used for a grammatical reason, something we will deal with in section 11.6. We have already seen how the various tones can convey attitudes such as surprise or irony as well as other information such as the fact that the utterance is nearly complete. We can also use intonation to draw attention to a particular element of an utterance, either for contrastive purposes or because the speaker wants to make sure the listener pays attention to something important.

We have also seen that intonation can indicate the particular function of a grammatical structure. (We touched on this point in section 11.4.) If, for instance, you compare the tonic syllables in the following three examples you will see how intonation can indicate function even though each example takes the same declarative form:

1 *It's ˎcold in here*
2 *It's 'cold in here*
3 *It's ˌcold in here*

The falling tone on *cold* in example 1 indicates that the declarative is functioning as a statement while the rising tone in example 2 turns the declarative into a *yes-no* question. In example 3, the fall-rise on *cold* could give the utterance a directive function, with the speaker implying that someone should do something about the cold.

Another important aspect of intonation is that certain intonation patterns are linked to different styles and genres. This is a complex area and we will only touch briefly on it here. To take one simple example, there are different ways of telling a story. We adopt one intonation pattern when we relate an anecdote spontaneously to a group of friends but a quite different pattern if we read a short story aloud. The latter would in turn differ depending on whether we are reading to children or to adults. Some varieties of English have very distinctive intonation patterns. Examples include the reading of the football results on radio or television, announcements at railway stations or airports, and sports commentaries.

11.6   GRAMMATICAL FUNCTIONS OF INTONATION

In contrast to the way in which intonation can convey meaning, some intonation features have a grammatical function. This is a salient example of the way in which language levels interact with each other. We have already seen that the positioning of stress can be related to word class. The position of a tonic stress can also signal the difference between a compound noun and a premodifier plus a head noun as in these *French teacher* examples:

Martin employed a <u>French</u> teacher	compound noun
Martin employed a French <u>tea</u>cher	premodifier + head noun

Assuming the speaker did not want to assign any particular emphasis to either *Martin* or *employed* in the above examples, then the intonation pattern of the first example with the tonic stress on *French* would indicate that Martin employed a teacher of the French language. By contrast, the second example, with the tonic stress on *teacher* implies that Martin employed a teacher who was French. Many meanings which would be ambiguous in writing can be clarified in speech by the use of specific intonation patterns.

Another clear instance of how intonation can give grammatical information relates to relative clauses. You may remember from Chapter 6 that a relative clause postmodifies a head noun:

This is the picture <u>which I prefer</u>

However, there are in fact two types of relative clause: **restrictive** and **non-restrictive**. Restrictive relative clauses distinguish one person, item or group from another whereas non-restrictive relative clauses simply give additional information about the noun in question. Compare the following examples:

The students <u>who had completed their work</u> were given prizes
The students, <u>who had completed their work</u>, were given prizes

The first example implies that prizes were only given to some students. The relative clause *who had completed their work* is restrictive here because it is separating the students with finished work from those with unfinished work. The second example, where the relative clause is more like an aside, implies that all the students had finished their work. The relative clause here is non-restrictive and functions as a means of providing additional information about all the students.

In the second example, the fact that the relative clause is non-restrictive is signalled by the use of commas. (An alternative way to show this would be to place the relative clause in brackets or between dashes.) In speech, we signal the difference between a restrictive and a non-restrictive relative clause by the way we organise the tone groups in the utterance:

restrictive
| *The students who had completed their ˌwork* | *were given ˌprizes* |

non-restrictive
The ˌstudents | *who had comˌpleted their work* | *were given ˌprizes* |

The non-restrictive relative clause is treated as a separate tone group while the restrictive relative clause occurs in the same tone group as the head noun which it postmodifies. Intonation is the means here by which the restrictive or non-restrictive status of a relative clause is indicated and thus the phonological level of language is operating in conjunction with the grammatical level.

> ☐ compound words ⇨ 3.5
> ☐ noun phrases ⇨ 5.2
> ☐ relative clauses ⇨ 6.13

11.7 OTHER SUPRASEGMENTAL FEATURES

Finally, we will consider some prosodic features which are more peripheral than stress, rhythm and intonation. These are **voice quality**, **volume** and **tempo**. Each of these aspects may have an effect on the meaning of what we say or they may be incidental to it. Since they are less central than the other prosodic features covered, we will discuss them only briefly.

Voice relates to the vibration of the vocal cords in the larynx. **Voice**

quality refers to the various effects which are brought about depending on the state of the vocal cords and the extent to which the glottis is open or closed. This can lead to a contrast with the regular quality of our speaking voices since we may speak in a breathy voice or a creaky voice or a whispered voice, to name just three possibilities. Sometimes voice quality is irrelevant to what is being said: if, for example, you have a very sore throat and your vocal cords are swollen, this will inevitably affect the way you sound. On the other hand, you may choose to adopt a particular voice quality because it seems appropriate to what you are saying. For instance, if you are telling someone a secret you might speak in a whisper. If you are reading a child a horror story you might adopt a creaky voice.

Volume relates to how loudly or softly someone speaks. Some speakers are typically louder or quieter than the majority of speakers and the volume of the voice may also be related to physical size. We have already seen that one way to give prominence to a syllable is to give it greater volume. We often increase the general volume of our speech when we are angry or trying to get someone's attention. By contrast, we often decrease the volume if we are trying to be gentle or show sensitivity. Volume is measured in decibels and special equipment is of course required for this.

Finally, **tempo** is the speed at which we speak. We can measure tempo in words per minute although sometimes syllables per minute may be more appropriate. There is a contrast between regular spoken tempo and a tempo which is adopted for a particular purpose. For instance, a sports commentator describing a horse race is likely to increase their tempo as the race draws to a conclusion, whereas someone who is dictating or explaining something very carefully will normally decrease the speed of their speech. In unbroken speech, speakers can easily utter an average of one hundred and fifty words per minute. Some speakers will of course utter far more and others typically fewer.

Phonetic and Other Symbols

THE CONSONANTS AND VOWELS OF RECEIVED PRONUNCIATION

Consonants		Vowels			
		Monopthongs		Diphthongs	
/b/	bead	/æ/	bat	/aɪ/	buy
/d/	deed	/ɑ/	bard	/aʊ/	bough
/ʤ/	jet	/e/	bet	/eɪ/	bay
/f/	feed	/ɜ/	bird	/ɛə/	bear
/g/	get	/ə/	about	/əʊ/	beau
/h/	heed	/i/	bead	/ɪə/	beer
/j/	yet	/ɪ/	bit	/ɔɪ/	boy
/k/	keep	/ɒ/	bomb	/ʊə/	tour
/l/	let	/ɔ/	board		
/m/	met	/u/	food		
/n/	net	/ʊ/	book		
/ŋ/	ring	/ʌ/	but		
/p/	pet				
/r/	reed				
/s/	seed				
/ʃ/	shape				
/t/	tape				
/ʧ/	cheat				
/θ/	thin				
/ð/	then				
/v/	vet				
/w/	win				
/ʒ/	measure				
/z/	zone				

OTHER USEFUL SYMBOLS

Brackets

/ /   slant brackets are used for phoneme symbols and for broad transcriptions

[ ]   square brackets are used for narrow transcriptions

< >   angled brackets are used for letters

Other consonant and vowel symbols

/ ʔ /   a glottal stop, as might occur in butter where it replaces /t/ (*bu'er*)

/ x /   a voiceless velar fricative, such as a Scots speaker might use at the end of *loch*

/ o /   the vowel sound in the French *beau*

[l]   clear *l*

[ɫ]   dark *l*

Diacritics

~   above a vowel symbol indicates nasalisation, e.g. in [restərɒ̃n] *restaurant*

ı   below a consonant symbol indicates a syllabic consonant, e.g. in [bʌtn̩] *button*

ʰ   superscript and after a consonant indicates that the consonant is aspirated, e.g. in [kʰʌp] *cup*

ː   after a vowel symbol indicates that the vowel is long, e.g. in [kɑː] *car*

Word stress

aˈmuse   a superscript vertical line indicates that the following syllable is stressed

ˌcontraˈdict   a subscript vertical line indicates that the following syllable has secondary stress (in contrast to the primary stress of the other stressed syllable here)

Tones

-	a level tone
`	a falling tone
′	a rising tone
^	a rise-fall tone
ˇ	a fall-rise tone

Miscellaneous symbols

*	before an example indicates that the example would not normally or naturally occur in English
?	before an example indicates that the example might occur but it may not be accepted by all speakers
Ø	indicates ellipsis (the omission of a retrievable or understood item) or an empty position
C	before a vowel symbol indicates that it is a cardinal vowel

Glossary

(All entries are nouns, unless stated otherwise)

A

absolute   *(adjective)*
The absolute form of an adjective is its unmarked form, without comparative or superlative inflections.

abstract noun
A noun which refers to a concept or thing which has no material existence, e.g. *truth*.

accent
The pronunciation of a language or dialect.

accidental gap
A combination of sounds (such as /stw-/) which could occur but doesn't.

accusative case
In traditional grammar, the object role, which requires a particular inflection.

acronym
A word formed from the first letters of a sequence of words, e.g. *scuba* from *self-contained underwater breathing apparatus*.

active articulator
Any part of the vocal tract used in articulating speech sounds which can change position. The active articulators are the lips, the tongue and the velum.

active verb
A verb phrase whose subject is also the agent of the activity denoted by the verb.

active voice
The voice of a clause whose verb element is active.

adjective
An open class word, usually having a descriptive function within a sentence, but normally identified grammatically by its ability to occur both attributively and predicatively, and in comparative and superlative forms.

adjective phrase
A phrase which has an adjective as its head word.

adjunct
A type of adverb or adverbial element. Adjuncts typically indicate manner, place, time or degree.

adverb
An open class word, but less central than nouns, verbs and adjectives. Adverbs perform a variety of functions: some indicate manner, place, time or degree (adjuncts) while others provide comment on a statement (disjuncts) or link sentences to each other (conjuncts).

adverb of degree
An adverb which indicates extent, e.g. *particularly, too.*

adverb of manner
An adverb which indicates how something is done or occurs, e.g. *carefully.*

adverb of place
An adverb which indicates location or direction, e.g. *abroad* or *backwards.*

adverb of time
An adverb which indicates when something occurred, how long it lasted or how often it happened, e.g. *tonight, forever, nightly.*

adverb phrase
A phrase which has an adverb as its head word.

adverbial clause
A clause which functions as an adverbial element of another, superordinate clause.

adverbial element
The least obligatory element of a clause and one which gives information in a comparable way to an adverb.

affected
The element of a clause (normally a noun phrase referent) on which the verb is performed. In an active clause, the affected is in object position, but in a passive clause it is in subject position.

affirmative clause
A clause whose truth or proposition is not denied, the opposite of a negative clause.

affix
A bound morpheme which is used to form a new word. Affixes can be subdivided into prefixes, infixes and suffixes.

affixation
The process of adding affixes to a base word-initially or word-finally to form a new word.

affricate
A speech sound which is produced with a plosive-fricative sequence. The two affricates in English are /ʧ/ and /ʤ/.

agent

The element of a clause (usually a noun phrase referent) which is carrying out the action of the verb. In an active clause, the agent will be in subject position. In a passive clause, the agent may be indicated with a *by*-phrase.

aggregate noun

A noun which refers to a collection of people (e.g. *police*) or things (e.g. *goods*) and which normally takes the plural form of the verb.

airstream

The flow of air through the vocal tract which is used in the production of speech sounds.

allomorph

The surface form which occurs in the realisation of a morpheme.

allophone

The surface form which occurs in the realisation of a phoneme.

alveolar   (*adjective*)

Of a consonant, articulated with the tongue against the alveolar ridge.

alveolar ridge

The hard ridge which runs above and inside the upper teeth.

anaphor   (*adjective:* **anaphoric***)*

A linguistic element which refers back to another item already introduced, e.g. *he* in *Harry knew he was making a mistake.*

anglicise   (*verb*)

To adapt a word derived from another language to an English form, e.g. *contemptuous* from Latin *contemptuus.*

antecedent

The linguistic element to which an anaphor refers. In the following example, *Harry* is the antecedent of *he: Harry knew he was making a mistake*

anticipatory assimilation

The assimilation of a speech sound to a following one in anticipation of a feature of that sound.

anticipatory *it*

The dummy item *it* when it signals the removal of a subject or object element to a position later in the clause or sentence.

antonym

A word whose meaning is opposite (usually by being at one extreme of a scale) to that of another word with which it might be paired, e.g. *black* is the antonym of *white.*

apposition

The placing of phrases of the same type, and with the same referent, side by side, e.g. the first two noun phrases in *Tony Blair, the Prime Minister, arrived in Geneva this evening.*

approximant
A speech sound which is produced by a partial closure of the vocal tract. The four approximant sounds in English are /w, l, r, j/.

arhythmic   (*adjective*)
Without a regular rhythm.

articulator
Any part of the vocal tract which is used in the production of speech sounds.

articulatory phonetics
The branch of phonetics concerned with the production of speech sounds.

aspect
A feature of a verb phrase indicating whether the state or action referred to is complete (perfect aspect) or on-going (progressive aspect), e.g. *I have read the book* is perfect aspect while *I am reading* is progressive.

aspirate
The speech sound /h/, which is a glottal fricative.

aspiration
The uttering of the aspirate sound /h/, particularly as a feature of a stop consonant preceding a vowel.

assimilation
The adjustment to a surface form of a phoneme which results in that form becoming more similar to another surface form.

attributive   (*adjective*)
The attributive position is that immediately preceding a head noun (but following any determiners within a noun phrase).

auxiliary
A type of verb but belonging to a closed class and occurring in a verb phrase before the lexical verb. This very small class can be subdivided into modal auxiliaries and primary auxiliaries.

auxiliary verb
An alternative term for an auxiliary.

B
back vowel
A vowel whose articulation includes the raising of the back of the tongue towards the soft palate.

back-formation
A word-formation process in which an affix is removed from an existing word and the resulting word belongs to a different word class, e.g. *television* (noun) gives rise to *televise* (verb).

bare infinitive
The infinitive form of the verb without the particle *to*.

base

A unit to which another morpheme may be added to create a new word, e.g. *origin* is the base of *original* and *original* is the base of *originally*.

base form

The form of a verb without any inflections.

bilabial   (*adjective*)

Of a consonant, articulated at the lips.

blend

A word formed through merging part of one word with part of another, e.g. *brunch* is formed from *breakfast* and *lunch*. Blends are also known as portmanteau words.

borrowing

An alternative term for a loanword.

bound morpheme

A morpheme which cannot stand alone and therefore is not a word in its own right.

broad transcription

A phonetic transcription which does not provide detailed information about allophonic realisations.

by-**phrase**

In a passive clause, a *by*-phrase can be used to indicate the agent of the verb, e.g. *Gill's garden was admired <u>by everyone</u>.*

C

cardinal numeral

A whole number in its counting form, e.g. *one, two, three.*

cardinal vowel

A member of a set of vowels used to map out tongue positions.

case

The role adopted by a noun (or pronoun) according to its clause function and normally indicated by an inflectional ending. Case is more relevant to highly inflected languages than to English.

cataphor   (*adjective:* **cataphoric**)

A linguistic item which refers forward to another item not yet mentioned, e.g. *this* in *This is what I want you to do: go to the shops, buy ...*

central adjective

An adjective which can occur in both attributive and predicative position.

central approximant

The approximant /r/, so called because the air escapes down the centre of the mouth in its articulation.

central determiner
A member of the largest group of determiners, identified according to their inability to co-occur with other central determiners.

central vowel
A vowel whose articulation involves the tongue being flatter than it is for front and back vowels.

centring diphthong
A diphthong which glides towards schwa during its articulation.

citation form
The form of a word which is used for reference purposes or in which a word is entered in a dictionary.

class-changing   (*adjective*)
An affix is class-changing if, when added to a base, it creates a new word of a different class from the base, e.g. adding *-ly* to an adjective such as *kind* creates the adverb *kindly*.

class-preserving
An affix is class-preserving if, when added to a base, it creates a new word of the same class as the base, e.g. when *-dom* is added to the noun *king* a further noun *kingdom* is formed.

clause
A unit of syntactic structure larger than a phrase and normally containing an overt subject element, a verb element, and any verb complementation.

clear *l*
In English, the allophonic form of the phoneme /l/ when it occurs word-initially.

cleft sentence
A restructured sentence consisting of the dummy subject *it*, followed by the verb *be* and then the focus of the sentence followed by a relative clause or a *that*-clause, e.g. *It is Terry who plays jazz piano.*

clipping
A word-formation strategy in which a new word (but of the same class as the original) is formed by shortening an existing one, e.g. *cred* from *credibility*. A word formed in this way is also termed a clipping.

close vowel
A vowel which is produced with a relatively small cavity between the tongue and the palate.

closed class
A class of words which is relatively small and changes very slowly. The closed classes are pronouns, determiners, auxiliaries, prepositions and conjunctions. The words of the closed classes are also known as grammatical words or function words.

closed syllable
A syllable which ends in at least one consonant.

closing diphthong
A diphthong whose finishing position has less distance between the tongue and the palate than its starting position.

closure
The process of blocking off the airstream in the articulation of a consonant sound.

coalescence
An alternative term for coalescent assimilation.

coalescent assimilation
Assimilation in which two speech sounds merge into one.

coda
In syllable structure, any consonant(s) which follows the vowel at the syllable peak.

cohesion
The process whereby a range of linguistic strategies signal that sentences belong together as a text and in a particular sequence.

collective noun
A noun which refers to a group but which can take both singular and plural forms, e.g. *family, herd.*

collocation
A typical or habitual combination of words or lexemes, or the process of combining words in this way, e.g. *rancid* collocates with *butter* but not with *wine.*

combining form
A unit of word-formation which is neither a typical affix nor a typical root or base, e.g. *technophobe* consists of the combining forms *techno-* and *-phobe.*

common case
A term used to refer to any noun, singular or plural, not in the possessive form.

common noun
A noun other than a proper noun, and which in isolation can be preceded by the definite article.

comparative
A form taken by adjectives and adverbs when they are used for purposes of comparison, e.g. *taller, faster.* The comparative inflection is *-er.*

comparative clause
A type of subordinate clause expressing comparison and typically introduced by the subordinators *than* or *as.*

complement element
The element of a clause which follows a copular verb such as *be* or *seem.*

complementary   (*adjective*)
Two words whose meanings are mutually exclusive are complementary to each other, e.g. *dead/alive.*

complex preposition
A preposition consisting of two or three words, e.g. *according to, on behalf of.*

complex sentence
A sentence in which at least one of the elements of the superordinate clause is realised by a subordinate clause.

complex tone
A tone which involves at least one rise and at least one fall in pitch.

complex word
A word which is formed of at least two morphemes or, more specifically, through affixation. Complex words may be contrasted with simple words and compound words.

complex-transitive verb
A verb which is followed by both an object and an object complement.

compound sentence
A sentence in which at least two independent clauses are joined by a coordinating conjunction.

compound word
A word constructed from at least two free morphemes, e.g. *sketchpad.*

compound-complex sentence
A sentence which contains coordinated clauses and at least one subordinate clause functioning as a clause element.

compounding
The process of forming compound words.

concessive clause
A subordinate clause which normally begins with *although, though* or *while,* and expresses a qualification of the truth stated in the main clause.

concord
The agreement in singular or plural number which exists between a verb and its subject.

concrete noun
A noun which refers to something measurable or perceptible through the senses.

conditional clause
A subordinate clause which normally begins with *if* (or conjunctions such as *provided, unless*) and expresses a condition.

conditional *wh*-pronoun
A pronoun belonging to the subset of *wh*-pronouns and which is used to introduce a *wh*-conditional clause.

conjugation
A set of verb forms consisting of the 1st, 2nd and 3rd person both singular and plural and in present or past tense.

conjunct
A type of adverb or adverbial element which performs the function of linking one sentence to another, e.g. *however, nevertheless.*

conjunction
A closed class word with either coordinating or subordinating properties.

connected speech
Speech which consists of strings of words as opposed to words uttered in isolation.

connotation   (*adjective*: **connotative**)
The association (positive or negative) of a particular word, e.g. *darkness* could have a positive or negative connotation depending on context.

conservative RP
The variety of Received Pronunciation associated with older royals and the upper classes.

consonant
A speech sound which is produced through a temporary closure (partial or complete) of the vocal tract.

consonant cluster
A sequence of at least two consonants.

content word
Any word which belongs to an open class (in contrast to a function word).

continuum
A linguistic scale.

contraction
The form resulting from the shortening of a word as part of the process of being joined to a preceding word, e.g. *n't* from *not*, or the form of the two elements together, e.g. *can't.*

contrastive stress
Stress which is placed on a syllable or word which is greater than the natural stress and serves the purpose of emphasising that syllable or word.

converse   (*adjective*)
A converse relationship exists between the meanings of pairs of words such as *lend/borrow* and *learn/teach.*

conversion
A strategy for creating a new word by changing the class of an existing word, e.g. the noun *access* has given rise to the verb *access.*

coordinating conjunction
A conjunction which joins two elements of equal status. The three main coordinating conjunctions are *and, but* and *or.*

coordination
The process of joining linguistic elements of an equal status with a coordinating conjunction.

coordinator
An alternative term for a coordinating conjunction.

copula
A copular verb, particularly the verb *be.*

copular verb
A verb which is followed by a complement element. There are only a few copular verbs, e.g. *be, seem, appear, become.*

co-referential   (*adjective*)
Of two linguistic items, denoting the same referent.

correlative   (*adjective*)
Of conjunctions, operating in pairs, e.g. *either/or.*

count noun
A noun which can refer to more than one and which therefore has a plural form.

D

dark *l*
The allophone of the phoneme /l/ as it is realised at the end of a syllable where it is more palatalised.

declarative   (*noun* & *adjective*)
The sentence type whose order is the subject followed by the verb and any verb complementation.

definite article
A specific term for the central determiner *the.*

deixis   (*adjective*: **deictic**)
The use of a word whose meaning is relative to the speaker or to the context of utterance, e.g. *mine* and *yours, here* and *there, this* and *that.*

demonstrative pronoun
Any of the pronoun set which consists of *this, that, these* and *those.*

denotation   (*adjective*: **denotative**)
The meaning or referent of a word (as opposed to any connotation it may possess).

dental   (*adjective*)
Of a consonant, articulated with the tip of the tongue between the front teeth.

dependent clause
A clause which cannot stand alone. This is an alternative term for a subordinate clause.

dependent form
The form of possessive pronouns which cannot stand alone but must qualify a following noun, e.g. *my, their*.

derivational morphology
The branch of morphology concerned with the formation of new words, particularly through affixation. Derivational morphology is sometimes used as an alternative term for lexical morphology.

derived word
A word formed through the process of affixation.

descriptive   (*adjective*)
A descriptive approach to language study is one which is concerned with open-mindedly describing a language and how it is used (rather than prescribing or judging use).

determiner
A closed class word which occurs only at the beginning of noun phrases and which has a function distinct from that of other noun premodifiers.

deverbal adjective
An adjective derived from a verb by the addition of the suffix *-ed* or *-ing*, e.g. *confused, confusing*. A deverbal adjective is sometimes referred to as a participle.

deverbal noun
A noun derived from a verb by the addition of the suffix *-ing*, e.g. *dancing*. A deverbal noun is sometimes referred to as a participle.

diacritic
A mark used in phonetic transcription to give additional information about the pronunciation of speech sounds.

dialect
The vocabulary and grammar of a language variety be it regional or non-regional.

diminutive
A suffix which, when added to a base, creates a word denoting a smaller version of the original, e.g. *-ette, -ling*. A word which is formed in this way may also be termed a diminutive.

diphthong
A vowel sound which is produced by gliding from one vowel position to another.

direct object
The object element following a ditransitive verb which occurs after the indirect object, e.g. *a present* in *Judith promised Matthew a present*.

directive
The typical function of an imperative sentence.

discourse
The largest unit of language construction in that it consists of one sentence or more. Text is an alternative term. Sometimes, discourse is used specifically to refer to conversation.

disjunct
A type of adverb or adverbial element whose function is to comment on the content of a sentence or to indicate the 'voice' in which it is said, e.g. *fortunately, frankly*.

disyllabic   (*adjective*)
Containing two syllables.

ditransitive verb
A verb which is followed by both a direct object and an indirect object.

dummy subject
It or *there* in subject position but when they have no co-reference.

dynamic verb
A verb which refers to an action or physical process, as opposed to a stative verb which refers to a state or condition.

E

-*ed* participle
A non-finite verb form which in regular verbs consists of the base plus an -*ed* inflection but which has an equivalent form in irregular verbs, e.g. *summoned, taken*.

egressive pulmonic airstream
An airstream which flows outwards from the lungs.

elision
In connected speech, the omission of one or more speech sounds.

ellipsis
The omission of a phrase or clause element whose existence can be inferred from the semantic and grammatical context.

embedding
The occurrence of one linguistic unit in a dependent position within another unit, e.g. the prepositional phrase *of the journey* is embedded in the noun phrase *the end of the journey*.

end focus
The positioning of the part of a sentence whose content is of most importance at the end of that sentence.

endophoric reference
Anaphoric or cataphoric reference which relates to another linguistic item as opposed to the context of use.

end-shift
The removal of a subject element to the end of its clause or sentence.

eponym
An open class word derived from a proper noun, e.g. *hoover*.

eponymy
The use of a proper noun to refer to an object or action.

Estuary English
The supposedly classless accent which is now associated with London and the south-east.

etymology   (*adjective*: **etymological**)
The historical origin of a word or words, or the study of word origins.

exclamation
The typical function of an exclamative sentence.

exclamative
A sentence form which begins with *what* or *how*, and in which this *wh*-word is attached to a clause element (and fronted if necessary), e.g. *What a lovely day it is*.

existential *there*
The dummy subject *there* when used to state the existence of whatever is referred to by a noun phrase in complement position, e.g. in *There is a raven flying towards us*.

exophoric reference
A reference which relates to the context or situation and not to another linguistic element.

explicit   (*adjective*)
Explicit (as opposed to implicit) knowledge about language is conscious, and usually achieved through studying the language.

extraposition
The moving of a linguistic item (normally a subordinate clause) out of its normal clause position and the placing of it later in the clause or sentence.

F
falling tone
A tone which falls from a higher to a lower pitch.

fall-rise tone
A tone which falls from a higher to a lower pitch and then rises again.

field
The combined purpose, context and subject matter of a text.

final consonant position
In syllable structure, one of the consonant positions following the vowel and which can be filled by the greatest number of singly occurring consonants.

finite clause
A clause in which the verb phrase is marked for tense.

finite verb
A verb or verb phrase which is marked for tense.

focus
The part of a sentence whose content is of most importance.

form
The shape or structure taken by a linguistic unit.

formal register
The register associated with more overtly polite usage, often adopted where there is inequality of status between participants.

fraction
A numeral which refers to a number which is not whole, e.g. *half, three-quarters*.

framework
A systematic structure or model used in the study of language.

free morpheme
A morpheme which can stand alone as a word.

fricative
A speech sound which is produced through friction at the place of articulation.

front vowel
A vowel whose articulation involves the raising of the front of the tongue towards the alveolar ridge and the hard palate.

fronting
The process of moving an element to the beginning of a clause or sentence in order to draw greater attention to it.

full verb
An alternative term for a lexical verb.

function
The role or purpose of a linguistic unit, as distinct from its form.

function word
An alternative term for a closed class word.

G

generic pronoun
A pronoun which refers to people in general as opposed to a specific person or sex, e.g. *one, they*.

genitive case
In traditional grammar, a particular role and form of a noun (or pronoun) used primarily to show possession. In modern grammar, genitive case is sometimes used to refer to a noun in its possessive form.

genre
The type of a particular text, e.g. letter, speech, telephone message.

glide
A vowel sound which is produced by gliding from one vowel position to another. Glide is an alternative term for a diphthong.

glottal   (*adjective*)
Of a consonant, articulated at the vocal cords and the glottis.

glottis
The opening between the vocal cords.

gradable   (*adjective*)
Adjectives and adverbs are gradable if they can be preceded by intensifiers or take comparative and superlative forms.

grammar
The set of rules in a language which enable a speaker to construct any well-formed sentence in that language. Grammar is subdivided into syntax and inflections.

grammatical word
Any word which belongs to a closed class (in contrast to a lexical word).

H
half-close vowel
A vowel which is articulated with the tongue a little less close to the palate than it is for a close vowel.

half-open vowel
A vowel which is articulated with the tongue a little less low in the mouth than it is for an open vowel.

hard palate
The roof of the mouth.

head word
The pivotal or only word in a phrase. The class of the head word typically correlates with the phrase type, e.g. the head of an adjective phrase is an adjective.

homograph
A word which takes the same written form as another word, e.g. *bank*.

homonym
A word which takes the same word-form as another word but has a different, unrelated meaning, e.g. *rent* (*payment* and *rip*).

homophone
A word which has the same sound as another word but a different meaning and written form.

hypernym
A name for an overarching category, e.g. *fruit* is the hypernym of *apple, pear, banana* etc.

hyponym
A member of a lexical set or category, e.g. *apple* is a hyponym of the lexical set of *fruit*.

I

idiom
An expression or group of words whose meaning is not retrievable from the individual elements in the idiom, e.g. *pay through the nose.*

idiomatic   (*adjective*)
Containing lots of idioms. Idiomatic English could more generally refer to the natural language use of a native speaker.

imperative
A sentence form which usually lacks an overt subject and in which the verb takes the base form. An imperative typically functions as a directive, e.g. *Stop!*

implicit   (*adjective*)
Implicit (as opposed to explicit) knowledge about language is subconscious, and is possessed by all speakers.

indefinite pronoun
A pronoun which typically does not have an identifiable referent and is not therefore functioning as a noun or noun phrase substitute.

independent clause
A clause whose verb element is marked for tense and which can stand alone. This is an alternative term for a main clause.

independent form
The form of possessive pronouns which can stand alone as a noun phrase, e.g. *mine, theirs.*

indicative mood
The normal mood of a verb phrase in English, as opposed to the subjunctive mood.

indirect object
The object element which occurs first after a ditransitive verb and which can be restructured into a prepositional phrase with *to* or *for*, e.g. *Matthew* in *Judith promised Matthew a present.*

infinitive

The uninflected form of a verb, sometimes preceded by the infinitive particle *to*, e.g. *to go*. This is an alternative term for the base form of a verb.

infinitive particle

The linguistic item *to* when combined with the base or uninflected form of the verb.

infix

An affix which occurs word-medially, although this is not found in English.

inflection

A grammatical word ending which indicates features such as number, possession, person and tense.

inflectional morphology

The branch of morphology concerned with grammatical word endings or inflections.

informal register

The register employed for relaxed, often colloquial usage.

***-ing* participle**

A non-finite verb form which consists of the base plus the inflection *-ing*.

ingressive pulmonic airstream

An airstream which is drawn inwards to the lungs.

initial consonant position

In syllable structure, one of the positions preceding the vowel and which can be filled by almost every consonant of English.

initialism

A word which, like an acronym, is formed from the first letters of a sequence of words but the letters themselves are pronounced, e.g. *BBC*.

intensifier

A type of adverb (belonging to a subset of adverbs of degree) which premodifies another adverb or an adjective and which indicates a point on an imagined scale, e.g. *slightly, very*.

interjection

A member of a minor word class consisting of emotive or spontaneous words which do not enter into syntactic structures, e.g. *wow, gosh*.

International Phonetic Alphabet

An alphabet used for transcribing speech in which one symbol is assigned to each speech sound.

International Phonetic Association

An association formed in 1886 for the purpose of improving the teaching and learning of foreign languages.

interrogative
A sentence form in which the subject and the first element in the verb phrase are inverted and which is typically used to ask a question.

interrogative pronoun
A pronoun belonging to the subset of *wh*-pronouns and which is used to form a question.

intonation
The way in which pitch rises and falls in speech.

intransitive verb
A verb which requires no complementation.

intrusive *r*
The speech sound /r/ when it appears between two words, where the first word doesn't end in /r/ nor does the second word begin with it.

IPA
The International Phonetic Association, or the International Phonetic Alphabet which this association devised.

L

labio-dental   (*adjective*)
Of a consonant, articulated with the upper front teeth placed against the lower lip.

larynx
The voice box, or section of the trachea which contains the vocal cords.

lateral approximant
The speech sound /l/, so-called because the air escapes down the side of the mouth in its articulation.

length
A feature of some vowels, particularly those which can occur in open syllable structure.

level tone
A tone which retains a constant pitch.

levels of language
The various layers of linguistic construction, such as lexis, grammar and discourse.

lexeme
The abstract, representative form of a word.

lexical cohesion
Cohesion produced by the related meanings of words.

lexical item
An alternative term for a lexeme.

lexical level
The layer of language structure related to the lexis or vocabulary of that language.

lexical morphology
The branch of morphology concerned with strategies for the formation of lexical words.

lexical set
A group of words belonging to the same word class and closely related by their meanings, e.g. the names of fruits.

lexical verb
A verb other than an auxiliary verb.

lexical word
Any word which belongs to an open class (in contrast to a grammatical word).

lexicon
The full set of words or lexemes in a language. Lexicon can also refer to a type of dictionary.

lexis (*adjective*: **lexical**)
An alternative term for vocabulary, or the words of a language.

liaison
The appearance or addition of speech sounds (usually /r/ in English) at word boundaries.

linking *r*
In a non-rhotic accent, the articulation of /r/ at the end of a word where it would not normally be pronounced but appears because it precedes a vowel.

lips
Active articulators used in the production of bilabial and labio-dental consonants, and which affect the production of vowels depending on whether they are rounded or unrounded.

liquid approximant
Either of the consonants /l/ and /r/.

loanword
A word which is brought wholesale into one language from another, e.g. *tortilla, feng-shui.*

lungs
The organs which are crucial to voice production in that the airstream flows from them.

M
main clause
In a sentence, a clause whose verb element is marked for tense and which, in contrast to a subordinate clause, can stand alone.

main verb
An alternative term for a lexical verb.

mainstream RP
The less class-based variety of Received Pronunciation, the variety more likely to be heard in the media.

manner of articulation
The way in which a consonant sound is produced, e.g. a plosive or fricative.

minimal free form
The smallest unit of language which can stand alone and still be meaningful.

minor sentence
A semantically complete unit but one which is incomplete as far as clause elements are concerned, e.g. *Pint of bitter* said to a barman is complete in meaning although it is just a noun phrase.

modal auxiliary
One of nine possible auxiliary verbs from the set *can, could, shall, should, will would, may, might, must.*

mode
The medium of discourse, normally speech or writing, but signing is also a mode.

monophthong
A vowel which involves no change in mouth shape in its articulation, unlike a diphthong.

monosyllabic   (*adjective*)
Containing one syllable only.

monotransitive verb
A verb which, in contrast to a ditransitive verb, is followed by one object element only.

morpheme
A minimal and abstract unit of word construction.

morphology
The formation of words or the study of the formation of words.

multi-word verb
A lexical verb which consists of two or three elements and whose meaning is usually partly or wholly idiomatic, e.g. *run up, play down.*

N

narrow transcription
A phonetic transcription which provides detailed information about allophonic realisations.

narrowing
The degrees of closure involved in the articulation of speech sounds.

nasal
A type of stop consonant in which air is released through the nasal as well as the oral cavity during articulation.

nasal cavity
The section of the vocal tract from the velum to the nostrils.

nasalisation
The release of air through the nasal cavity during the articulation of a vowel, giving that vowel a nasal quality.

negative clause
A clause in which the negative particle *not* denies the truth asserted.

nominal clause
A clause which occurs in a position normally occupied by a noun phrase, typically as a subject or object.

nominal relative clause
A clause which occurs pronominally and which begins with a *wh*-word for which the antecedent is implicit, e.g. *Where to go was quite a problem.*

nominal relative pronoun
A pronoun belonging to the subset of *wh*-pronouns and which is used to introduce a nominal relative clause.

nominative case
In traditional grammar, the subject role, which requires a particular noun (or adjective) inflection.

non-count noun
A noun which cannot refer to more than one of its referent and so has no plural form, e.g. *hockey, music, furniture.*

non-finite clause
A clause in which the verb element is not marked for tense.

non-finite verb
A verb which is not marked for tense.

non-fluency features
Features of spoken language such as hesitations and false starts which interrupt the flow of speech and are superfluous to it.

non-restrictive relative clause
A relative clause which gives additional information about the referent(s) of the noun which it postmodifies.

noun
An open class word characterised by its naming function and normally possessing the property of being able to be preceded by *the*.

noun phrase
A phrase which has a noun (or pronoun) as its head.

noun phrases in apposition
Adjacent noun phrases which have the same referent.

nucleus
An alternative term for the tonic syllable in a tone group.

number
The grammatical distinction between singular and plural.

numeral
A word which refers to a number, be it a pronoun, a determiner or a noun.

O

object complement
A complement which gives more information about the object of the clause, e.g. *unhappy* in *She made her friend unhappy*.

object element
The element of a clause which follows a transitive verb and which is typically the affected element in the clause, e.g. *three eggs* in *Julia broke three eggs*.

object predicative
An alternative term for an object complement.

objective form
The form a pronoun normally takes when it is in the object position in a clause, e.g. *me, him, us*.

obligatory   *(adjective)*
An obligatory linguistic element is one that cannot be omitted from a particular structure.

of-construction
A prepositional phrase with *of* as its head used to indicate possession or association, e.g. *the end of a journey*.

Old English
The earliest phase of English, dating from approximately AD 450–1100.

onomatopoeia   *(adjective: onomatopoeic)*
The mimicking of a sound by a word, although the representation is only approximate.

onset
In syllable stucture, any consonant(s) which occurs before the vowel.

open class
A class of words which is too large to count and is constantly changing. Nouns, verbs, adjectives and adverbs are all open class words.

open syllable
A syllable whose vowel is not succeeded by a consonant.

open vowel
A vowel which is articulated with a relatively large cavity between the tongue and the palate.

operator
The first (or only) auxiliary in a verb phrase.

oral cavity
The section of the vocal tract from the larynx to the lips, and excluding the nasal cavity.

ordinal numeral
A numeral which is used to count in rank order, e.g. *first, second, third.*

P

palatal   (*adjective*)
Of a consonant, articulated with the tongue against the hard palate.

palato-alveolar   (*adjective*)
Of a consonant, articulated with the tip of the tongue against the alveolar ridge, while the front of the tongue is raised towards the hard palate.

paradigm
A systematic set of inflected forms, especially of nouns and verbs.

parallelism
The repetition of a grammatical structure, e.g. subject and past tense verb in *I came, I saw, I conquered.*

part of speech
A traditional term for a word class.

participle
A non-finite verb form ending in either *-ed* (or taking an equivalent form in irregular verbs) or *-ing.*

particle
A member of a very small and minor word class, which includes the negative particle *not* and the infinitive particle *to.*

passive articulator
Any part of the vocal tract used in articulating speech sounds which cannot change position. The passive articulators are the teeth, the alveolar ridge and the hard palate.

passive verb
A verb phrase whose subject is the affected element of the lexical verb and which is constructed by using a form of the verb *be* as an auxiliary, e.g. *was surrounded* in *The castle was surrounded.*

passive voice
The voice of a clause whose verb element is passive.

past perfect
The aspect constructed using the auxiliary *have* in the past tense and by placing the lexical verb in its *-ed* participle form, e.g. *had walked.*

past perfect progressive
The aspect constructed using the auxiliary *have* in the past tense, the auxiliary *be* in its *-ed* form, and by adding *-ing* to the lexical verb, e.g. *had been walking.*

past progressive
The aspect constructed using the auxiliary *be* in the past tense and by adding *-ing* to the lexical verb, e.g. *was walking.*

past tense
One of the two tenses in English (the other being the present), signalled in regular verbs by an *-ed* inflection, e.g. *walked* in *Rasheed walked to college.*

peak
The vowel at the heart of a syllable.

perfect aspect
An aspect constructed using the auxiliary *have* and denoting completion of the activity referred to by the lexical verb, e.g. *has read* in *She has read this book.*

performative verb
A verb which, in the first person present tense, performs the action to which it refers though the actual speaking or writing of the verb, e.g. *promise* in *I promise.*

perseverative assimilation
Assimilation in which a feature of one speech sound continues into the next sound.

person
A grammatical category distinguishing between 1st, 2nd and 3rd person.

personal pronoun
A member of the set of pronouns distinguishing between 1st, 2nd and 3rd person (singular and plural) and taking either a subjective or an objective form, e.g. *I, me, you, they, them.*

pharynx
The section of the vocal tract between the uvula and the larynx.

phoneme
A distinct speech sound in its representative, abstract form.

phoneme inventory
The set of phonemes which represents all the distinct speech sounds of a particular language.

phonetic transcription
The writing down of speech using the phonetic alphabet to indicate pronunciation.

phonetics
The study of speech sounds.

phonology
The sound system of a language or the study of that system.

phonotactics
The systematic possibilities for combining distinct speech sounds in a particular language.

phrasal verb
An alternative term for a multi-word verb or, more specifically, a multi-word verb consisting of the lexical verb and an adverb, e.g. *give away*.

phrase
A unit of linguistic construction smaller than a clause, consisting of a head word and any other words dependent on that head word, and having the capacity to fill a clause element slot.

pitch
The apparent height of the voice, ranging from low to high.

place of articulation
The point in the vocal tract where complete or partial closure occurs in the articulation of a consonant.

plosive
A consonant which is produced by a complete closure at some point in the oral cavity and the sudden release of the pressurised air at this point.

plural form
The form taken by a noun, usually through adding an inflection, when it refers to more than one of its singular referent, e.g. *books, addenda*.

politeness marker
A linguistic element which is often peripheral to a clause but which is used to show respect for the addressee, e.g. *please*.

polysemy   *(adjective:* **polysemous***)*
With regard to a word, the state of having more than one meaning, e.g. *mouse*.

polysyllabic   *(adjective)*
Containing three or more syllables.

portmanteau word
An alternative term for a blend.

possessive form
The form taken by a noun when an inflection has been added to indicate possession or association, e.g. *Susan's* in *Susan's brother* or *journey's* in *the journey's end*.

possessive pronoun
Any pronoun used to indicate possession, whether it is in the dependent or

independent form (although those in the dependent form are sometimes classified as determiners), e.g. *my, mine, your, yours.*

postdeterminer
One of a handful of determiners which succeed any central determiner in a noun phrase.

post-final consonant
In syllable structure, any consonant(s) (one or two) which follows a final consonant.

post-initial consonant
In syllable structure, any consonant which follows an initial consonant.

postmodification
In phrases, modification which follows the head word.

postnominal   (*adjective*)
Occurring after a noun.

post-nucleus
The part of a tone group which follows the nucleus, usually shorter than the pre-nucleus.

predeterminer
One of a handful of determiners which precede any central determiner in a noun phrase.

predicate
In a clause, the verb element and any obligatory elements which follow it.

predicative   (*adjective*)
The predicative position is the one following a copular verb where a complement element occurs.

predicator
An alternative term for the verb element in a clause.

pre-final consonant
In syllable structure, any consonant which precedes a final consonant.

prefix
An affix which occurs word-initially or at the beginning of a base.

pre-initial consonant
In syllable structure, any consonant which precedes an initial consonant.

premodification
In phrases, modification which precedes the head word.

pre-nucleus
The part of a tone group which precedes the nucleus, usually longer than the post-nucleus.

preposition
A closed class word often used to express the relationship between two

elements and typically complemented by a noun phrase to form a prepositional phrase.

prepositional complement
The phrase or clause which follows a preposition and which, together with
that preposition, forms a prepositional phrase.

prepositional phrase
A phrase which has a preposition as its head. The preposition occurs at the
beginning of the PP and is followed by the prepositional complement, which
is most typically a noun phrase.

prescriptive   (*adjective*)
A prescriptive approach to language study is one which is concerned with
prescribing how the language should be used and often leads to judgemental
attitudes towards users of the language.

present perfect
The aspect constructed using the auxiliary *have* in the present tense and by
placing the lexical verb in its *-ed* participle form, e.g. *have walked.*

present perfect progressive
The aspect constructed using the auxiliary *have* in the present tense, the auxiliary *be* in its *-ed* form, and by adding *-ing* to the lexical verb, e.g. *have been
walking.*

present progressive
The aspect constructed using the auxiliary *be* in the present tense and by
adding *-ing* to the lexical verb, e.g. *is walking.*

present tense
One of the two tenses in English (the other being the past) indicated normally
by a zero inflection on the verb but with an *-s* inflection in the 3rd person
singular.

primary auxiliary
Any of the verbs *be, have* or *do* when functioning as an auxiliary rather than a
lexical verb.

primary cardinal vowel
One of a set of eight vowels used to map out tongue positions and moving
from spread to rounded lips through the sequence.

primary pronoun
A member of the group which includes personal, possessive and reflexive
pronouns.

primary stress
The most prominent stress in a word, in contrast to any secondary stress.

productive   (*adjective*)
Of any linguistic process, leading to new forms.

progressive aspect
An aspect constructed using the auxiliary *be* and denoting that the activity referred to by the lexical verb is continuous or on-going.

pronominal   (*adjective*)
Occurring in place of a noun.

pronoun
A closed class word which occurs in the same position as a noun and which sometimes acts as a co-referent with a noun or noun phrase.

proper noun
A noun which names someone or something which is unique, e.g. *Jane, London*. Proper nouns are conventionally written with a capital letter at the beginning.

prosodic features
The features of speech covered by prosodics.

prosodics
The suprasegmental aspects of speech, namely pitch, intonation, stress, volume, tempo and voice quality.

purpose clause
A subordinate clause normally introduced by *so that* or *in order that* and expressing motive.

Q
question
The typical function of an interrogative sentence.

question tag
A unit formed from an auxiliary verb followed by a pronoun, and which is added to a declarative sentence to form a tag question, e.g. *isn't it* in *It's hot, isn't it?*

R
reason clause
A subordinate clause normally introduced by *as, because, for* or *since* and providing explanation.

Received Pronunciation
The non-regional accent which is taken to typify British English and which is taught to foreigners.

recursion
The occurrence more than once of a structural pattern, particularly as seen in embedded structures.

reduced relative clause
A postmodifying non-finite clause which has the potential to be expanded to

a full relative clause, e.g. *the storm <u>brewing at sea</u>* could become *the storm <u>which is brewing at sea</u>*.

reduplication
A word formation strategy involving the total or partial repetition of an element, e.g. *no-no, flip-flop*.

referent
The person(s) or thing(s) to which any linguistic item refers.

reflexive pronoun
A member of a set of pronouns formed from a personal or possessive pronoun and *self* (singular) or *selves* (plural), e.g. *myself, themselves*.

register
The degree of formality and the appropriate style adopted in discourse according to topic, purpose, mode, genre, participants and context.

relative clause
A type of subordinate clause which postmodifies a noun and is introduced by a relative pronoun, adverb or determiner.

relative pronoun
A pronoun belonging to the subset of *wh*-pronouns and which is used to introduce a relative clause, or the pronoun *that* when it fulfils the same function.

repetition
The recurrence of any linguistic feature.

restrictive relative clause
A relative clause which distinguishes the referents of the noun it modifies from another person, item, or group.

result clause
A subordinate clause normally introduced by *so* and expressing outcome.

rhotic   (*adjective*)
A rhotic accent is one where /r/ is pronounced where it would not be realised in RP, e.g. in *floo<u>r</u>*.

rhyme
The part of a syllable containing the vowel, which is the peak, and any following consonants, which make up the coda.

rhythm
The pattern of stressed and unstressed syllables in connected speech.

rise-fall tone
A tone which rises from a lower to a higher pitch and then falls again.

root
The part of a word which is at the heart of its construction and meaning, e.g. *-pel* in *impel, expel* and *compel*.

root morpheme
An alternative term for a root.

RP
The abbreviation for Received Pronunciation.

S
-s plural
The regular plural form occurring on nouns.
schwa
The neutral vowel which is represented in the IPA by the symbol /ə/.
secondary cardinal vowel
One of a set of eight vowels used to map out tongue positions and, in contrast to the primary set, moving from rounded to spread lips through the sequence.
secondary stress
A degree of syllable prominence greater than that of an unstressed syllable but less than primary stress.
segment
A distinct speech sound.
segmental phonology
The branch of phonology that deals with the distribution of phonemes in a language.
semantic field
A theme or topic created by the occurrence of words of associated meanings within a text.
semantics
The meaning of linguistic elements, or the study of meaning.
semi-consonant
An alternative term for an approximant, also known as semi-vowel.
semi-vowel
An alternative term for an approximant, also known as semi-consonant.
sentence
The largest unit of syntactic construction, consisting of one clause or more.
simple preposition
A single-word preposition, e.g. *under, through, into.*
simple sentence
A sentence which has no elements realised by a subordinate clause.
simple tone
A level, rising or falling tone.
simple word
A word constructed from one free morpheme only.
slang
Vocabulary which has a short linguistic shelf-life and which is used very informally, often by specific groups of users.

soft palate
The back part of the roof of the mouth, also known as the velum.
sonority
The volume of speech, often greatest in connected speech at a syllable peak.
speech sound
A distinct sound realising any of the phonemes of a language.
Standard British English
The standard variety of English used specifically in the British Isles.
Standard English
The non-regional dialect of English which is regarded as typifying the language in terms of vocabulary and grammar.
statement
The typical function of a declarative sentence.
stative verb
A verb which refers to a state or condition, in contrast to a dynamic verb which refers to an action or physical process.
stop
A nasal or a plosive sound, both of which involve momentary total closure in the vocal tract.
stress
In speech, the means by which some syllables are given prominence.
stressed syllable
Any syllable in a word or in connected speech which is given prominence (in contrast to an unstressed syllable).
stress-timed language
A language such as English where the stressed syllables occur at roughly equal intervals.
stricture
The process of blocking off the airstream in the articulation of a consonant sound. An alternative term for closure.
strong form
The stressed pronunciation of a grammatical word which in other contexts is unstressed.
subject complement
A complement which gives more information about the subject of the clause.
subject element
The element of a clause which precedes the verb and which is often the agent of an active clause, e.g. *Julia* in *Julia has broken three eggs*.
subject position
The clause position in front of the verb element which is filled by the subject.

subject predicative
An alternative term for a subject complement.

subjective form
The form a pronoun normally takes when it is in the subject position in a clause, e.g. *I, he, we, they.*

subject–operator inversion
The inversion of the subject element and the first auxiliary of a verb phrase used in forming an interrogative sentence.

subject-specific lexis
Lexis which relates to a specific field or topic.

subject–verb inversion
An alternative term for subject–operator inversion or, more specifically, the inversion of the subject element and the verb *be* when *be* is the lexical verb and there are no auxiliaries in the verb phrase, e.g. <u>*Is he*</u> *ready?*

subjunctive mood
A feature of a verb phrase (rare in English) which may be contrasted with the indicative mood. It is found chiefly when the base form of the verb occurs instead of an inflected form, e.g. *be* in *anxious that he be caught.*

subordinate clause
A clause which cannot stand alone and is therefore subordinate to or dependent on some other element(s).

subordinating conjunction
A conjunction which introduces a subordinate clause.

subordinator
An alternative term for a subordinating conjunction.

substitute pronoun
Any pronoun when it is used to replace a noun or noun phrase.

suffix
An affix which occurs word-finally or at the end of a base.

superlative
A form taken by adjectives and adverbs when they indicate the most of something, e.g. *tallest, fastest.* The superlative inflection is *-est.*

superordinate clause
In a complex sentence, the independent clause on which the subordinate clause(s) is dependent.

suppletion
The process by which a particular word-form is supplied by a seemingly unrelated form rather than by an inflectional ending, e.g. *went* as the past tense of *go.*

suprasegmental phonology
The aspect of phonology concerned with prosodic features such as stress, pitch and intonation.

syllable
A unit of a word's pronunciation with a vowel at its peak.
syllabic consonant
A consonant which functions as the peak of a syllable in place of a vowel.
syllabification
The way in which a word divides into syllables.
syllable template
The internal structure of a syllable.
synonym   *(adjective:* **synonymous***)*
A word which has the same meaning as another word in the same language, e.g. *sight* meaning the same as *vision*, although it is arguable that there are no true synonyms.
syntactic rule
A rule relating to word order.
syntax
Word order, or the rules which govern word order. Syntax is an aspect of grammar, the other being inflections.

T
tag question
A question formed from a declarative sentence followed by a question tag.
tempo
The speed of speech, usually measured in words per minute.
tenor
In discourse, the relationship between the writer or speaker and their audience which determines the level of formality.
tense
A grammatical feature of verbs, indicated by inflections and having both a present and a past form in English.
text
An alternative term for discourse.
textuality
The fact of being a cohesive text, spoken or written.
***that*-clause**
A subordinate clause introduced by *that* and having a pronominal function or postmodifying a noun.
***to*-infinitive**
The infinitive form of the verb preceded by the particle *to*, e.g. *to write*.
tone
The pitch contour on a single syllable, although this may extend to adjacent syllables.

tone group
A unit of connected speech which contains a tonic syllable or nucleus, usually towards the end of the group, and usually a pre-nucleus and post-nucleus. A tone group is likely to have some degree of grammatical completeness.

tone unit
An alternative term for a tone group.

tongue
The most important active articulator, comprising the tip, blade, front, back and sides.

tonic syllable
The syllable in a tone group on which there is the most noticeable change in pitch.

trachea
The windpipe, which carries air from the lungs to the mouth.

transitive verb
A verb which requires an object element to follow it.

tree diagram
A method of representing a linguistic analysis diagrammatically using vertical and horizontal lines to show branching.

triphthong
A vowel sequence in which a diphthong is followed by a further vowel, usually schwa. Speakers may realise triphthongs as one syllable or two.

trisyllabic   (*adjective*)
Containing three syllables.

U

unstressed syllable
A syllable which is given no prominence and in which the vowel is often realised as /ə/ or /ɪ/.

upper teeth
The passive articulators used in the production of labio-dental sounds.

uvula
The piece of flesh at the tip of the velum which hangs down at the back of the mouth.

V

velar   (*adjective*)
Of a consonant, articulated with the back of the tongue against the soft palate.

velum
The soft palate.

verb
The most central type of open class word, identified by its ability to make a contrast of present and past tense.

verb complementation
The obligatory element(s) which follows a particular lexical verb.

verb element
The most obligatory element of a clause and which is always a verb phrase.

verb phrase
A phrase which has a lexical verb as its head.

verbless clause
A linguistic unit which does not contain a verb element but resembles a full clause, particularly in its potential to be expanded into a clause, e.g. *if available* could be expanded to *if it is available.*

vocabulary
An everyday term for the words in a language, or a subset of those words.

vocal cords
The two muscles essential for speech situated in the larynx.

vocal folds
An alternative term for the vocal cords.

vocal tract
The oral and nasal cavities, and the upper section of the trachea as far as the larynx.

voice
The contrast in verb phrases between active and passive.

voice box
The section of the trachea which contains the vocal cords. It is also known as the larynx.

voice quality
A type of spoken voice, e.g. *creaky* or *husky.*

voicing
The vibration of the vocal cords in the articulation of a speech sound.

volume
The degree of softness or loudness with which speech is produced.

vowel
A speech sound which is articulated without any closure of articulators in the vocal tract so that the airstream flows through freely.

vowel mutation
A vowel change for grammatical purposes and occurring instead of the addition of an inflection, e.g. *sang* as the past tense of *sing.*

W

weak form

The unstressed pronunciation of a grammatical word which in some contexts may have full stress.

***wh*-pronoun**

A pronoun beginning with *wh-*, one of a larger set of *wh*-words.

***wh*-question**

A question formed with a *wh*-word at the beginning.

***wh*-word**

An adverb, determiner or pronoun which begins with *wh-* (or *how*).

word class

A category of words whose members are identified by their grammatical similarities.

word stress

The pattern of stressed and unstressed syllables in a word.

word-final   (*adjective*)

Occurring at the end of a word.

word-form

The form a lexeme takes when it is realised in speech or writing.

word formation

The process of forming or creating words.

word-initial   (*adjective*)

Occurring at the beginning of a word.

word-medial   (*adjective*)

Occurring in the middle of a word.

Y

yes-no question

A question formed through subject–verb inversion without the addition of a *wh*-word, and which could be answered simply with yes or no.

Z

zero inflection

An absent inflection where an inflection might normally occur, e.g. the plural of *sheep* has a zero inflection.

zero relative pronoun

A relative pronoun absent from a relative clause but understood, e.g. in *the man Ø I saw*.

Index